A Gui
NORTHERN '
and the Ancient of
Lanna

A Guide to
NORTHERN
THAILAND

and the
Ancient Kingdom
of
Lanna

MICHAEL FREEMAN

First published and distributed in
the USA and Canada by
Weatherhill, Inc.
41 Monroe Turnpike
Trumbull, CT 06611

British Library Cataloguing-in-
Publication Data.
A catalogue record for this book is
available from the British Library.

ISBN 0 8348 0508 1

Publisher Narisa Chakrabongse
Editor Hilary Barker
Advisor Viwat Temibhandu
Design Bradbury and Williams
Production Supervision Paisarn
Piemmettawat
Maps and plans Charoenkwun Klinphut

Printed and bound in Thailand by
Amarin Printing and Publishing Public Co. Ltd

CONTENTS

ART AND CULTURE

Northern Thailand, known for the last few centuries
as Lanna, was until recently a quite independent
political entity. The physical isolation of its valleys,
hemmed in by forested ranges, kept it apart: a
collection of small, self-governing principalities that
developed their own culture, art and architecture.
Lanna's political independence ended in the late
nineteenth century when it was incorporated into
Siam, but its cultural personality to this day remains
distinct.

*In a village wat near Chiang Mai, a monk hangs his robe to dry in
the winter sun.*

LAND AND PEOPLE

Northern Thailand begins where the broad plains of the Chao Phaya River and its tributaries give way to the hills. The grain of the land is north-south, but the complexities of hill and valley are such that until the arrival of the railway in the 1920s, it was largely a world apart. The convoluted topography that first channeled the settlement of migrating peoples from the north was also responsible for keeping them quite isolated from the rule of the Siamese. Known from at least the sixteenth century as 'Lanna', which translates as 'a million rice fields', the region was a composite of small principalities known as *muang*, and was largely self-governing but also prone to endless conflicts.

The topography is a mixture of hills that occasionally make the grade to mountain (the highest peak, Doi Inthanon, reaches 2595 metres – 8514 feet) and valleys that are seldom broader than about 20 kilometres. Water and fertile land determined the settlement, which followed the main rivers of Lanna: the Ping, Wang, Yom and Nan, which all flow south into the Chao Phraya, the Kok and the Ing, which drain north into the Mekong, and the Pai and Yuam in the far west, tributaries of the Salween. Separating these rivers – very effectively until the construction of 20th century roads and railway – are the three principal ranges: the Daen Lao Mountains, the North and West Thanon Thongchai Mountains and the Phi Pan Nam Mountains.

The settlement of Lanna is principally the story of the Tai Yuan, one of the main Tai ethno-linguistic groups who migrated south across the Mekong River and into the narrow valleys of these highlands. Exactly

Ranges of hills separating parallel valleys, seen here near Pai, are typical of Lanna's topography. They channelled settlement and encouraged individual principalities.

when this movement to the south occurred is still debated, but certainly most of it had already taken place by the middle of the 13th century. The basic pattern was established as follows: the Tai Yuan, who called themselves *khon muang* or 'The People of the Principalities', dominated Lanna, and the Siamese (another Tai group) occupied the basin of the Chao Phraya to the south. 'Thai', incidentally, refers to the nation and the language of Thailand, and is distinct from the ethno-linguistic description 'Tai'.

The actual way in which the valleys were settled, however, was far from simple. To begin with, the Lanna highlands already had an indigenous population, even though little is known about it. There was a substantial prehistory, as evidence artefacts from cave sites near Mae Hong Son dated to around 6000 BC, from Chiang Saen and other locations. By the beginning of the region's documented history, around the 8th century, at least part of the area was settled by an Austro-Asiatic group, the Lawa. Although there remain some 10,000 of this ethno-linguistic group in Lanna, only a few traces of their early habitations remain: for example, the circular fortified settlement called Muang La Maing immediately west of Chiang Mai at the foot of Doi Suthep which can be detected in aerial photogaphs.

The first movement of peoples into the Lanna valleys for which there is evidence was that of the Mon. Surprisingly little is known about this large and important group - also Austro-Asiatic - who created the major civilising culture of the lower Irrawaddy and Chao Phraya basins between the 5th-6th and 13th centuries. Dvaravati was the name of the loose confederation of states in the Chao Phraya valley that included Nakhon Phathom, U Thong, Khu Bua and Lopburi, and it was from Lopburi that Mon settlers moved north into the Ping, Wang and Yom valleys. Here they built towns fortified with oval ramparts and moats at what are now Lamphun, Lampang and Phrae, occupying this southern part of Lanna from possibly the 8th century.

The Mon displaced the Lawa in these valleys, but they in turn came into contact with the expansion of the Khmer empire in the 7th century. However, despite accounts in the local chronicles that the rule of Angkor extended north of Chiang Saen, there are no archaeological remains north of Si Satchanalai on Lanna's southern border, and probably no Khmer settlement either. By the end of the 13th century it was principally the Mon that the Tai had to deal with.

The Tai, who now number more than 80 million, are believed to have originated in central, or possibly eastern China around 2000 BC, and migrated gradually towards the southwest, eventually establishing themselves in what is now Yunnan. From the middle of the 8th to the

The valley floors, often narrow, provided the essentials for settlement: water and fertile soil for growing rice.

The Mon from the coastal plains of what are now Thailand and Burma founded small states as far north as Lanna. Their facial features, recorded in many terracotta sculptures like this, in Lamphun's museum, were broader than those of the Tai.

The appearance of the Tai, who settled Lanna from the north, is recorded faithfully in the distinctively realistic mural paintings of northern wats.

Rural pursuits still dominate life in the northern valleys.

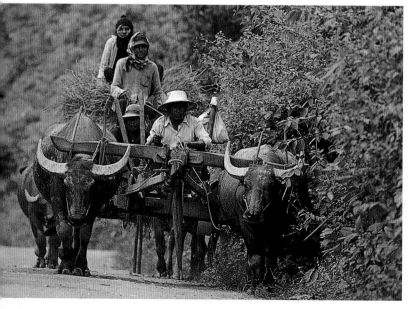

middle of the 13th centuries the major state in this area was Nanchao, with its capital Dali by Lake Erhai, and while this was a Tibeto-Burman speaking kingdom, the Tai settled here and to the south. Over an unknown period of time they spread outwards, becoming differentiated as they did so into more than a dozen groups, six of them still within China and the others scattered from Assam in the west to Vietnam in the east and the Malay peninsula in the south.

The four Tai groups that had an involvement with Lanna were the Siamese, who passed through and settled initially in central Thailand, the Tai Yuan who form the bulk of Lanna's population, the Shan (also called the Tai Yai or Tai Khün) who settled mainly in the west, and the Tai Lü, who are distributed patchily but mainly in the northeast, in Nan province. These last two were relative latecomers. The Tai migrations were not single, distinct events, but rather a gradual and small-scale process of infiltration along valley routes. The complex topography helped to ensure that settlement took place in overlapping layers, with groups of settlers moving up one tributary valley but not another, accumulating in greater or lesser numbers according to all kinds of local cirumstances. The key historical event, however, was the capture of the Mon capital Haripunchai by the founder of the Lanna kingdom, Mangrai, in 1281, after which the Mon were largely absorbed and the Tai Yuan became the dominant people.

One increasingly important factor in the settlement of Lanna, right up to the late 19th century, was war. It had two collateral effects: refugee movements and forced re-settlement. Both were responsible for mass displacements of people - in the thousands - even though one was disorganised and the other state-directed. In the second decade of the 13th century, for example, unrest in southern Yunnan stimulated a major movement of the Tai southward into the region. Again, at the end of the 18th century, when the Siamese and the Tai Yuan had finally defeated the Burmese, Lanna was so ravaged and its population depleted that forced re-settlement was the only solution. Keng Tung and Sipsongpanna were accordingly raided for people, and the result was an even more patchy ethnic mixing.

Deciduous dipterocarp forest once covered most of Lanna, and its most valuable species was teak, which in turn brought Shan and British traders from Burma.

The settlement of the Shan and the Tai Lü is better known because they are more recent arrivals than the Tai Yuan, and so better documented. The Shan were found principally in the highlands drained by the upper Salween River (essentially the present-day Shan State of Burma). While the Pai and Yuam Valleys appear to have been under at least the nominal control of Lanna for most of its history, they were difficult to reach from Chiang Mai because of the mountains and offered little inducement in earlier times to Tai Yuan settlers. As a result, such little population as there was before the 19th century came from the north and west and was Shan. When Mae Hong Son began to attract attention as a centre for the capture and training of elephants in the 1830s, this far west of Lanna began to develop, the more so as the teak industry became important. More Shan moved into the area, accompanied by the British, whose experience with teak in Burma gave them an advantage in controlling the trade, to other logging centres in Lanna, notably Chiang Mai, Chiang Rai, Lampang, and Phrae.

The Tai Lü were originally from Sipsongpanna (Xishuangbanna in Chinese) in Yunnan, but moved into Lanna mainly as refugees from wars and civil disturbances. The first recorded migration was in the 17th century to Keng Tung and Luang Prabang, and in 1804 more were taken from Sipsongpanna to help re-populate Lanna, Nan, Phayao, Chiang Saen and Chiang Khong. They are notable for their social cohesion and for maintaining their traditions, including the distinctive architectural style of their monasteries.

The Shan, the men with their distinctive turbans, settled mainly in the north-west part of Lanna in the 19th century.

A BRIEF HISTORY

An eighteenth century map of Southeast Asia (then known as Indo-China) by P. Santini.

The detailed events that concern the cities, towns and wat of Lanna are dealt with later, in the valley-by-valley descriptions that begin on page 60. The purpose of this abbreviated account is to set the overall scene and to put into an historical context the movements and interactions of the Lanna peoples that we have just seen. As through out this book, the sources vary in reliability. The various local chronicles are certainly entertaining, but often imaginative, and where there is no corroboration they are quoted with qualifications. Perhaps even more confusing is the problem of dates, on many of which the various chronicles differ. For a fuller account and for the most reliable judgement on such matters of accuracy as dating, see David Wyatt's modestly titled *A Short History of Thailand.*

The known history of Lanna begins with the arrival of the Mon from the south to settle in the middle valleys of the Ping, Wang and Yom, founding Haripunjaya on the site of present-day Lamphun around the beginning of the ninth century. Although the date is uncertain, this was certainly the capital, and two other small cities were later built at Khelang (now Lampang) and Phrae. There continued a succession of rulers, one of whom, King Adityaraja, gained attention for his resistance to the expanding Khmer empire.

During the reign of the Suryavarman I at Angkor in the first half of the 11th century, the Khmers invaded the Chao Phraya valley, conquering Dvraravati. By 1025 they occupied Lopburi, then called Louvo, and launched attacks further north. The accounts are unreliable, but suggest that Haripunjaya was besieged two or three times, though unsuccessfully, and there is no evidence of direct Khmer rule or occupation. Only one of the chronicles claims Khmer hegemony extending north to the area around Chiang Saen, and this is unsupported.

However, the beginnings of the Lanna Tai kingdom were here on the west bank of the Mekong, and Ngoen Yang was a significant settlement close to present-day Chiang Saen and a natural crossing place for the Tai groups moving south from Yunnan. In 1230 the ruling family entered a marriage alliance with the rulers of Chiang Rung in southern Yunnan, resulting in the birth in 1239 of a prince, Mangrai, who went on to found the kingdom of Lanna. He succeeded his father in 1259, and three years later moved his capital to Chiang Rai. From here, he began expanding his rule through a combination of alliances and conquests, taking Chiang Khong on the Mekong in 1269, Fang in the upper valley of the Kok in approximately 1273, and the Mon city of Haripunjaya in 1281.

Mangrai was an astute, energetic and determined ruler, but this was not the only reason for his success in expanding his kingdom. The second half of the 13th century saw catastrophic changes in Southeast Asia, due principally to the Mongol invasions from the north, but also to the weakening of the Khmer empire. The combination meant that the Tai who had settled in the Chao Phraya basin and in the Lanna highlands had no powerful foreign forces to contend with, and so had the opportunity to create their own states. In the east, the once-powerful Khmer empire had begun to weaken after the death of its last powerful ruler Jayavarman VII around 1220. The time was ripe for the Tai to assert themselves, and in 1238 two Tai princes seized Sukhothai and its sister city Si Satchanalai from the Khmer governor. In 1253 the Mongols captured Nanchao, the state in the north of Yunnan, and within four years had subdued all of Yunnan. By 1287 they had seized Pagan, and the city fell into anarchy. That year, Mangrai made a pact of friendship with Ram Kamhaeng, third Tai ruler of Sukhothai, and Ngam Muang, ruler of the smaller principality of Phayao (founded in 1096).

A Lanna couple on their wedding day.

In the following year Lampang also fell within the compass of Lanna rule, but Phrae was absorbed into the expanding kingdom of Sukhothai. Mangrai, seeing the importance of the broad middle valley of the Ping, moved his capital to Wiang Kum Kam, less than 20 kilometres from Haripunchai. This was a temporary move, and with the help of Ram Kamhaeng and Ngam Muanghe, he carefully chose the site of Chiang Mai, which he founded in 1296. By 1298, the year in which Ram Kamhaeng died, the Lanna kingdom included Lampang, Lamphun and as far as Tak in the south, the Pai valley in the west, and Muang Nai, Keng Tung and Jing Hong in the north. Sukhothai controlled most of the area to the east, including Phrae, Phayao, Nan & Luang Prabang.

Mangrai died suddenly in 1317, leaving a succession dispute. His second son Chai Songkhram succeeded him briefly, handing over the throne to his son Saen Phu and retiring to Chiang Rai in 1318. However, Mangrai's youngest son, who had been sent to rule Muang Nai on the upper Salween, decided to claim the throne for himself and in 1319 seized it from his nephew, who retreated to Chiang Rai to join his father. Three years later, Saen Phu's brother, Nam Thuam, overthrew the usurper, and in 1324 Saen Phu was re-installed on the throne of Chiang Mai by his father, and ruled for another decade until his death in 1334. His son Kham Fu succeeded him but lived for only three more years, when the throne passed in turn to his son Pha Yu, who moved the capital for a few years to Chiang Rai. In 1339 Chiang Mai once more became the capital of Lanna, this time for good. Sukhothai, meanwhile, had fallen into decline with the death of Ram Kamhaeng, and control of Phayao passed to Lanna.

Lanna's troubles began with the founding of Ayutthaya in 1347. This aggressive new state on the lower Chao Phraya successfully extended its rule, south to the peninsula and eventually east to Angkor. Almost immediately, in 1349, it made Sukhothai into a vassal (annexing it in 1438), and by the 1380s it was making repeated assaults on Chiang Mai, which in 1390 was forced to submit to the Ayutthayan King Ramesuan. As if one warlike neighbour were not enough, Ayutthaya's impending confrontation with Burma would make Chiang Mai a pawn in what was to be the major struggle of the region.

Building of the Northern railway, c. 1900.

Nevertheless, the Lanna kingdom continued to prosper. During this period, three kings in the Mangrai dynasty ruled - Ku Na, Saen Muang Ma and Sam Fang Kaen - and despite the military struggles, art flourished and several important religious foundations were made around Chiang Mai. Then, in 1441, the able and devout King Tilokaraj ascended to the throne, ushering in Lanna's cultural golden age. Under his command, Chiang Mai forces were able to reverse Lanna's military fortunes, and after capturing Nan in 1449, seized Si Satchanalai in 1459 and Sukhothai two years later. Although their third assault on Ayutthaya was unsuccessful, peace between the two states followed for three decades.

War resumed with Ayutthaya a few years after the death of Tilokaraj in 1487, and although under King Muang Kaeo Chiang Mai forces were able to take Sukhothai and Kamphaeng Phet, they were driven back and defeated near Lampang in 1515. However, these struggles with Ayutthaya were the forerunner of an even more serious conflict, with ultimately disastrous consequences for both kingdoms. Ayutthaya's expansionist policy inevitably brought it to challenge Burma, and with the foundation of a powerful state in Pegu, the Burmese were able to respond. In 1551 the warlike King Bayinnaung was crowned there and immediately set about subjugating the surrounding states.

Unfortunately for Lanna, a sequence of succession disputes beginning in 1538 weakened the rule of Chiang Mai, so that it was ill-equipped to meet the new threat. It began with King Chettarat being deposed by his son. He re-took the throne in 1543 but was assassinated two years later, following which King Setthathirat of Luang Phrabang was invited to rule. He left a couple of years after the death of his father, and Lanna was plunged into a civil war. Lanna was poorly placed to resist Bayinnaung's attacks, and by 1558, Chiang Mai and the rest of Lanna had been conquered, beginning two centuries of Burmese suzerainty. Nor was this a peaceful subjugation, because the Burmese used Lanna as a base for prosecuting its war with Ayutthaya, and mounted punitive expeditions against the north when Chiang Mai proved uncooperative, as in 1564. In 1578, the three-century Mangrai dynasty came to an end with the death of Princess Wisutthithewi, and the Burmese king placed his son on the throne of Chiang Mai. Rebellions, reprisals, attacks and counter-attacks punctuated the next two hundred years, with Chiang Mai changing hands between the two warring states. It was re-captured by Ayutthaya in 1598, but when Chiang Rai revolted against Burmese rule in 1614, it provoked an expedition in which the Burmese took both cities. In 1661 Ayutthaya once more re-captured Chiang Mai, but only briefly. Other Lanna cities fared no better. Chiang Saen was placed under direct Burmese rule at the beginning of the 18th century, and at the same time, in 1703, the Burmese sacked Nan.

Finally, after eight years of assaults by the new Burmese King Alaungpaya, Ayutthaya itself fell in 1767 and was so thoroughly destroyed that it was abandoned. This total catastrophe for the Siamese was, however, the turning point in Lanna's misfortunes. The Siamese forces re-grouped downriver at what is now Bangkok, and under the

Elephants hauling logs, c. 1900.

new King Rama I began a series of ultimately successful campaigns against the Burmese. Within a few years, in 1774, the Burmese were decisively defeated in Lampang by a combination of Siamese forces and troops under the command of Phraya Chaban of Chiang Mai and Chao Kawila of Lampang. Two years later, in 1776, Chiang Mai was re-taken, but after the ravages of war over this long period, it was subsequently abandoned. Chiang Rai was taken in 1786, followed by the other cities, with Chiang Saen the last to fall in 1804. It was razed on the orders of the Siamese as a defensive measure.

As the century turned, Lanna's revival began, but not independently. The price it paid for Siamese help in driving out the Burmese was Siamese suzerainty, which led eventually to Siamese rule. The speed of its recovery was aided by the capability of its ruler, Chao Kawila; with Mangrai and Tilokaraj, he was the third of the notable Chiang Mai rulers who directed the key periods in Lanna's history. As Prince of Lampang he helped defeat the Burmese, and was appointed to over see Chiang Mai's recovery by the Siamese King Taksin. The city was formally occupied in March 1796, and Kawila re-settled it by raiding Keng Tung and other areas for part of their population. He died in 1815.

The seventh ruler of Chiang Mai, King Intra Vijayanonda (1870-1897).

Lanna's recovery continued throughout the 19th century, at times with the help of more forced re-settlement. Chiang Rai was re-founded in 1844, and Chiang Saen in 1881. Mae Hong Son in the west grew as an elephant centre for the princes of Chiang Mai, and teak became an important commodity that attracted British interests. British involvement in the region began with its 1824 war with Burma, which it eventually made a colony; parallel French activity in Indo-China meant that European empire-building became the new threat to Siamese sovereignty. Partly because of this, the Siamese extended their control over Lanna, appointing a high commissioner in 1874 and incorporating it into Siam as the administrative unit of Monthon Phayap in 1892. The British threat was contained by concessions which included being able to trade in teak, which in turn brought Burmese workers and merchants to the main cities of Lanna. Siam was less fortunate with the French,

King Prajadhipok (Rama VII) during his visit to Chiang Mai in 1921.

however, and was forced to cede two large parts of Lanna: the east bank of the Mekong in 1893 and the west bank downriver from Wiang Kaen in 1904.

Communications helped the continuing integration of Lanna, the telegraph reaching Chiang Mai in 1885 and the railway in 1921. King Rama VII, who was Siam's last absolute ruler, was the first ever to visit Lanna in 1926. Nan was the last Lanna principality to be incorporated into Siam in 1931, and the following year, when a coup ended the absolute monarchy, Chiang Mai became a province. As a political entity, Lanna ceased to exist.

LANNA ART & ARCHITECTURE

A common theme throughout Lanna decoration is the life of the forest, with its once-numerous species of animals and plants.

This viharn at Wat Chiang Man in Chiang Mai typifies the northern monastery building: small scale and sweeping roof lines, all in teak.

As elsewhere, Lanna art was religious in inspiration and function, and for this reason it is essential to consider the architecture of its monuments and monastic buildings at the same time as its sculpture and mural painting. Difficulties arise, however, in devising a chronology that covers all religious art and its local variations, and due to insufficient evidence, this continues to be disputed by art historians. Here, we have chosen to follow the system used at the National Museum, Chiang Mai, but it is important to be aware that there is no general agreement over the dating of what some refer to as the early Chiang Saen style.

The main events shaping the stylistic changes were first the conquest of Haripunchai by the Tai; second, the creation and growth of the Lanna kingdom; third, the success of Sukhothai and increasing relations between it and Lanna; and finally the Burmese conquest, which brought most artistic production to a halt. These events applied equally to the building of *chedi* and founding of monasteries, together with all their decorations, but while sculpture never recovered from the two-century Burmese inter-regnum, architecture and architectural decoration continued, and even underwent a 19th-century revival. The architecture also absorbed more foreign influence at this time, particularly Burmese and European, and some Chinese.

The 20th century, on the other hand, has seen the gradual

replacement of Lanna style by central Thai style, as new monastic buildings are commissioned and others restored. Most new building design and decoration is heavily adulterated, showing little restraint, and is normally executed in concrete. There are nevertheless some talented craftsmen working in the region, particularly in woodcarving, and in a few instances their skills have been put to good use in architectural decoration that draws on traditional Lanna motifs.

Lanna art is almost exclusively within the Theravada Buddhist canon. Some Brahmanic imagery certainly exists, and in particular the *naga* which play such an important part in the monastic buildings, but apart from these creatures there is less of it in Lanna than in central Thai art. One reason is that this region was much less under the influence of the Khmer, whose art had a well developed Brahmanic iconography based on the state worship of Shiva (and to a lesser extent Vishnu) for most of its empire's history. Another is that in Siam, Brahmanism was deliberately used to reinforce the status and power of royalty, as can be seen for example at Wat Phra Kaeo in Bangkok, while Lanna only began to come under Siamese rule in the 19th century. Indigenous animism also enters into Lanna art, particularly in the decoration of monastic buildings. Motifs from the forests are particularly characteristic, including animals large and small, and the *khrue thao* vine motif of scrolling and looping vegetation.

Our view of what constitutes Lanna style is unavoidably skewed in the direction of what remains. One notable feature was the extensive use of teak wood from the once-abundant forests. Being strong, straightforward to carve and particularly resistant to termites and rotting, it was a natural choice, not only for buildings but also Buddha images. Unfortunately, not even this excellent wood can survive more than a very few centuries' exposure to the elements, and the bulk of early Lanna carving is lost to us. The teak work that you can see today is principally from the 19th century, the revival period of Lanna art. However, on the positive side, this is at least in the earlier Lanna idiom (other than buildings and carving done in specifically Burmese or European style). Only bronze, stucco, terracotta and brick remain from the earlier centuries, but it is important to remember that these are not wholly representative. Nor, in the case of important *chedi,* are they actually visible, because it was normal practice to enlarge these structures for the purposes of making merit, and this meant encasing the original and introducing stylistic changes. Stone was little used, due to the lack of types suitable for carving.

The periods listed below were neither clear-cut nor homogeneous. In architecture in particular there were anomalies; witness the *chedi* of Wat Chet Yot in Chiang Mai, inspired by the Indian Mahabodhi

The oldest surviving style is that of the Mon, who built this stepped, four-sided chedi at Wat Ku Kut near Lamphun.

A stucco-on-laterite head of the Buddha in Mon style, now at the national Museum in Lamphun.

Temple and an individual expression of the will of King Tilokaraj rather than a progression of style. There were also countless idiosyncrasies, inevitable when so much was created in communities that were to an extent isolated and quasi-independent. Over most of Lanna, the decoration of monastic buildings was vernacular, undertaken by local craftsmen to the best of their varying skills, using their imaginations and local details to supply the references. In fact, it is this variety and individualism that gives Lanna art, taken as a whole, so much of its character.

Haripunjaya: The Last Mon Art
From the 8th to late 13th centuries: the founding of Haripunjaya to its sacking by King Mangrai, 767–1281.

This period preceded the arrival of the Tai from Yunnan and the north, when Haripunjaya (now Lamphun) was the northern outpost of the Austro-Asiatic Mon peoples. Little remains from this culture, the principal state of which was Dvaravati, located further south around Lopburi, U Thong and Nakhon Pathom. Haripunjaya lasted longer than Dvaravati, and the two chedi near Lamphun are the country's principal Mon architectural remains.

In sculpture, the Mon used stucco, terracotta, stone and bronze, and most Buddha images are standing and symmetrical. The broad-browed face is fleshy with a wide, flat nose and full, half-smiling lips, lowered eye and arched eyebrows that meet in the middle. There is sometimes a suggestion of a moustache in the form of an incised line. The hair curls are small, ending in sharp points, and the ushnisha is smooth and conical. The gesture is usually the *vitarka mudra*, with both hands if standing, and the *uttarasanga* (robe) covering both shoulders, falling without pleats. Sculpted heads of monks, disciples and others show a tendency towards exaggerated features and even caricature, such as lively expressions and bulging eyes.

Lanna First Period: The Founding of the Kingdom
From the 13th (but possibly earlier) to mid-14th centuries: the foundation of Chiang Mai by King Mangrai in 1296, the early Tai settlements on the west bank of the Mekong, through the reign of King Pha Yu 1355.

A bronze Buddha in the posture of touching the Earth, in the Chiang Saen style, now in the National Museum, Chiang Saen.

There is an unresolved problem of dating what some believe to be the earliest Tai images of the Buddha: a series of sophisticated and distinctive bronze castings found in the area of Chiang Saen that show the clear influence of the Pala and Sena schools of northern India (8th to 12th centuries). Their importance lies in the fact that they may mark the beginning of independent Lanna art; in the most traditional view of Thai art history they define the Early Chiang Saen Period.

The Buddha images of this early period are noted for their plastic qualities. The face is round with lowered eyes: arched and clearly separated eyebrows; sharp nose and small, fleshy lips; hair rendered in large curls; smooth knob above the hemispherical *ushnisha*. The upright body has broad shoulders and a full chest ("like a lion's", as one of the 32 distinguishing characteristics has it) and is usually seated in the *vajrasana* (full-lotus) position with hands in the *bhumisparsa mudra* subduing Mara. In attire, the *uttarasanga* (robe) typically leaves the entire right breast uncovered, while the *sanghati* (shawl) hangs down from the shoulder only a short way, to just above the left breast, and the *antaravaska* (undergarment) is rendered as an outline only. The technical quality of the bronze castings is superb.

It is likely that images of the Buddha from the Pala and Sena schools in northern India reached the area in the hands of Buddhist missionaries travelling through Burma, or during the reported campaign of King Anawratha in the mid-11th century, for the influence of this Indian art style can be seen in such features as the smooth knob on top of the *ushnisha*, the large hair curls and the full body. One distinction is that while in Pala statues the right hand rests on the calf of the leg, here it is on the knee, and the right arm is held out from the body.

The architecture, which is little and confined to *chedi*, was influenced by Haripunchai & Burmese styles. Theravada Buddhism forged an affinity between the settled Mon and the immigrant Tai. The conquest of Haripunchai notwithstanding, Mon Buddhist art appears to have been enthusiastically adopted by the Tai, as witness the copies of the Mahapol Chedi from Wat Chamathewi, made at Wat Kum Kam in this period and elsewhere later.

Sukhothai-style Buddha images in bronze, one in meditation, the other walking, at Wat Phaya Pu, Nan.

Lanna Second Period: The Influence of Sukhothai
Mid-14th to mid-15th centuries: reigns of King Ku Na, King Saen Muang Ma and King Sam Fang Kaen 1355-1441.

This period was influenced by Sukhothai style, due not only to the flowering of Sukhothai art at this time, but also to the growing prosperity of Lanna that encouraged the Chiang Mai rulers to look beyond their own kingdom for religious inspiration. In particular, Ku Na invited the famous Sukhothai monk Sumana to Lanna, and had built for (or because of) him Wat Phra Yeun in Lamphun, Wat Umong Suan Puthatham, Wat Suan Dok and Wat Phra Boromathat Doi Suthep in and around Chiang Mai. Saen Muang Ma began the construction of Chedi Luang, and some of the *chedi* in Chiang Saen were also built at this time.

In sculpture, which more clearly shows Sukhothai influence, this period corresponds with the beginning of what is also known as Late Chiang Saen, or Chiang Mai Period, which continues through until the Burmese conquest. The significance of Sukhothai art on Buddha images, which became distinctive in the early 14th century, was profound. As Jean Boisselier wrote, Sukhothai sculptors strived for spiritual expressionism rather than realism: "It was their purpose to create not a lifelike figure but a hieratic image of otherworldly mien, and to this end they emphasized everything that made the Exalted One a pre-destined man of destiny."

Buddha images are, as before, seated and shown in the attitude of subduing Mara, the *bhumisparsa mudra*, but in the *virasana* (half-lotus).

A classic bell-shaped Sukhothai-style chedi at Wat Umong Suan Putthatham near Chiang Mai.

They betray their Sukhothai influence in the oval face, slimmer body and more stylised overall treatment. The mouth remains small and fleshy, the eyes lowered, eyebrows separated and hair in large curls, but the *ushnisha* is distinctively topped with a flame finial. This increasing stylisation, applied to the more human Pala faces, sometimes results in a slightly disdainful expression. In attire, the *uttarasanga* exposes less of the right breast, to just below the nipple, and the *sanghati* hangs lower, to just above the navel.

Lanna Third Period: The Golden Age

Mid-15th to mid-16th centuries: reigns of King Tilokaraj to King Muang Kaeo 1441-1526.

This was the peak of Lanna art, which flourished in all forms during the economic prosperity of these reigns; under royal patronage important *wats* were founded and new monastic buildings constructed. King Tilokaraj commissioned the building of Wat Chet Yot in Chiang Mai, based on the design of the Mahabodhi Temple in Bodh Gaya, India, and organised the Eighth World Buddhist Council here in 1477. Military successes included the capture of Sukhothai and Si

Two of Lanna's finest chedi feature a small bell, three prominent circular mouldings, and a heavily redented square base. That of Wat Phra That Sri Chom Thong (above) was built in 1452, and that at Wat Phra That Haripunchai (right) in 1447.

Satchanalai, enabling Tilokaraj to bring craftsmen back to Chiang Mai and so add their skills to the local artisan base, as well as more Sukhothai stylistic influence. Tilokaraj also established direct contact with Sri Lanka, then the centre of Theravada Buddhism, and Lanna art so acquired some Sri Lankan characteristics.

In sculpture, this period corresponds with the continuation of Late Chiang Saen (Chiang Mai), as described under the Second Period above. Here, the Sukhothai influence continues, and traces of Ayutthaya and U-Thong styles begin to be seen, among them some images dressed in royal attire and crowned. Beyond the Lanna capital, centres such as Phayao, Nan and Fang began to develop local stylistic variations.

A number of Lanna's most important *chedi* were built or enlarged during this period. They include those at Wat Chet Yot, Wat Phra Boromathat Doi Suthep, Wat Chedi Luang, Wat Phra That Haripunchai, Wat Phra That Lampang Luang and Wat Phra That Sri Chom Thong. The Emerald Buddha, discovered in Chiang Rai, was brought to Chiang Mai and installed at Wat Chedi Luang at this time.

Various naïve local styles of art are preserved from the 17th and 18th century. This standing Buddha (left) with arms held straight down, is typical of the Nan valley.

One of the few fine religious buildings constructed during the Burmese occupation was Wat Phumin in Nan, built in 1596 and restored in the 19th century.

Bat-like ears and sharp nose on the Buddha image at Wat Phumin, Nan, are evidence of the influence of Laotian art from the 16th century on.

Lanna Fourth Period: Decline and Burmese Occupation
Mid-16th to mid-18th centuries: 1525-1774 (reign of King Chettharat to the end of the Burmese suzerainty).

These two centuries were the period of decline, beginning with succession disputes that were followed by the subjugation of Lanna by Burmese forces under King Bayinnaung. Court patronage of the arts ceased and economic hardship was the inevitable result of battles, skirmishes, rebellions and reprisals. Art became a local matter, and there is evidence of Lan Xang and Burmese influence. A notable exception of excellence in religious architecture was Wat Phumin in Nan, built in 1596 during a period of relative peace following the death of the Burmese king.

Fewer Buddha images were created in this artistically depressed period. For the Laotian kingdom of Lan Xang, however, this was its heyday, with the founding of Vientiane in 1564 and some of the characteristics of its statuary, such as 'bat' ears and sharply pointed, ridged nose begin to be seen in Lanna images.

Lanna Fifth Period: The Revival
Late-18th to 20th century: reign of Chao Kawila to direct Siamese rule.

The tiny, elegant viharn of Wat Buppharam in Chiang Mai is typical of 19th century teak architecture.

The end of the Burmese occupation heralded the revival period of Lanna art. Kawila re-settled Lanna extensively, and this included the city of Chiang Mai, which after the ravages of war was abandoned from its recapture in 1776 until 1796. Simply by virtue of being the most recent, and for the reasons given above, the architecture from this period makes up the bulk of what can be seen today. Earlier Lanna architectural and decorative styles were copied.

Burmese influence is marked because of the influx of Burmese teak merchants accompanying the British logging initiative of the 19th century, who commissioned *wat* for their own use, while the western part of Lanna, now the province of Mae Hong Son, was settled almost exclusively by Shan.

The Shan, who arrived in the 19th century, brought the Burmese style of chedi, as here at Wat Sri Chom Ruang in Phayao.

The terms Burmese and Shan are often used interchangeably, but the people who moved here for teak were Shan ethnically, even though by the 19th century many had absorbed mainstream Burmese tastes in religious architecture. The influence of the British can be seen mainly in domestic architecture, with a European distribution of living space and gingerbread decoration. Finally, as Lanna came more and more under the control of Bangkok, Rattanakosin influences began to creep into the religious architecture.

Colonial gingerbread architecture was introduced by British teak traders, seen here at its finest at Ban Wongburi in Phrae.

Wood carving

Plant motifs form the basis of most carved temple decoration throughout Thailand, and Lanna is no exception, with both sharing the *kanok* leaf-like motif and the *khrue thao* vine motif, although the Lanna treatment tends to be more curved and freer in its loops and

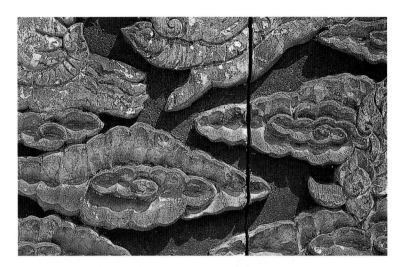

Lanna is justly famous for its wood carving. One of the finest pediments still in situ is at Wat Duang Di, Chiang Mai (above). A recurring Lanna pediment style employs rectangular panels, as at Wat Pa Daet, Mae Chaem (right), while Chinese design influence occasionally makes itself felt, as in the 'floating clouds' carving at Wat Pratu Pong, Lampang (above right).

spirals. In addition, there are particular designs unique to the North, such as the sunflower (dok tan tawan) and the pineapple (dok sabparot). Cloud motifs are unique to Lanna, being strongly influenced by Chinese style, and the mek lai ('floating cloud') was both a symbol of coolness and happiness, and an invocation for abundant, timely rains.

Animals feature particularly strongly in Lanna wood carving, partly because of the Chinese-influenced belief in the zodiacal animals and partly because of the local importance of the forest with its variety of wildlife. Over and above this, the naga is prominently and imaginatively incorporated into carved decorations.

Geometrical designs also play a part. The most common way of dividing the gable area in Lanna is into rectangular panels, while on a smaller scale lozenges, half-lozenges and cartouches appear. One specific Chinese introduction, normally seen as a strip below the pediment, is a cross-weave design known as prachae chin.

TOWN, VILLAGE, HOUSE

Town

The principal Lanna settlements, most of which are now the provincial capitals, were the *chiang* or *wiang:* the seats of power for small principalties or city-states known as *muang*. The Tai Yuan called themselves *khon muang*, or 'People of the Principalities' and each of these usually covered a valley or else its most fertile, habitable part. The *muang* took its name from the capital city, and if this was where the king or an important prince lived, it was called a *chiang*. Otherwise, if it were simply a fortified settlement, it was known as a *wiang* (the word actually means a fortified wall or palisade). These principal settlements were located on the valley floor next to the main river, ideally with hills behind, and it was such towns as Chiang Rai, Chiang Saen, Lampang, Lamphun, Phayao, Phrae, Nan and (most important of all) Chiang Mai where the most sophisticated expressions of Lanna culture flourished.

The morning market scene in Phrae in early 1900. Note the city wall can be seen at right. (River Books Archives)

In size and structure, however, they were very different from today. A town plan or aerial view of Chiang Mai, Lamphun, Lampang or Phrae, which still have their city walls (or at least the outline), gives an immediate impression of how much the population has grown, mainly within the last century. In addition, the original form of the settlement was highly structured, not least by the defensive walls. The dense, demarcated pattern of buildings helped to maintain a tightly knit community with conservative traditions and a social hierarchy that was reflected in the architecture.

The growth of both population and economy has inevitably changed all this, and none of the provincial capitals could now be considered traditional. Another change over the last century has been the growth of former villages into small towns, and these are almost completely non-traditional in their structure. Nevertheless, some capitals have changed less than others – Phrae, for example – and throughout there remain pockets of the community that for one reason or another have kept much of their original structure, such as parts of Chiang Mai's old city, Thanon Talat Gao in Lampang and the area south of Wat Phra Kaeo Don Tao, among others.

Varoros Market in Chiang Mai in 1920. (River Books Archives)

Important towns were fortified, originally with a moat enclosing earthen ramparts (the former providing the material for the latter), for which water would be diverted from a stream or the main river. Wooden palisades with wooden gates were probably built on the ramparts, then eventually superseded by brick walls. Mon settlements (now Lamphun, Lampang and Phrae) were laid out within roughly oval fortifications, while the Tai style, as in Yunnan

The Prince of Lampang's teak palace, now preserved at Ancient City, near Bangkok (above).

The village shrine, san chao muang, at Ban Muang Pon, near Mae Hong Son (right).

The city pillar, lak muang, of Phrae (below).

and the north, was square (as in Chiang Mai) or rectangular (as in Chiang Saen). Near the centre was the town square, also the location of the city pillar, the *lak muang* (or *jai muang:* 'heart of the country'). Variations on a single pillar were a *lak muang* surrounded by four posts, as can still be seen in Yunnan, and a group of three pillars, as those in Lampang between 2.5 and 4 metres tall. Under the influence of the Shivaite Khmer, a number of the country's city pillars took the form of a *linga*, some with faces carved on the head and known as *mukhalinga*, as in Nan. Traditionally, when there was a single pillar, its height should be that of the ruler, and the diameter 5, 7 or 9 times that of his fist.

Also close to the centre were the ruler's palace (later superseded by the governor's mansion), the principal wat, and a reservoir. The main road usually bisected the town, passing through the main gate and the centre, lined with clusters of houses which, with time, were increasingly converted into shophouses. Minor roads led on either side to other clusters within the town, skirting hills (as in Chiang Rai) and following river banks (as in Lamphun and Lampang). Markets of

The basis of rural northern life is rice, grown on the flood plain in a pattern of fields surrounding the village, maintained by weir and channel irrigation.

different sizes served different sections of the community. Near the outskirts of the town was the *ho seua*, or spirit house, the shrine for the spirits protecting the community and the ruler, built as a miniature house raised on six posts, under a large tree and enclosed by a fence.

Although recent urban development has masked much of this, many of the indvidual elements still exist (except the reservoir, which is often superseded by mains water supply). The picture of a traditional Lanna *muang* is an historical one, and to see more of the old way of life in the North we need to visit the villages, particularly those away from the main highways.

Village

In the face of 20th century changes, it is the village that best preserves Lanna community traditions. A typical Lanna village is located on the valley floor, by a stream or river, and surrounded by its rice fields. The road entering the village is its main thoroughfare; from it, lanes lead to clusters of houses, often sharing a common yard, and these are the basic units that make up the village. As in larger settlements, there is a village pillar, the *lak ban* or *jai ban*, made from a tree-trunk, in the village square, or *khuang ban*.

One of the surviving customs of village life: the dawn offering of food to monks from the local monastery.

Some, but not all villages have a *wat*, which can be located anywhere in the settlement, and if a few villages share a common *wat*, it may be built apart from them, either in its own tree-shaded enclosure among the rice fields or on the top of a small hill

At the edge of the village is the community's spirit house, the *ho seua*; like that of a town, it is set in its own fenced, sacred enclosure, ideally in the shade of a large tree, and takes the form of a small house raised on six wooden posts. Here, villagers make food and other offerings at an annual ceremony, which in former times was a serious matter. Holt Hallett,

a British engineer who visited Lanna in 1876, observed that "northern Thai villages were traditionally fenced and forbidden to strangers on the occasion of the sacrifice to the village tutelary spirit at the new year."

Tai Lü villages in particular are likely to preserve this tradition, and the offering ceremony varies in length, but is normally between one and three days, and during this period, boundary markers are set up around the area. In Tha Wang Pha in Nan, for example, the offering ceremony has been altered so that it takes place three times a year, each lasting three days. There is also another annual ceremony at the village pillar.

Field shacks, theng na, provide shelter and storage space during the working day, and are essential structures when the rice fields are a long walk from the village.

By custom, the village is surrounded by a *pa phae* ('goat forest') for domestic animals to forage in, although this once-essential common land is tending to disappear. Lanna tradition sets great store by trees and the forest for all kinds of practical and symbolic reasons. They give shade and keep the village cool and moist, provide food and building materials, protect the sources of streams in the hills, are inhabited by many spirits, good and evil, and are an inspiration, as we have seen, for the arts and crafts. In Lanna's hilly topography they were the dominant part of the landscape, essential for the survival of an agrarian people.

The rice harvest is one of the most important times of the Lanna agricultural year.

Beyond the *pa phae* are the village's fields, irrigated by channels and connected by narrow paths on the raised dykes at their edges. Scattered among them are field huts: simple shelters raised on piles consisting of an open platform and a thatch roof, used for resting and

taking lunch. Beyond the fields is the *pa ton nam* ('watershed forest'), stretching up into the hills, which are a home for wildlife that is used to supplement the diet and a protection, as its name indicates, for the upland water sources.

In whatever Lanna community, the houses are a constant, and the traditional design follows certain fixed principles. Even the differences between houses of the main ethno-lingustic group, the Tai Yuan, and those of the Shan and Tai Lü, are relatively small. All the important building activities connected with the house, from constructing a new house to digging a well, are by custom performed according to astrological calculations, involving various rites.

Ruen Kalae

The archetypal Lanna dwelling is teak-built and, because of a distinctive decorative feature at the top of the gable, is known as a '*kalae* house'. The *kalae* is a V-shaped design in wood, decoratively carved, that appears as an extension of the barge boards, and in fact was originally just that; the name means 'glancing crow'. It was unique to the North and found particularly around Chiang Mai, but because it is so identified with Lanna style, the *kalae* has been adopted as a motif for many modern buildings, and is as likely to be seen adorning a concrete petrol station as a traditional house. Nevertheless, in its pure form it is a part of the Lanna tradition, and denoted the house of an important member of the community. For this reason, it was never the most common type of dwelling, but its features embody the canon of Northern domestic architecture. For the same social reason, it is today found less and less in the North, since those people who would traditionally have built a teak house to such high standards now prefer modern, quasi-Western designs.

The well-preserved ruean kalae at the Old Chiang Mai Cultural Centre has two principal and one secondary building, each with the projecting roof carving that gives this Lanna house-style its name.

The old style of bedroom in a reuan kalae, which contains the "Auspicious Pillar" and the "Pillar of the Female Spirit."

The house platform, chan, is raised high above ground level and is a multi-purpose area for drying produce and bedding, and for relaxing in the evening.

Also on the house platform is a roofed shelf carrying jars of drinking water for guests.

A typical *ruen kalae* (*heuan kalae* in Northern dialect) comprises two pitched-roof buildings side by side, with a terrace, all raised high above the ground on wooden piles. The construction is skeletal, so that the pillars and frame bear all the weight and the walls are essentially prefabricated screens. On the longer sides of the buildings these walls slope outwards, in contrast to inward-sloping in central Thailand, and are in a single piece rather than panels (as is the case in central Thai houses). The windows have single shutters, and these open inwards. There is no ceiling, and from the beams is hung a wooden storage structure called a *khwan* for keeping various containers and utensils. The rooves are of either terracotta tiles or wooden shingles, with barge boards at the ends to prevent these being blown off the ends in a high wind, and gables that are traditionally aligned north-south; the opposite orientation is considered inauspicious, probably because it would be the same as the alignment of religious buildings, which usually face east.

The main staircase is in one of two styles: either at right angles up to a front terrace, or else sloped against the wall beneath the eaves, which are supported by a free-standing post called *sao laeng maa* ('post for leashing a dog'). At the bottom of the steps there is a water jar and dipper for washing feet before entering (shoes are always removed here). The terrace, typically decorated with potted plants, is surrounded by a balustrade and is an area used for drying chillies, garlic and the like, and for relaxing in the evening after the sun has lost its strength. Here also is a shelf at about waist-level, known as a *ran nam,* for terracotta water jars (*mo nam*) and ladles (*kra buey*) where

guests can drink, indicative of Lanna hospitality.

A step above the terrace and facing onto it is a roofed verandah known as a *toen*, part of the main building and in practice the principle living area of the house. Guests are received here, meals are eaten, male members of the family often sleep here, and so on. There is normally no furniture in the *toen* other than one or two low pedestal trays, as the floor itself is used for sitting (and is kept spotless). On one wall is an altar in the form of a shelf projecting from the wall; it carries a Buddha image and often a *tua peng*: a picture symbolising the year of birth of the house-owner.

A door from the *toen* leads to the main building's inner room, which is completely enclosed and private, being also the residence of the ancestral spirits. Guests may not cross the raised threshold without special invitation, and a carved wooden panel known as the *ham yom* over the door protects against evil. Inside is the bedroom for all family members except perhaps the son and father, who may sleep on the

Raised a step above the platform is the toen, the main living area, with an altar. This large house is in San Kamphaeng, near Chiang Mai.

Kalae and Ham Yon – buffalo symbols

Traditionally, the buffalo is an essential partner in the Thai farmer's life, and prosperity depends on its efforts. Consequently, the two decorative elements in a Lanna house symbolise the animal. The *kalae* is thought to represent a pair of buffalo horns, and indeed the form of the house has been likened to a broad-shouldered buffalo standing on strong legs. The *ham yon* wooden lintel over the entrance to the inner room has even more direct significance, the two roundels depicting the testicles of the buffalo (*ham* is an old Lanna word for testicles and *yon* derives from the Sanskrit *yantra*, a magical diagram for protection against evil). A new lintel had to be carved for each new owner with appropriate

offerings to ensure its magical power, and if there was an old lintel it had to be beaten to rid it of its accumulated magic. Interestingly, the size of the *ham yon* lintel, and so the width of the door, was either three or four times the length of the owner's foot - by association imposing a form of superiority on all those entering.

A kalae in the cross-shaped style, carved as a single attachment (above).

A ham yon lintel (left), the two circular motifs symbolising the buffalo's testicles.

A traditional Lanna kitchen at Ban Fai, Phrae, with its raised hearth in the form of a wooden tray packed with earth.

toen, with the northeast corner reserved for the most respected members. The individual sleeping areas are laid out with mat, mattress and hanging mosquito net, arranged so that the head is to the east (the sacred direction, in contrast to west, the direction of death, and the auspicious north; south is neutral). Clothes and personal items are kept at the foot of the mattress, usually in a free-standing cabinet, and there may also be a floor-level dressing table with mirror.

As the inner room also houses the ancestral spirits (a tradition derived from the Tai Yuan's Chinese origins), there is an Ancestral Shelf on which are placed offerings in the form of candles and flowers to the *phi pu ya* ('grandfather and grandmother spirits'). At the Thai New Year, the end of Buddhist Lent and on special occasions such as a marriage, special offerings are made, such as a chicken and money. Close to this shelf are the two most important pillars of the house, known respectively as the *sao mongkhon* ('auspicious pillar') and the

sao nang ('lady pillar'), which are
responsible for the fortune, wealth
and happiness of the household.
The sao mongkhon is the first pillar
erected when the house is built,
and the rituals accompanying this
were traditionally directed by an
individual known as a phor mor.
This pillar would have been carved
from a carefully selected tree,
carried and raised by villagers with
auspicious names such as Kham
('gold') and Ngoen ('silver'), and at
the base of its hole gold leaf, silver
coins and leaves of the jackfruit
tree would be placed.

The under-house area, between the teak
pillars, is used principally for storage,
and also certain chores.

   The second building, which is
sometimes slightly smaller, usually houses the kitchen, or is
occasionally used as a storage area. Standing side by side with the main
building, it is normally so close that the eaves almost meet, in which
case a gutter joins them so that rainwater can be collected and fed to a
large jar, and the walk space underneath is sunk 20-30 centimetres to
allow people to pass without stooping. In some Lanna houses, the two
buildings are joined to make one continuous area, and in this case a
long beam known as a mai paen tong separates the two floor sections
so that anyone walking around the kitchen area early will not vibrate
the boards in the sleeping area. In the kitchen, the traditional hearth in
Lanna is a raised tray, lined with zinc sheeting and packed with earth,
on which are charcoal-burning earth stoves or three stones enclosing
an open fire. Shelves carry jars of preserved foods and cooking
utensils, and containers hang from the beams. There may be a second
set of steps leading directly from the kitchen down to the yard for
carrying water, and possibly a rear extension to the terrace for food
preparation.
   The space underneath the house is a general working area; if there is
a loom, for example, it will be used here. In the yard is likely to be a

Shan houses are distinct from the
mainstream Lanna style, and generally
simpler. A 19th century mural (below
left) depicts basic pitched roofs, while
the twin-gabled house in the Yuam
valley (below) features extended eaves
and a thatch of large dried leaves.

rice granary (although occasionally there may just be a large rice basket in the second, kitchen building), raised high on piles for protection from water and animals, and sometimes with carved walls. Chickens and pigs may be kept below. There is also a well (possibly two) and there may be an open-sided barn for storing agricultural implements and straw, and for pounding rice in a large wooden mortar hewn from a tree trunk.

Ruen Mai Ching

A step below the *ruen kalae* in the community hierarchy is the standard teak house lacking the *kalae* decoration (although, as already mentioned, the traditional rules for using it are no longer followed, and we are looking rather at how Lanna houses used to be). Called simply a *ruen mai ching* ('real-wood house'), it is essentially a modest variation of the *ruen kalae*: smaller, lacking some features and constructed more simply, with less or no decoration. Other than this, all the principles of Lanna domestic architecture just described apply.

Ruen Mai Bua

The simplest and poorest Lanna dwelling (and still built for reasons of cost and simplicity in rural areas) is known as *ruen mai bua* ('bamboo house'). As its name suggests it has little or no wood, using instead bamboo for structure, floor and walls, and large dried *bai thong teun* leaves for roof thatching. It is usually a single building, containing the kitchen, and no larger than absolutely necessary for the family, although there are occasional exceptions, such as the double-gabled bamboo houses at Hang Dong and Mae Rim, near Chiang Mai.

Shan houses

There are a number of points of difference between Shan and Tai Yuan houses, although on average there are more similarities. The more substantial houses, like the *ruen mai ching*, have two buildings next to each other, but they are more likely to be of unequal size: a particular Shan belief. Most noticeable, however, is the gambrel roof, hipped with sloping ends that leave a small gable above. Also characteristic are the extended eaves, often on one side only, that reach almost to the ground and may shelter the rice granary. Given the size of this roof, there is usually no terrace, and the verandah is much more enclosed than the Tai Yuan *toen*.

Inside the house, the altar, known as the *keng pha la*, is usually more elaborate than the Tai Yuan equivalent. In some houses it is in a box-like structure called a *keng* that protrudes from the outer wall.

MONUMENTS AND MONASTERIES

The term *wat* is used in Thai to describe the majority of religious enclosures, and there is no completely satisfactory English term for it. The closest description is a Buddhist monastery, but most *wat* are also places of worship, and some have no monastery. In any case, the concept of monastery is rather different in Buddhism from Christianity, as all Thai males should be ordained into a *wat* at some time in their lives, if only for some weeks, and many still do. The *wat*, therefore, has inherently strong connections with the lay community, and is in constant use (the exception is the few forest *wat* which function as meditative retreats). As used here, the word applies equally to a monastery and to an archaeological monument.

A typical *wat* in Lanna, as elsewhere, is a walled enclosure containing a number of buildings with specific religious functions. Its size and the number of buildings depends partly on the community it serves and partly on its perceived importance, which could be influenced by a particularly sacred relic enshrined there or by an auspicious foundation. At one end of the scale, a small village *wat* with no wealthy donors may consist of one simple assembly hall and living quarters for a few monks; at the other, a major foundation such as Wat Phra That Haripunchai in Lamphun may have more than a dozen buildings and much ornate decoration. There is also, as elsewhere in

Footwear is always removed before entering the buildings of a monastery, here the main viharn at Wat Phra That Haripunchai in Lamphun.

The principal structures in a large monastery precinct, like Wat Phra That Lampang Luang, are the chedi, one or more viharn, and an ubosot.

One of the largest chedi in Lanna is the heavily gilded 46-metre Phra Maha That Chedi at Wat Phra That Haripunchai in Lamphun. The complex redenting of the high base is typically Lanna.

Thailand, a tradition of 'forest *wat*', built and used by the more reclusive *arannavasi* sect, for whom meditation and isolation are a key to Enlightenment, preferring not to be distracted by engaging in the daily life of the community. On occasion, the power of a sacred relic demanded that it be enshrined outside the city precincts. The Thai word for 'forest' is *pa*, so that names such as Wat Pa Sak and Wat Pa Phao indicate this kind of foundation, even when the monastery no longer functions in the same way. The traditional distance for locating a forest wat was 500 bow-lengths from a settlement: approximately one kilometre.

The sacred enclosure, or *putthawat*, is usually bounded by a rectangular wall, with the main entrance in the middle of the east side. Often, this wall may be lined on the inside with a cloister, or *phra rabieng*, and this is sometimes used as an informal shelter for Buddha images and for occasional religious furniture. The main monastic buildings and the Buddha images within them usually face east, in the direction of the rising sun, which is the direction in which the Buddha himself faced when he achieved Enlightenment, although in Lanna there are many valley-by-valley variations, particularly in the valleys of the Wang, Yom and Nan. The entrance may be guarded by *singh*, the mythical lion, and these are not uncommonly in the Burmese style. Very occasionally in Lanna, a *wat* would be fortified as a *wiang*, as at Wat Suan Dok in Chiang Mai and Wat Phra That Lampang Luang. Formerly, worshippers would remove their shoes at the entrance to the *putthawat*, as is still the case at Wat Lai Hin near Lampang, but now this is normally restricted to the *ubosot*.

The principal structure (when present) is the reliquary monument, or *chedi*. This is a *stupa*, the primary function of which is to enshrine a sacred Buddhist object. The most sacred are relics of the Buddha himself – a hair, for example, or a piece of bone – and a *chedi* containing such is called a *phra that*. With such a sacred structure, the base is often enclosed by a railing or wall, not only to guide ritual circumnambulation (always clockwise, which is *wien tien tang khwa* in Thai and *pradakshina* in Sanskrit) but to guard it from defilement. Women, for this reason, may be barred from the inner area. There are, of course, many more *phra that* than there are possible relics of the Buddha – more than two dozen in Lanna alone – and legend plays a rôle in the description. Another type of relic is what is called an 'indicative reminder' (*utthesik*), such as a Buddha image or footprint.

The normal position for a *chedi* is in the centre of the enclosure or offset slightly to the west, behind the viharn. Being always of durable material, usually brick, and usually in a conical or pyramidal shape that resists collapse, *chedi* tend to be the longest surviving of all religious structures. Lanna *chedi* are both distinctive and varied, combining many influences from outside the region, from as far as Sri Lanka and China, with native invention to create a rich diversity of form. The more important *chedi* are plated with thin sheets of *chang-go*, which are gilded copper sheets.

Western architectural terminology is poorly suited to describe the various parts of a *chedi*, which has no equivalent in Christianity, so that terms are often used rather haphazardly. This is further complicated by the fact that all the possible parts are not always present. Nevertheless, the full complement in Thailand is as follows, in descending order:

1. The *hti*, or sacred umbrella, found mainly on Burmese-style *chedi*.
2. The spire, often in the form of diminishing annulets (circular mouldings).
3. The shaft. When present, it occupies just a short section, and is slimmer than the spire above.
4. The *harmika*, a short square structure representing the throne of the Buddha.
5. The bell, which is the relic chamber. Note, however, that important *chedi* are often enlarged, or rather encased in a new structure, in which case the relic may be left in the original, smaller chedi.
6. The mouldings, often circular or octagonal, in a diminishing series. Traditionally these are in three groups, commemorating the Traiphum, or Three Worlds.
7. The base, which in Lanna *chedi* is distinctively large, often square and redented at the corners.
8. The plinth, consisting of one or more steps supporting the base.
9. A terrace or platform, sometimes with an enclosed walkway for ritual circumambulation.

While the ultimate origin of the *chedi* was the early Indian burial mound, the source of the form was Sri Lanka, in particular the *dagoba* of Anuradhapura and Polonnaruwa. As the religion spread throughout Asia, the shapes were modified in every conceivable way, even borrowing from Brahmanic temples, such as those built by the Khmer. By the time Lanna was settled, there was a tremendous variety of sources to draw on. The earliest *chedi* were built by the Mon, settled around Lamphun (Haripunjaya), Lampang and Phrae, and the type example remaining is the Mahapol or Suwan Chang Kot Chedi at Wat Ku Kut (*see page 118*): square in plan, stepped and with diminishing tiers, each lined with niches containing images. This became an icon for the early Tai builders, who made several copies.

As the Lanna kingdom expanded from the end of the 13th century onwards, *chedi* design developed, drawing on the bell-shape from Sri Lanka as modified at Sukhothai, sometimes surrounding the base with the foreparts of elephants (another Sinhalese invention to represent the animals supporting Mount Meru). A general Lanna trend,

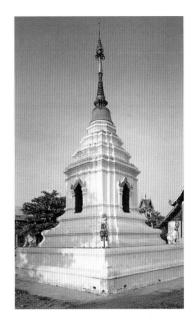

Plastered brick chedi of Wat Muan Ngoen Kaung in Chiang Mai, featuring a miniature bell and large redented base, with niches on all four sides.

Gilded chedi at Wat Nantharam in Chiang Mai, in which the circular mouldings representing the Three Worlds of Buddhist cosmology have been enlarged, and the bell reduced.

Ribbed spire, summit parasol and splayed, multi-tiered base are typical of a Burmese-style chedi, as at Wat Saen Fang in Chiang Mai.

The principal viharn at Wat Phra That Lampang Luang displays the pure Lanna features of open sides and a flaring multi-tiered roof.

however, was to increase the size of the base relative to the mouldings, bell and spire. The beginnings of this trend can be seen in the late Sukhothai period, as at Wat Chedi Soong where the base is high, square and redented at the corners, and this combination became quintessentially Lanna.

Redenting was a notable feature of Khmer architecture, particularly in the 12th century, when it was used to spectacular effect at Phimai, Angkor Wat and elsewhere to create distinctive towers, and is achieved by cutting back the corners into a series of angles. In a Lanna *chedi*, the redenting not only articulates the monotony of a plain cube, but adds a strong vertical component to increase the apparent height, at the same time helping to integrate the base with the round *chedi* above by reducing its corners. This technique was further developed by redenting the corners so much that the base became virtually octagonal, and in some *chedi* this octagonal plan was extended all the way to the top. The square and octagon add a directional element, sometimes re-inforced by niches containing images of the Buddha, and the alignment is to the cardinal points. The octagon also recalls the Brahmanic *dikpala*, or guardians of the eight directions, and the eight directions and gates of Chinese cosmology.

Also distinctive of Lanna is the Burmese influence, nowhere more evident than in the *chedi*. It dates, not from Burmese rule in the 16th-18th centuries, but from the influx of Burmese teak industry workers in the 19th century. The typical form, of which the classic example is the Shwedagon Pagoda in Rangoon, is round, splayed at the base and tapering strongly in two concave sweeps to an attenuated ribbed spire, topped with a *hti*, or multi-tiered gilded parasol. Gilded parasols also typically mark the corners of the *chedi*'s terrace, and in attendance may be Burmese-style guardian lions (*singh* in Thai but *chinthe* in Burmese) and some of the 37 *nat* spirits. The late-settled valleys of the Pai and Yuam Rivers have exclusively Burmese *chedi*.

A few exceptional *chedi* designs in Lanna have Indian and possibly Chinese origins. Wat Chedi Yot in Chiang Mai and a copy in Chiang Rai are loosely based on the Mahabodhi Temple in Bodh Gaya, India, although possibly via the copy in Pagan rather than directly. Three *chedi* in Chiang Mai (at Wat Rampoeng, Wat Phuak Hong and Chedi Prong) have circular diminishing tiers, which may or may not reflect Yunnanese influence.

A constant in Lanna *wat* is the gabled hall known as the viharn. If there is only one monastic building it is likely to be this multi-functional structure, used as an assembly hall for the laity as well as for monks, and usually containing the *wat*'s principal Buddha image at the far end. A notable feature of Lanna *wat* is that the viharn is larger than the ubosot – the consecrated hall for monks – whereas in Siamese Thailand the rôles are usually reversed. The reason for this is that historically, and to some extent even today, Lanna people placed greater store by the ordination of novices (which can take place in a *viharn*) than the full ordination of monks (which must use the *ubosot*). This may well be a Burmese influence, and one local belief is that the *ubosot* itself was an import from Ayutthaya.

The floor plan is rectangular, redented to follow the roof tiers and portico; the roof is gabled with a single ridge, and you enter from the end facing the Buddha image. The *viharn* is typically on the main axis of the enclosure and so usually facing east, the first building you see on entering. *Viharn* in Lanna have many special features that set them apart from those in central Thailand, which tend to follow, with few changes, an Ayutthayan model established in the 18th century. Lanna structures, in contrast, tend to be more dynamic, more 'homely' and more varied. The walls are particularly low, which by bringing the eaves closer to the ground makes the overall proportions more squat and broad further enhanced by the roof-line.

A typical roof has three superimposed tiers, of which the lowest is over the portico, but the

A village viharn near Chiang Mai, with a three-tiered roof and panelled gable, the entrance guarded by two naga balustrades.

Naga balustrades at Wat Chet Yot flank the steps. The two mythical snakes issue from the mouths of makara water beasts.

A distinctive Lanna detail of façades is the eyebrow pelmet (top).

The projecting board under the eaves, the phaeng lae, carved with the shape of an elephant at Wat Rampoeng, Chiang Mai (above).

number can vary from one to four. In addition, each tier has an upper and lower section. In the classic Lanna style, both of these sections have a gentle concave curve and the lower section is at a shallower angle. The combination of all this and the low sides is a flaring, ground-hugging roof-line, often likened to a mother hen spreading her wings to protect her chicks: *hang mae*. The tiers and sections all overlap by a small amount, and the gaps may be open for ventilation, or panelled or stuccoed.

There are other distinctively Lanna features around the portico. The short staircase is typically flanked with a balustrade in the shape of an undulating naga – *nak sadung* – and the treatment of this mythical serpent often shows considerable flair and variation. The heads of the *naga* rear up flamboyantly, and quite commonly resemble dragons more than snakes, probably drawing on Chinese influences. On closer inspection, the mouth of another creature can be seen at the *naga's* neck; this is the mythical water beast known as a *makara*, combining features of a crocodile, elephant and fish, and it is disgorging the *naga*. This motif derives from the Khmer, who also used *naga-makara* combinations as entrance balustrades, with the cosmological significance of a 'bridge' between the secular and sacred worlds. Between the two inner pillars of the portico at the end of these balustrades is a pelmet known as the *kong khieu* ('eyebrow pelmet'), representing the eyebrows of the Buddha, and this is often repeated left and right on the winged gables known as the *na ban pik nok* ('bird wing gable'). Occasionally this has a hanging projection in the middle that is seen by some as the Buddha's nose.

Yet another extra area available for decoration is the side panel under the eaves of the tiered roof, known as the *phaeng lae*; this again is unique to Lanna, as central Thai tiered roofs do not have an interval of this depth between them. The floor plan at the front of the viharn is redented because of the two reductions of the portico and staircase. The door may often be framed by an elaborate decorative arch, usually in stucco, called a *sum* or *sum khong:* another Lanna feature.

Inside, the lower Lanna proportions give a greater feeling of intimacy than in a typical central Thai viharn, and the roof beams are nearly always exposed, so that you can easily see the building's beam frame structural system, derived ultimately from China. The teak pillars are decorated with paint, gold-leaf or glass mosaic, or a combination of the three. The Buddha images sit on an altar at

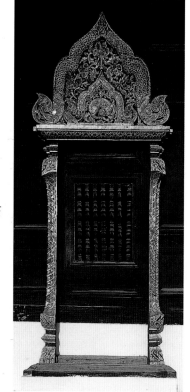

An elaborate sum over a window of the viharn at Wat Phan Tao, Chiang Mai (right).

the far – usually west – end, and may be flanked by a *thammat*, or pulpit, and *sattaphan*, or candle holder, both decorated. A special Lanna feature found in some *viharn* in place of an altar is a *ku*, a reliquary for a Buddha image resembling an ornate miniature *chedi*. This tends to be for principal images that are small and is a way of enhancing their presence; *ku* means a sacred cave or grotto and the term refers to the small space for the Buddha image at the heart of the structure. If there are murals, they usually depict scenes from the *jataka* tales, with the wall over the main door often reserved for the Defeat of Mara (*see page 102*). Even in the traditional open-sided design of building, wooden panels descend from the roof to just below eave-height, and these often carry murals.

The quantity and style of decoration on the outside of the viharn is yet another Lanna characteristic, mostly carved wood but also including inlaid coloured glass (a possible Indian or Burmese influence) and stucco. In more wealthy *wat*, gilding is used extensively. The principal decorated space is the front gable and the winged gables on either side, including the *kong khieu*, where they exist. The designs are many and varied, reflecting local tastes and the abilities of the carvers, and idiosyncrasy is a common and entertaining feature. The tendril motif of intertwining plants is extensively used, as are geometrical patterns and the inclusion of animals from the Chinese 12-year cycle. Many gables are divided into rectangular panels.

Roof decorations, some of which are structural, follow the pattern of all Thai viharn, though with some Lanna distinctions. The bargeboard, or *pan lom*, which covers the end of the gable, has the function of preventing loose tiles or shingles from falling off, and is either plain – which is generally regarded as the pure Lanna form – or treated decoratively as the downward sloping body of a *naga*, with the head rearing upwards at the end. In the latter case, the crested projections in a row along the upper edge are called the *bai raka*, and the lower roof finials in the form of upturned *naga* heads are known as *hang hong*, although occasionally they may be plain and rounded in the *tua ngao* style of domestic architecture. The end roof-ridge finial is the enigmatically titled *cho fa* ('sky cluster'), and although often highly

The highly decorated gable of the ubosot at Wat Chai Sri Chum, Chiang Mai.

The bargeboard typically ends in the reared head of a naga (left).

A less common alternative bargeboard design ends in the leaf-like *tua ngao*, as in the *ubosot* at Wat Phra Singh, Chiang Mai (above).

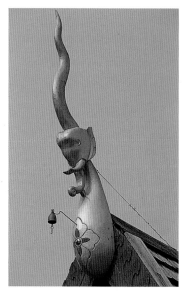

Cho fa roof ridge finials are in various degrees of abstraction, from stylised versions of a garuda with its beak curved down (left) to a representational carving of the strange *hasadiling* (far right), a swan with the head of an elephant.

stylised it usually represents a *garuda*; the full symbolism is that this mythical bird grasps the tails of its mortal enemy, the *naga* on the bargeboard. This finial often has a beak-like projection and is known properly as a *cho fa pak krut* ('garuda beak finial'), but Lanna invention once again comes into play, and the *cho fa* may even be depicted as a different creature, such as a *makara* or *hasadiling* (an elephant-headed bird). Occasionally the roof ridge has a central finial in the form of an umbrella of state.

Lanna eave-brackets, which are in a row along each outer long wall, are distinctive and different from those in central Thailand, which tended to use the *kanok* vine motif. In Lanna there are two types: the *hu chang* ('elephant ear') design, which is a triangular piece of wood,

and the several designs of a specific figure. The latter is most commonly a *naga*, the design being called *nakkhatan* in Northern dialect, but others include the monkey king Hanuman, *kinnari*, and zodiacal animals. When many *naga* are intertwined, this is known as *nak kieo* ('coiled *naga*')

Traditionally, wood was used throughout the building – pillars, beams, panels and the entire roof construction including the shingles – and the sides were open except at the rear. Although restoration has in many cases changed this by substituting concrete pillars for teak, ceramic tiles for shingles, and adding walls, there are still a few *viharn* in this original style, notably the Viharn Nam Tam at Wat Phra That Lampang Luang, probably the oldest surviving wooden building in Lanna. With open-sided buildings, the roof reaches closer to the ground for protection against wind and rain.

The roof-line and proportions are the most distinctive characteristics of Lanna *viharn*, but as there are no surviving wooden buildings older than 500 years, their architectural origins are not obvious. However, they do contrast with central Thai buildings and with the ancient tall brick *viharn* of Ayutthaya and Sri Lanka, and are strikingly similar to gabled buildings north of here: the *sim* of Laotian wat and Yunnanese Buddhist buildings. This alone suggests that the low sweeping roof in concave overlapping sections may have come with the Tai from China.

In appearance similar to the *viharn*, the *ubosot* is the consecrated ordination hall, used exclusively by monks. Women may not usually enter, and the building may even be locked; it is normal to ask permission to visit, and shoes must always be removed. Daily prayers are held here, as well as other ceremonies including the ordination of new monks, and there is one or more Buddha images at the far end. The consecration of an *ubosot* involves burying nine stone spheres called *luk nimit* to demarcate the sacred space: one at the centre, four at the corners and four at the cardinal points in the middle of each

Eave brackets are an excuse for decorative woodwork, which in Lanna normally features a coiled naga. At Wat Thon Kwain near Chiang Mai (above left), a garuda is included, while the bright colours of the series at Wat Tha Fa Thai in the upper Yom Valley (above) are typical of Tai Lü design.

At Wat Bun Yeun in the lower Nan valley, each individual bracket incorporates a different figure.

An eave bracket at Wat Phan Tao, Chiang Mai, carved in a floral design that makes the shapes of a parrot's head (above).

A luk nimit, or sacred marker sphere for an ubosot, waiting to be buried at an inauguration ceremony at Wat Hua Wiang, Mae Hong Son (above right).

The elegant library ho trai at Wat Phra That Haripunchai, Lamphun.

side. In this way, the eight compass directions and the axis are covered. The Central Thai custom of placing upright stone slabs called *bai sema* over the spheres that surround the building has now spread to Lanna, and they make it easy to identify.

All the stylistic features of *viharn* apply to the *ubosot*, which is also known as the *bot*. When there are both types of building in the enclosure, the *ubosot* is likely to be smaller because it needs only accommodate the resident monks, not the laity. It is most typically placed to the left of the *viharn* as you face it and set back: that is, usually on the south side and offset to the west. One special type, or rather location, is a *bot nam* ('water bot'), built on piles in the middle of a pond.

One of the most exquisite structures, although normally found only in important *wat*, is the library or scripture repository, known in Thai as the *ho trai*. Its original function, no longer needed since printed texts became available, was the safe storage of hand-written and illustrated Buddhist manuscripts. These were written on long strips of dried palm leaf bound together in bundles. Placed in decorated manuscript chests or cabinets, they were stored in this small building raised high off the ground as protection from the ravages of termites and damp, either on piles or on a brick base. *Ho trai* are often roofed as if miniature *viharn*, and their scale made it easy to lavish detailed decorative attention on them.

There are a number of other monastic buildings which may or may not be present in any particular enclosure. One, usually very small, is the *ho rakhang*. A bell is struck to call monks to devotions, to announce noon (after which the monks cannot eat) and to toll the end of the day's work, and may be housed in a free-standing belfry (*rakhang* means 'bell') or simply hung from a pole.

Another reminder of the Buddha in a few *wat* is a stylised Footprint, a *Phra Putthaba*t, usually in stone and

The ho trai of a village wat in the Mae Chaem valley, Wat Pa Daet.

often based on legendary prints such as that on the summit of Adam's Peak in Sri Lanka. Very occasionally, as at Wat Phra That Doi Tung, it is in the open air, but normally it is enshrined in a small chapel, commonly called a *Ho Phra Putthabat*. There is no standard form for this building; that at Wat Si Khom Kham, Phayao, is a small gabled chapel paired with the ubosot, while that at Wat Phra That Lampang Luang is a raised square brick structure.

In central Thailand, larger *wat* may have a preaching hall, called a *sala gan parian*, gabled like a *viharn* and open-sided, but there are only a few of these imports in Lanna. The most notable is at Wat Suan Dok, Chiang Mai. Then, sheltering a variety of devotional images, often of purely local significance, there may be a *mondop*, which is a pavilion, usually open-sided, square in plan and with a multi-tiered pyramidal roof rising to a central peak. In Lanna, *mondop* often show Burmese influence; there is a fine example at Wat Phra Kaeo Don Tao, Lampang.

Finally, there are the monks' living quarters, traditionally in the form of small, one-roomed buildings known as *kuti*. More and more, however, these are being replaced by ordinary modern buildings. Again traditionally, the kuti were in an area of the *wat* known as the *sanghawat*, outside the *putthawat*.

The monastery bell, sometimes as simple as this, is used to sound the times of work, devotion and eating.

Monks' robes hanging to dry below the raised platform of a Shan monastery in Phrae.

Phrae style

Travelling across Lanna, it is easy to see the many small variations from district to district and *wat* to *wat*. Nevertheless, the political and cultural dominance of Chiang Mai over the centuries has meant that the art and architecture of the central Ping valley has virtually become synonymous with Lanna style. Certainly the buildings just described, and in particular the design of the *viharn* and *ubosot,* are the most common, but the valleys to the west and east have their own, less noticed, traditions. The valley of the Yom, being two watersheds distant from Chiang Mai and more easily reached from Uttaradit and Sukhothai, developed some distinctive features of its own. These are described more fully in the valley description later, but the most

A distinctive feature of the Phrae style, as in this viharn, is the substitution of a row of vertical 'wind gaps' for windows.

A carved guardian figure of a yak on a pillar of the ho trai of Wat Luang, Phrae, in the brightly painted local naïve style.

notable is the use of thick walls without windows: an alternative way of dealing with the heat to the open-sided low-eaved design of Chiang Mai. In place of windows, the buildings traditionally have what are called *chong lom* ('wind gaps') – vertical slits separated by thick, square balusters – and small cross-shaped openings. Whitewashed inside and out, the buildings stay cool, with more illumination than you would expect. The influence of Sukhothai can be seen in some of the Buddha imagery, and of central Thai architecture in taller proportions to the monastic buildings. The preference for painting the carved decorations in a number of colours, however, is local.

Tai Lü wat

The ethnic sub-group that emigrated from Sipsongpanna in Yunnan, the Tai Lü, brought their own architectural ideas, and these can be seen in particular in the upper Nan valley, as well as in isolated pockets around Lanna where the Tai Lü arrived after forced re-settlement. A classic Tai Lü building, which often combines both *viharn* and *ubosot*, is recogniseable for the use of a hipped roof on the lower one or two tiers, with just a small pitched roof at the top and so a small gable. The eaves are decorated with an open fretwork strip, or *choeng chai*, in a water-drop design, and a feature of the gable is a mirror, intended to drive away evil forces by reflection, in the Chinese manner.

As in Phrae, the walls tend to be thick, with small windows. The gaps between the tiers are usually left open for ventilation rather than being closed off with panels as in the normal Lanna style. Inside, long woven cloth banners known as *tung* hang from the ceiling or the pillars. The most popular colours for these are red, black and white, and often include horizontal strips of animals such as horses, elephants or *hong*. The pedestal for the Buddha image is distinctive, typically a large masonry structure with encircling *nagas* known as *nak ballang*.

The Tai Lü viharn at Wat Ton Laeng in the upper Nan valley.

Shan monasteries

While Burmese *chedi* were in many instances built in the grounds of Lanna *wat,* some monastic enclosures are purely in the Burmese style, built by and for Shan immigrants, most of them in the second half of the 19th century. Although there may sometimes be an *ubosot*, it is more traditional for there to be just one monastic building: a multi-functional structure for prayer, preaching, monks' living quarters, school and museum. Raised on piles and customarily built of unpainted and minimally decorated wood, the multi-functional Shan monastery is normally rectangular in plan and open-sided. Its different functions are confined to specific areas which are demarcated by both walls and different levels. Also, there is no tradition of orienting it towards the east.

At another Tai Lü monastery, Wat Nong Daeng, the space below the eaves is decorated with a fretwork strip, and mirrors to ward off evil.

From a distance, its most distinctive feature is the complex, multi-tiered roof. As the entire building is often made up of several adjoining structures, all on piles, there are often several interlocking rooves, sometimes in a variety of shapes. At first glance there seems to be little order to this, and a large monastery may have many superstructures, each with multiple tiers of roofs. However, the basic design is a lower hipped roof – or a set of interlocking hipped roofs at the same height – with one principal superstructure in the centre in the form of a false storey. This is usually pitched, with west and east-facing gables, and in two or three tiers.

Embellishments to this basic form can include extensions to the superstructure facing out in different directions, each with multiple tiered rooves, and smaller superstructures surrounding the central one. Then again, there may be pitched or hipped rooves that are slightly separate from the main roof, and sometimes the upper pitched rooves are at right angles, so that the gables face north and south. One common result of all this is a large number of tiny roof sections.

Despite such a decorative appearance, there is a highly practical basis for Shan *wat* rooves in dealing with the heat. The principal roof over the altar allows a very high ceiling, and windows in the upper walls draw hot air upwards. The subsidiary multi-tiered roofs are in fact false storeys, and have purely this heat-extracting function.

The height of all these superstructures is sufficient to warrant a certain amount of decoration to their outer walls, and this is typically geometric, with redented rectangular outlines enclosing a roundel or flower head design. The rooves themselves are traditionally shingled, but the Shan eagerly embraced the use of corrugated iron to the point where this almost has a tradition of its own, and is often painted. The eaves and bargeboards are traditionally fringed with intricate fretwork, but this is gradually being replaced with filigree in a zinc-tin alloy. Yet another roof type makes an appearance on some monasteries: the *pyatthat*, which features a tall series of diminishing tiers (as many as nine in some instances), topped with a spire and representing Mount Meru. It may grace a mondop or an entrance staircase.

Whether elaborately or simply roofed, the staircase leads up to a verandah furnished with benches. A short step up from this is the building proper, and standing in front of the Buddha images, you can appreciate the wonderful contrast between an exterior of plain,

A classic example of a Shan monastery in teak – Wat Chom Sawan, Phrae – with multi-tiered pyatthat over the entrance porches.

The elaborately decorated ceiling at Wat Chom Sawan.

untreated wood and the lavishly decorated interior. The coffered wooden ceiling above the first level is low enough to display intricate carvings and an exuberant use of glass inlay. Ahead, the altar and images are directly under the tallest part of the roof, and the high ceiling may also be beautifully decorated.

There are usually three levels in the building, each separated by a step of some 20 centimetres. Basically, the lowest level is for the laity, the next for the monks, and the highest for the Buddha images at the heart of the building complex. In practice, the distinctions are not rigidly kept, and while the second level in front of the altar is where the monks sit during ceremonies and on festival days, for the rest of the year the laity can use it to approach the Buddha images. The living accommodation for the monks usually surrounds the central area, while the abbot has his own area, often at the same level as the altar, with a private room.

The flaring, bell-shaped chedi in Burmese style at Wat Chetawan, Chiang Mai.

ICONOGRAPHY

Lanna has always been strongly Theravada Buddhist, even more so than Siam, the monarchy of which adopted Brahmanic traditions to help strengthen its rule by divine association. Theravada, which means 'Doctrine of the Elders', is the form of Buddhism practised today in Southeast Asia and Sri Lanka, and stresses that the path to enlightenment be followed by individual observance and effort, and most effectively in a monastic life. The other major form, Mahayana ('Great Vehicle'), which is practised in the Himalayas and East Asia is less rigorous, and admits enlightened beings – *bodhisattva* – that can assist man. The only *bodhisattva* recognised by some (but not all) Theravada Buddhists is the Future Buddha, Maitreya, who is waiting in the Tushita Heaven before descending to Earth.

Fulfilling some of the rôles of *bodhisattvas* in the iconography illustrated in monasteries are the previous incarnations of the Buddha. Gautama, the historical Buddha, who lived in the sixth century BC (the Thais hold his death to have occurred in 543 BC), is believed to have had 27 previous lives, and these form the basis of the 547 *Jataka*, or birth tales. These are the main subject of religious murals, and are treated principally as morality tales.

Brahmanic motifs, some of which are always present in Lanna religious architecture, are subsidiary, and the Hindu gods are only rarely depicted, in contrast to the rest of the country, where gods such as Indra riding his three-headed elephant, and the man-bird Garuda, are common figures on gable decorations. A third source of occasional imagery is animism: mainly the local spirit world that derives from the forests and mountains, but also the Burmese pantheon of the 37 *nats*.

Buddhist Imagery

It is not certain when the Tai encountered Theravada Buddhism, but by the 11th century they were in contact with the Mon of Haripunjaya and with the Burmese of Pagan. Moreover, the centre from which they spread mainly southwards, Yunnan, was certainly on trade and cultural routes connecting China and India, and they were exposed not only to Mahayana Budhhism but to contemporary movements in India such as the art of the Pala and Sena in Bengal.

The primary source of Theravada Buddhist faith on the mainland of southeast Asia at the time when the Tai were moving into Lanna was the Mon, who occupied the lower valleys of the Irrawaddy and the Chao Phraya. They were early converts to Buddhism, and when the religion fell into decline in India, they kept contact with Kanchipuram in southern India and with Sri Lanka, which took on the mantle of the centre of world Theravada Buddhism. They had a refining influence in art and culture on both the Burmese and the Tai.

Another source of exposure may have been Burma. Pagan's King Anawratha, a fervent convert to Theravada Buddhism, conducted a campaign in Lanna at some time in the middle of the 11th century, according to the chronicles, and this may have introduced images of the Buddha to the area.

The figure of the Buddha is represented in one of a very few

Buddha images at Wat Suan Dok, Chiang Mai.

positions, or *sana*: seated, standing, reclining or walking. Overall, in Lanna, the most common is seated, with normally two variations: the full lotus position in which the soles of both feet are uppermost, and the half-lotus. In such Mon-Haripunjaya images that survive, those appearing in niches are usually standing in the *samapada asana*. The reclining position, which is usuallly treated monumentally, relates to the Buddha's passage into nirvana. Walking images were an invention of the Sukhothai school, and where they appear in Lanna art, as for example in 15th century Nan, they are evidence of Sukhothai influence.

Reclining Buddha, Phrae-style.

Of particular significance is the *mudra*, or ritual gesture in Pali, of the figure, which is usually related to an event in the Life of the Buddha, and is called *pang* in Thai. There are six main gestures: *abhaya*, giving reassurance, in which the palm of the right hand is held outward with the fingers extended upward; *bhumisparsa*, or touching the Earth ('*bhumi*'), with which the Buddha at his Enlightenment called the Earth-goddess to witness his victory over Mara and the forces of evil; *dharmachakra*, the gesture of teaching, or turning the *Dharmachakra* (the Wheel of the Law), in which the right hand is held in front of the chest, its thumb and index finger joined and touching one finger of the left hand, the palm of which is turned inwards; *dhyana*, the attitude of meditation, in which both hands, fingers extended, rest in the lap, right above left; *vara*, signifying benediction, in which the right hand is extended palm outwards; and *vitarka*, the gesture of preaching and giving a sermon, performed with one hand or both by joining thumb and forefinger, palm held outwards. The most common of these in Lanna art is the *bhumisparsa mudra*.

The normal attire for a Buddha image is that of a monk, which traditionally comprises three cloth garments, normally saffron yellow in Thailand. The *antaravaska* is the undergarment, tied at the waist with or without a belt. Over this is worn the *uttarasanga*, or robe, which covers both shoulders or just the left. Last comes the *sanghati*, a type of shawl, which folded is draped over the left shoulder, hanging down more at the back than at the front.

Having attained enlightenment, the Buddha became a *mahapurusa*, or 'great man', and as specified in early Sanskrit and Pali texts was distinguished by auspicious marks or signs (*laksana*). There are 32 principal signs, and the artist attempts to reproduce some or most of them as faithfully as possible. The strangeness of certain *laksana*, such as projecting heels, arms like an elephant's trunk, chin like a mango and a nose like a parrot's beak, makes a literal representation difficult, and the realism of sculpture, bas-relief and painting varies according to the art stye of the culture and period.

Offerings to a standing Buddha at Wat Phra That Doi Tung.

Brahmanic Imagery

The Brahmanic symbolism in Lanna *wat* comes from Khmer iconography, as is clear from motifs such as the *naga* balustrade, which occurred nowhere else prior to the Khmer empire. Many of the icons are drawn from a mythology of serpents and fantastic creatures which preceded their Brahmanic use, and can almost be considered animist.

Naga roof finial.

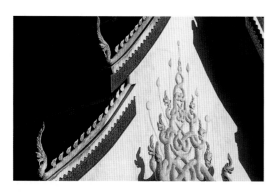

Stucco naga pediment.

Makara.

Naga

The most ubiquitous mythological creature is the *naga*, serpent-god who inhabits the watery underworld, deriving ultimately from ancient snake-worship that pre-dated the major religions. It is called *nak* in Thai, although we will continue to use the more familiar Sanskrit term. *Naga* appear extensively in Brahmanic art (individual *naga* play a rôle in two creation myths involving Vishnu) and were particularly admired for architectural decoration by the Khmer, who were one source of inspiration for Lanna. Nevertheless, the animistic origins of the creature are never far below the surface, and *naga*-worship was long practiced by the Shan, even up to the late 19th century.

They act as guardians – for the earth's treasure, water and prosperity – and are also associated with rainbows, which in turn are seen as a bridge between heaven and earth. For these reasons, the Khmer invented a special use for them as balustrades, not found in India. This idea was adopted by the Tai for balustrades flanking the entrances to the *wat* enclosure and to individual buildings, and is very much a Lanna feature. Moreover, Tai craftsmen took a particular delight in developing the *naga*'s appearance, extending the body into an undulating form, sometimes a few hundred feet in length, and embellishing the rearing head. Often, the *naga* in this rôle takes on the appearance of a dragon, and this probably betrays an early influence from China.

Naga guardians appear in Lanna monasteries as pairs of balustrades lining steps and entrances. They also sometimes feature as an arch to niches and doorways, following the Khmer use. Their other rôle in a *viharn* or *ubosot* is as roof decoration, both as lower roof finials with their bodies forming the barge-board, and as *khan tuey*, or eave brackets. Whereas the Khmer usually represented *naga* with several heads (always odd in number and as many as nine), in Lanna art they usually have a single head.

Makara

This composite marine monster also derives ultimately from India, where it appears in some temples such as the 7th-century Draupadi Ratha at Mamallapuram. It also appears in Sinhalese art, as at Abhayagiri Vihara and Ruvanveliseya Dagoba in Anuradhapura, and very commonly in Khmer architectural decoration. The *makara* is a mixture of animals including, with variations, the body of a crocodile, an elephant-like trunk, claws, scales and a large-jawed head, and has an intimate relationship with the *naga*. What at first glance appears to be just a *naga* framing an arch or flanking a staircase is, in fact, the pair of creatures, with the *makara* disgorging the serpent. They are so fused, however, that the *makara*'s head blends into the body of the *naga*. In bas-relief, as on arches, the *makara* is shown in profile.

Singh and chinthe

The mythical lion, or *singh*, is a distinctive Lanna guardian figure, sculpted large and in the round. The influence is Burmese, and they are usually treated in the Burmese style as a *chinthe*.

Kala

This guardian face derives from Khmer temples, where it was very popular as a central device on stone lintels. An adopted Indian motif, its menacing face with bared teeth and bulging eyes protects the entrance to a sacred building from evil spirits; its name comes from the Sanskrit for 'blue-black'. Another Sanskrit term for it is *kirtimukha* ('glory face'). In the act of devouring itself, it is usually depicted without a body, and from the Khmer treatment sometimes has tendrils of vegetation emerging from the corners of its mouth and grasped by its hands. Legend has it that Shiva was so enraged at the impertinence of this demon in demanding a victim to eat that he commanded the *kala* to devour itself, thus it appears without a lower jaw. Because of similarities in their histories, the *kala* is often confused with Rahu.

Rahu

In one of the most popular Brahmanic creation myths, the gods and demons, in a rare display of co-operation, churn the Ocean of Milk by pulling alternately on a giant serpent wound around Mount Mandara, in order to release *amrita*, the elixir of immortality. Vishnu commands the operation, which is nearly thwarted by the demon Rahu, who attempts to steal the *amrita*. Vishnu, furious, decapitates him, and Rahu's revenge has ever since been to try and swallow the sun and moon at the time of eclipses. When he appears as a guardian over a *viharn* entrance, he takes the place of a *kala,* and the only obvious difference is the disc of the sun or moon; the two tend to be confused. This is the original myth from India, and followed by the Khmer, but in Lanna there are more homely versions, such as one in which the Sun, Moon and Rahu are brothers. Rahu is humiliated by the other two on a visit to a *wat*, and takes his revenge for ever more once they have all died. Another similar version is Cinderella-like, with a cast of two sisters (the Sun and Moon) and a slave-girl whom they abuse.

Town and city pillar

The *lak muang*, or city pillar, is the abode of the guardian spirits of a Tai community. Occasionally, in cities, the pillar takes the form of a *linga*: the essence of the god Shiva from the Hindu Trinity. In turn, the *linga* derives from a phallus. This syncreticism is not a Lanna feature, however, and occurs elsewhere in the country, such as at Yala in the south. Its source is the Khmer Empire, where stone *linga* were installed in the central shrine of temples, mounted in a pedestal representing an abstract *yoni*, or female organ. Most Khmer *linga* had three sections to represent the Trinity; the lowest was square in section, representing Brahma, the middle octagonal representing Vishnu, and the top round, representing Shiva. Some, known as *mukha linga* ('face linga'), had one or more faces carved at the top.

Rahu.

Zodiacal Animals

The twelve years of the lunar cycle play an important part in Lanna culture, even to the point of being featured prominently in some wat. The chedi at Wat Phra That Lampang Luang, for instance, is dedicated to the Year of the Ox, and so is especially important to people born in that year. Where a building features one of the animals on the pediment, it is an indication that the person who commissioned it was born in that year. The twelve cyclical years, which derive from the Tai's Chinese heritage, are:-

1. Year of the Rat (pi chuad)
2. Year of the Ox (pi chalu)
3. Year of the Tiger (pi khan)
4. Year of the Rabbit (pi tho)
5. Year of the Dragon (pi marong)
6. Year of the Snake (pi maseng)
7. Year of the Horse (pi mamia)
8. Year of the Goat (pi mamae)
9. Year of the Monkey (pi wog)
10. Year of the Cock (pi raka)
11. Year of the Dog (pi cho)
12. Year of the Pig (pi kun), but in Lanna this becomes the Year of the Elephant (pi chang)

54

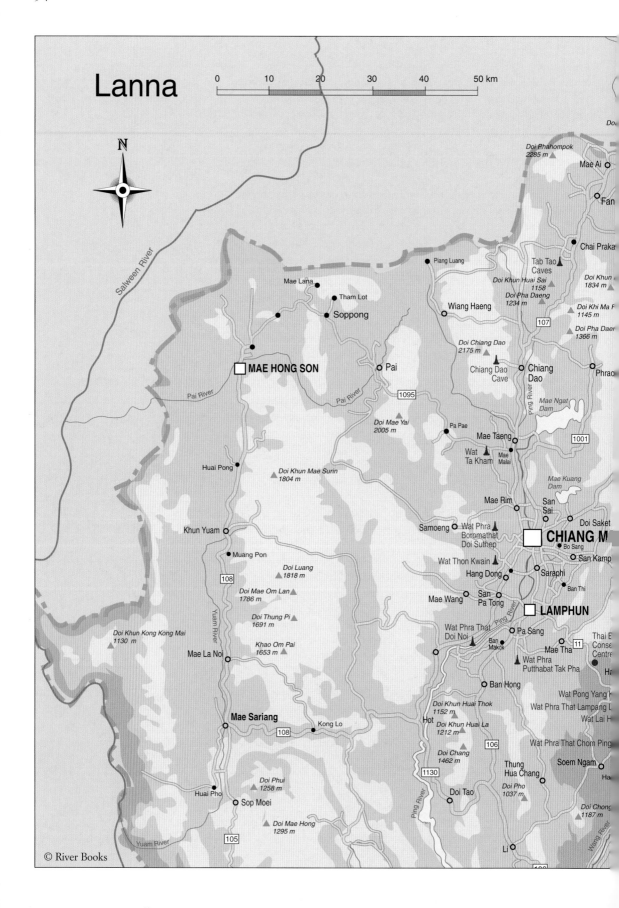

Lanna

0   10   20   30   40   50 km

N

Doi Phahompok
2285 m

Mae Ai

Fan

Chai Praka

Doi Phum

Tab Tao
Caves

Doi Khun Huai Sai
1158

Doi Khun
1834 m

Piang Luang

Doi Pha Daeng
1234 m

Doi Khi Ma F
1145 m

Mae Lana

Tham Lot

Wiang Haeng

107

Soppong

Doi Pha Daen
1366 m

Doi Chiang Dao
2175 m

Chiang
Dao

Phrao

MAE HONG SON

Pai

Chiang Dao
Cave

Doi Mae Yai
2005 m

Pa Pae

1095

Mae Ngat
Dam

Mae Taeng

1001

Pai River

Pai River

Wat
Ta Kham

Mae
Malai

Doi Khun Mae Surin
1804 m

Huai Pong

Mae Kuang
Dam

Mae Rim

San
Sai

Doi Saket

Khun Yuam

Samoeng

Wat Phra
Boromathat
Doi Suthep

CHIANG M

Bo Sang

Muang Pon

Doi Luang
1818 m

San Kamp

Wat Thon Kwain

Saraphi

108

Doi Mae Om Lan
1786 m

Hang Dong

Ban Thi

Doi Thung Pi
1691 m

Mae Wang

San
Pa Tong

LAMPHUN

Doi Khun Kong Kong Mai
1130 m

Khao Om Pai
1653 m

Wat Phra That
Doi Noi

Pa Sang

Thai E
Conse
Centre

Mae La Noi

Ban
Makok

Mae Tha

11

Wat Phra
Putthabat Tak Pha

H

Ban Hong

Wat Pong Yang

Doi Khun Huai Thok
1152 m

Wat Phra That Lampang L

Mae Sariang

Kong Lo

Hot

Doi Khun Huai La
1212 m

106

Wat Lai H

108

Wat Phra That Chom Ping

Doi Chang
1462 m

Soem Ngam

Thung
Hua Chang

1130

Doi Phui
1258 m

Doi Pho
1037 m

Ha

Huai Pho

Doi Tao

Doi Chong
1187 m

Sop Moei

Doi Mae Hong
1295 m

Li

105

Yuam River

© River Books

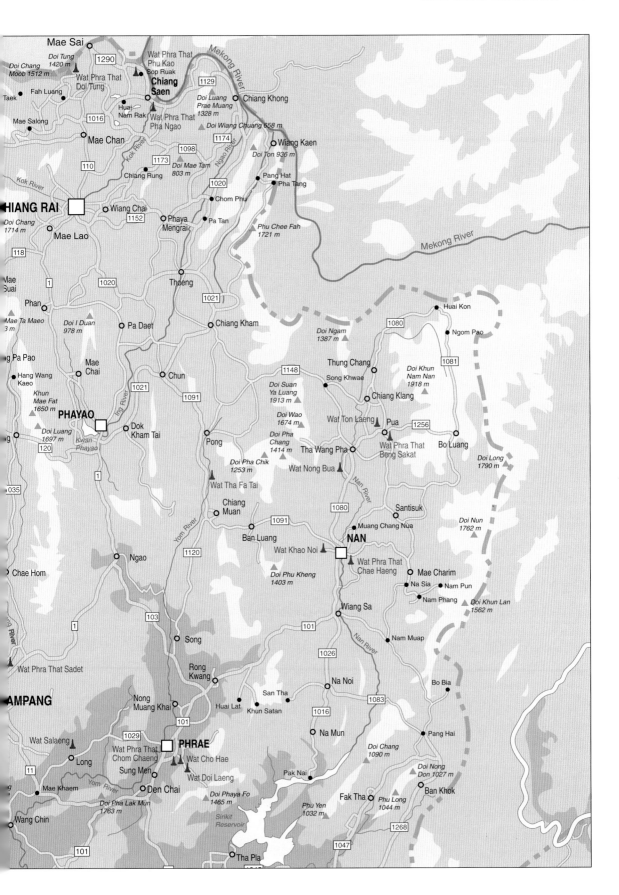

Mae Sai
Doi Chang
Moob 1512 m
1290
Wat Phra That
Phu Kao
Sop Ruak
Mekong River
Doi Tung
1420 m
Wat Phra That
Doi Tung
Chiang
Saen
1129
Chiang Khong
Doi Luang
Prae Muang
1328 m
Taek
Fah Luang
Huai
Nam Rak
Mae Salong
1016
Wat Phra That
Pha Ngao
Doi Wiang Chuang 658 m
Mae Chan
1098
1174
Wiang Kaen
110
1173
Doi Mae Tam
803 m
Doi Ton 936 m
Kok River
Chiang Rung
1020
Pang Hat
Pha Tang
HIANG RAI
Wiang Chai
Chom Phu
Doi Chang
1714 m
1152
Phaya
Mengrai
Pa Tan
Phu Chee Fah
1721 m
Mekong River
Mae Lao
118
Mae
Suai
1
1020
Thoeng
Phan
1021
Huai Kon
Mae Ta Maeo
3 m
Doi I Duan
978 m
Pa Daet
Chiang Kham
Doi Ngam
1387 m
1080
Ngom Pao
g Pa Pao
Mae
Chai
Chun
1148
Thung Chang
Doi Khun
Nam Nan
1918 m
1081
Hang Wang
Kaeo
Song Khwae
1021
Doi Suan
Ya Luang
1913 m
Chiang Klang
Khun
Mae Fat
1650 m
1091
Doi Wao
1674 m
Wat Ton Laeng
Pua
1256
Bo Luang
PHAYAO
Dok
Kham Tai
Pong
Doi Pha
Chang
1414 m
Tha Wang Pha
Wat Phra That
Beng Sakat
Doi Long
1790 m
Doi Luang
1697 m
120
Kwan
Phayao
Doi Pha Chik
1253 m
Wat Nong Bua
Nan River
1
Wat Tha Fa Tai
Chiang
Muan
Santisuk
Doi Nun
1762 m
035
1091
1080
Ban Luang
Muang Chang Nua
NAN
1120
Wat Khao Noi
Wat Phra That
Chae Haeng
Mae Charim
Ngao
Doi Phu Kheng
1403 m
Na Sia
Nam Pun
Chae Hom
Nam Phang
Doi Khun Lan
1562 m
Wiang Sa
g River
1
103
101
Nam Muap
Song
1026
Rong
Kwang
Na Noi
Bo Bia
AMPANG
Nong
Muang Khai
San Tha
Huai Lat
Khun Satan
1016
1083
Na Mun
Pang Hai
101
Wat Salaeng
1029
Wat Phra That
Chom Chaeng
PHRAE
Wat Cho Hae
Doi Chang
1090 m
11
Long
Sung Men
Wat Doi Laeng
Pak Nai
Doi Nong
Don 1027 m
Mae Khaem
Yom River
Den Chai
Doi Phaya Fo
1465 m
Fak Tha
Phu Long
1044 m
Ban Khok
Doi Pha Lak Mun
1763 m
Phu Yen
1032 m
Wang Chin
Sirikit
Reservoir
1268
101
Tha Pla
1047

SUGGESTED ITINERARIES

Within each valley, the descriptions that follow begin with the principal town, followed by its environs (if there is sufficient of interest) and then continue with excursions up and down the valley. Within each town, the various *wat* and other sites of interest are ordered in such a way that they can be visited with as little back-tracking as possible, beginning, where applicable, with the inner town. This will work best if you are based for a day or two in one of the provincial capitals. However, it would take a few weeks of dedicated travelling to cover all the places in this book, and the purpose of the itineraries shown here is to group parts of different valleys to make the best use of limited time.

Chiang Mai is for almost all purposes the most convenient entry point and, given the number of interesting places in and around the city as well as its infastructure, it is for most first-time visitors the best place to use as a base. Nevertheless, there are alternatives even for a short visit, if for instance you have specific interests (such as trekking or rafting) or want a less urban, tourist-oriented experience. Each valley and each town has its own character - and indeed this is a notable part of Lanna's attraction as a region - and the descriptions that form the main part of this book should help you to decide which will best suit your tastes.

If you have only a very few days, you may find that the best use of your time is to use one town as a base for excursions. If you have more time, consider the longer itineraries below. Given the size of Lanna and the intricacy of its topography, by far the best way to travel is with your own transport, whether a vehicle with driver, self-drive or motorcycle. Major tourist centres like Chiang Mai and Chiang Rai are organised for this, with more choice of vehicles and generally lower prices than less-frequented towns such as Nan or Phrae. Having a car with driver does not cost significantly more than self-drive (the driver always takes care of his own eating and sleeping arrangements, the latter often in the vehicle), and this choice will help you avoid the confusing and unpleasant repercussions of an accident (in which you as a foreigner will be at a disadvantage). That said, the countryside back roads of Lanna are among the country's quietest and easiest for driving, and self-drive allows a certain freedom to wander.

These itineraries are selections, naturally, and follow the interest of this book. For this reason, some destinations that feature prominently in package tours are absent here, or in a few cases grudgingly included. Places which, for reasons mentioned in the valley descriptions, you may wish to consider avoiding at all costs include the 'Golden Triangle', Mae Sai, hill-tribe villages with roadside souvenir stalls, San Kamphaeng and any stop along the road to it other than restaurants and Wat Bua Khrok Luang, and some but not all elephant centres. This last is a slightly difficult issue, because Thai elephants, who have very few occupations open to them other than pleasing tourists, are both supported and exploited by tourism. The balance, from so-called 'camp' to 'camp', varies, and we have eschewed individual judgement. The Elephant Conservation Centre and nearby Elephant Hospital at

Hang Chat west of Lampang can certainly be recommended, however, even though the riding experience is weak.

Half-day trips from Chiang Mai

1. Lamphun and Hang Dong: 61 km
Stage 1: Chiang Mai-Wat Chedi Liam and Wiang Kum Kam 8 km, Stage 2: Saraphi-Lamphun (Wat Phra That Haripunchai, National Museum, Wat Chamathewi) 15 km, Stage 3: Lamphun-Wat Ton Khwain, Hang Dong 28 km, Stage 4: Hang Dong-Chiang Mai 10 km.

2. Mae Taeng-Mae Rim-Samoeng-Hang Dong: 205 km
Stage 1: Chiang Mai-Wat Ta Kham 46 km, Stage 2: Wat Ta Kham-Mae Ta Man (elephant camp), 31 km, Stage 3: Mae Ta Man-Mae Rim 42 km, Stage 4: Mae Rim-Samoeng 36 km, Stage 5: Samoeng-Wat Ton Khwain, Hang Dong 40 km, Stage 6: Hang Dong-Chiang Mai 10 km.

Full-day trips from Chiang Mai

1. Mae Cham Valley: 269 km
Stage 1: Chiang Mai-Mae Chaem (passing Doi Inthanon) 111 km, Stage 2: Mae Chaem-Hot-Chom Thong (Wat Phra That Sri Chom Thong) 99 km, Stage 3: Chom Thong-Chiang Mai 59 km

2. Chiang Dao and Phrao: 208 km
Stage 1: Chiang Mai-Chiang Dao 71 km, Stage 2: Chiang Dao-Phrao 43 km, Stage 3: Phrao-Chiang Mai 94 km.

3. Phayao: 324 km (162 km each way)

4. Southern Loop (Chiang Mai, Lamphun, Lampang, Phrae and Nan): 340 km
Stage 1: Chiang Mai-Lamphun 22 km, Stage 2: Lamphun-Elephant Conservation Centre, Hang Chat-the *wats* around Ko Kha-Lampang 110 km, Stage 3: Lampang-Phrae 107 km, Stage 4: Phrae-Nan 125 km.

This trip, taking a minimum of 4 days and ideally 7, cuts right across the middle valleys of the Ping, Wang, Yon and Nan, and gives a wonderful impression of the way in which Lanna culture and settlement evolved, with its fertile but generally narrow valleys separated by the difficult terrain of forested watersheds. Including Chiang Mai, it also takes in the bulk of extant Lanna tradition, and we highly recommend it. The sole disadvantage is that it is a one-way journey, so that the vehicle's return must be organised, and this favours hiring a vehicle with driver. The reverse direction, starting in Nan, to which there are flights from Bangkok, has the particular recommendation of beginning in pleasant, backwater Lanna.

Central Circuit (Lamphun, Lampang, Phayao and Chiang Rai from Chiang Mai): 626 km
Stage 1: Chiang Mai-Lamphun 22 km, Stage 2: Lamphun-Elephant Conservation Centre, Hang Chat-the *wats* around Ko Kha-Lampang

110 km, Stage 3: Lampang-Jaeson and Sopli 66 km, Stage 4: Jaeson and Sopli-Wang Nua-Phayao 178 km, Stage 5: Phayao-Chiang Rai 94 km, Stage 6: Chiang Rai-Wiang Pa Pao 180 km.

Western Circuit (the Pai and Yuam Valleys from Chiang Mai): 597 km
Stage 1: Chiang Mai-Wat Ta Kham, Mae Taeng-Pai 133 km, Stage 2: Pai-Mae Hong Son 106 km, Stage 3: Mae Hong Son-Mae Sariang 168 km, Stage 4: Mae Sariang-Hot-Chom Thong 131 km, Stage 5: Chom Thong-Chiang Mai 59 km.

Northern Circuit (Chiang Rai and Chiang Saen from Chiang Mai): 616 km (692 km via Phayao)
Stage 1: Chiang Mai-Chiang Dao-Fang-Tha Ton 175 km, Stage 2: Tha Ton-Mae Salong-Doi Tung 110 km, Stage 3: Doi Tung-Chiang Saen 63 km, Stage 4: Chiang Saen-Chiang Rung-Chiang Rai 88 km, Stage 5: Chiang Rai-Wiang Pa Pao-Chiang Mai 180 km (alternatively, Chiang Rai-Phayao-Chiang Mai 256 km).

Phayao from Chiang Rai: 271 km, 1 day's round trip
Stage 1: Chiang Rai-Phayao 94 km, Stage 2: Phayao-Chun (Wat Phra That King Kaeng-Chiang Kham (Wat Nantaram) 80 km, Stage 3: Chiang Kham-Thoeng-Chiang Rai 97 km.

Upper Nan Valley: 323 km, 1 day's round trip from Nan
Stage 1: Nan-Tha Wang Pha (Wat Nong Bua) 39 km, Stage 2: Tha Wang Pha-Pua (Wat Ton Laeng)-Chiang Klang (Wat Nong Daeng)-Lao border 98 km, Stage 3: Lao border-Bo Luang 77 km, Stage 4: Bo Luang-Nan 109 km.

Complete Lanna Tour (round trip from Chiang Mai): 2035 km
Stage 1: Chiang Mai-Lamphun 22 km, Stage 2: Lamphun-Elephant Conservation Centre, Hang Chat; the *wats* around Ko Kha-Lampang 110 km, Stage 3: Lampang-Phrae 107 km, Stage 4: Phrae-Nan 125 km, Stage 5: upper Nan Valley, as above 323 km, Stage 6: Nan-Chiang Muan-Pong-Chiang Kham-Phayao 252 km, Stage 7: Phayao-Chiang Rai 94 km, Stage 8: Chiang Rai-Chiang Rung-Chiang Saen 88 km, Stage 9: Chiang Saen-Doi Tung-Mae Salong-Tha Ton 173 km, Stage 10: Tha Ton-Fang-Chiang Dao-Mae Taeng-Pai 232 km, Stage 11: Pai-Mae Hong Son 106 km, Stage 12: Mae Hong Son-Mae Sariang 168 km, Stage 14: Mae Sariang-Mae Chaem-Chom Thong 176 km, Stage 15: Chom Thong-Chiang Mai 59 km.

THE MOST INTERESTING SITES
In the valley descriptions, the *wat* and other sites are in bold type, and ranked according to interest. *** denotes major sites of the first rank architecturally and in religious importance, not to be missed and worth a complete journey. ** sites are of considerable interest, definitely worth seeing if in town and worth half a day's travelling time if outside. * sites are of general interest, and worth a detour. Unstarred sites are worth mentioning in the text but not necessarily worth stopping to see.

The major Lanna _wat_
Wat Phra Singh, Chiang Mai ***
Wat Phra Boromathat Doi Suthep, Chiang Mai ***
Wat Phra That Haripunchai, Lamphun ***
Wat Phra That Sri Chom Thong, Chom Thong ***
Wat Phra Kaeo Don Tao, Lampang ***
Wat Phra That Lampang Luang, Ko Kha ***
Wat Phumin, Nan ***

Sites of considerable interest
(In the same order as they appear in the following chapters)
Wat Mahathat, Chiang Mai **
Wat Pan Tao, Chiang Mai **
Wat Chedi Luang, Chiang Mai **
Wat Chiag Ma¬n, Chiang Mai **
Wat Saen Fang, Chiang Mai **
Old Chiang Mai Cultural Centre, Chiang Mai **
Wat Chet Yot, Chiang Mai **
National Museum, Chiang Mai **
Wat Buak Khrok Luang, Bo Sang **
Wat Chedi Lim, Saraphi **
Wat Thon Kwain, Hang Dong **
National Museum, Lamphun **
Wat Chamathewi, Lamphun **
Wat Ta Kham, Mae Taeng **
Wat Suchadaram, Lampang **
Wat Pong Sanuk Tai, Lampang **
Wat Pa Fan, Lampang **
Wat Pong Yang Khok, Ko Kha **
Elephant Conservation Centre, Hang Chat **
Wat Luang, Phrae **
Ban Wongburi, Phrae **
Wat Chom Sawan, Phrae **
Ban Fai, Phrae **
Wat Phra That Chae Haeng, Nan **
Wat Nong Bua, Tha Wang Pha **
Wat Si Khom Kham, Phayao **
Wat Nantaran, Chiang Kham **
Wat Phra Kaeo, Chiang Rai **
Wat Phra Singh, Chiang Rai **
Wat Phra That Doi Tung, Mae Fa Luang **
Wat Phra That Chedi Luang, Chiang Saen **
National Museum, Chiang Saen **
Wat Pa Sak, Chiang Saen **
Wat Chong Klang, Mae Hong Son **
Wat Phra That Doi Kong Mu, Mae Hong Son **

THE PING VALLEY

Lanna is defined by its valleys, and the most important of these has always been that of the Ping River; important not because of its length (the Nan is longer), but because in its middle reaches, around Chiang Mai and Lamphun, it broadens into a fertile plain. Since the eighth century, when the Mon Dvaravati civilisation made this their furthest outpost, this has remained Lanna's heartland.

Rice fields in the haze of the hot season, on the outskirts of Chiang Mai.

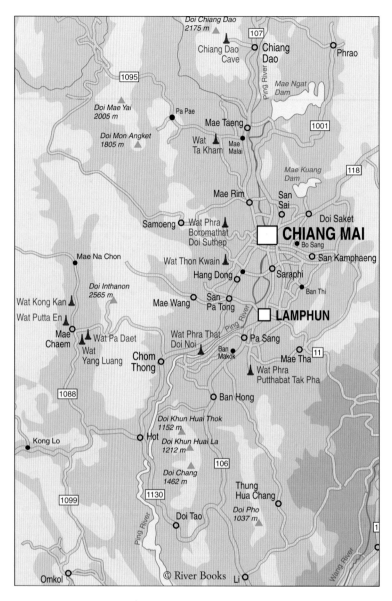

Map of the central part of the Ping Valley.

This area around Chiang Mai and Lamphun is the largest fertile flood-plain in Lanna; some 20 kilometres wide around Chiang Mai, it extends north as far as the gorges below Chiang Dao, and south as far as Nakhon Sawan. It has, therefore, always been a main centre of population, and so the Ping Valley is important not simply because of its size (the river is 590 kilometres long), but also politically and culturally. The greatest concentration of art and architecture is here, and for almost all of the region's documented history it has been the political centre. The Mon established their capital at what is now Lamphun in the 8th century, and King Mangrai made his capital here in 1288.

CHIANG MAI

"Temples decorated with dark red and gold, and picturesque monasteries, were set like gems in the beautiful fringes of foliage that skirted the banks." Holt Hallett, 1890.

Founded in 1296 by King Mangrai, the ruler who first consolidated the Lanna kingdom, Chiang Mai is both Thailand's second city and the capital of the North. Possibly built over an older Lawa settlement, it was Mangrai's third capital, after Chiang Rai (1262) and the nearby Wiang Kum Kam (1288).

Although it occupied an existing site, the processes involved in founding the city were by no means simply pragmatic. Mysticism and geomancy played important parts, and according to the Chiang Mai Chronicle, Mangrai himself spent a number of nights camped in the fields around the area "to seek a dream". The auspicious sign that he was looking for came when he saw two hog-deer standing their ground against a pack of wolves (some texts say hunting dogs). Elders of the local Lawa inhabitants confirmed that this was indeed a special place, and Mangrai began building in the vicinity of what is now Wat Chiang Man. He consulted with his two friends, Ram Kamhaeng of Sukhothai and Ngam Muang of Phayao, with whom he had formed an alliance in 1287, and they counselled a rather smaller city than he had been

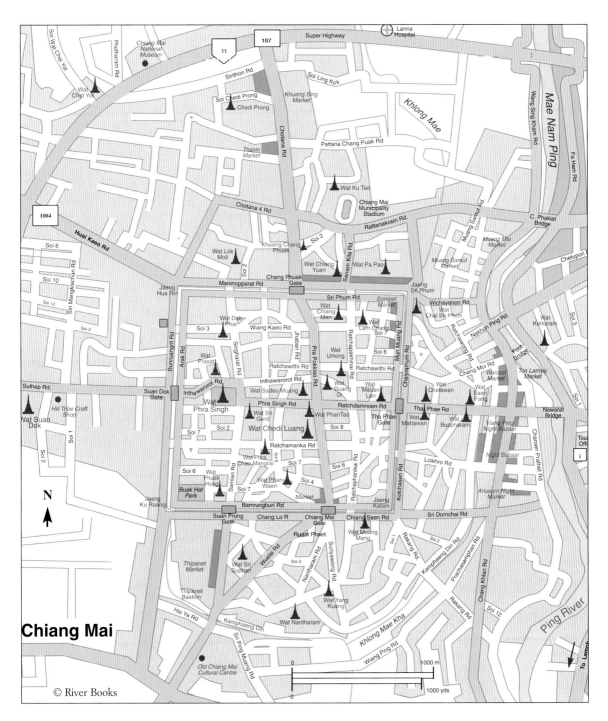

Plan of the city; the almost square moat defines the old city.

planning. He settled on "1,000 wa long and 400 *wa* wide", which is about 2 kilometres by 800 metres: quite different from the 1.8 by 2 kilometres of the existing walls. There is no obvious explanation for this discrepancy. Ultimately, it was decided that there were seven auspicious signs, of which three were quite practical ones concerning the water supply. Like Sukhothai, the city is located between hills on the west and a river on the east.

Construction and Development of the City

Chiang Mai was aligned almost exactly with the cardinal directions, for which there were numerous precedents, both Brahmanic and Mahayana Buddhist. The placing of the *lak muang*, or 'city pillar' near the centre, and the royal palace in its northern part (as in Khmer cities) was also traditional. In the city's magical geography, the city pillar represented the centre of the universe, Mount Meru, while the walls and moat represented the surrounding mountain ranges and sea. By the same token, the area to the west of the city was particularly sacred because it was the dwelling of the Amithaba Buddha, and it was here that the forest *wat* were later built: Wat Pa Daeng and Wat Umong Suan Putthatham, among others.

Chiang Mai's fortunes were those of Lanna, and until the beginning of the 16th century it prospered both materially and culturally, particularly under the autocratic and highly effective rule of Mangrai until 1317, and again under King Tilokaraj from 1441 to 1487. Nevertheless, the expenditure on great religious monuments was a drain on resources and contributed to the period of decline, which became marked after the death of King Muang Kaeo in 1526. By this time also, the chain of command had been weakened, and political in-fighting increased.

Burmese Occupation

After Muang Kaeo, there was no peaceful transfer of power between the successive rulers, and for four years the city had no ruler. When the Pegu Burmese began to expand aggressively, they found no resistance in Chiang Mai, and the city fell without a struggle in 1558.

At first, however, this was not a draconian military occupation. Rather, Chiang Mai was a vassal with some Burmese officials and a Burmese military commander, and the inhabitants seem to have reached a *modus vivendi* with the Burmese. The first westerner to visit Chiang Mai and write about it was a London merchant, Ralph Fitch, who travelled overland from Pegu in 1587, taking twenty-five days for the journey. He wrote, "Jamahey is a very fair and great town, with fair houses of stone [unlikely; he was probably extending his imagination], well peopled, and the streets are very large....Hither to Jamahey come many merchants out of China and bring great store of musk, gold, silver and many other things of China work."

Working against this was the continuing struggle between Ayutthaya and Burma, in which Chiang Mai became something of a pawn. Around 1600 and again in 1662 the city was occupied by Ayutthayan forces, and over the two centuries of Burmese rule over Lanna, intermittent warfare weakened both the region and Chiang Mai. In the end, it suffered badly in the fight to recapture it. A combined force of Siamese under General Taksin, local troops under Chao Kawila and the Prince of Lampang, succeeded in taking Chiang Mai from the Burmese defenders on Wednesday 15th February 1775.

The Burmese, however, re-attacked. The starving city was subjected to a siege which was only relieved at the end of that year by another Siamese army from the south. This time neither side prevailed. The devastated city was abandoned, and as the chronicle describes it, left to become "overgrown with weeds, bushes and vines. It was a place for

Detail of the chedi at Wat Saen Fang, off Tha Phae Road.

Preparing a northern Thai meal in the traditional kitchen of the Reuan Saw Hong, in the south-west of the city.

rhinoceros and elephants and tigers and bears, and there were few people." It remained in this state for twenty years, and it was not until March 1797 that it was formally re-occupied by Chao Kawila. To speed up the re-settlement, he had raids conducted in Shan territories, from where whole villages were moved to the south side of the city, and from Sipsongpanna in Yunnan, founding new villages in the north-east and east of the city.

Chiang Mai ceased to rule its own kingdom when the North was incorporated into Siam in 1892 as Monthon Phayap, and in 1931 it became the provincial capital it remains. The biggest physical changes to the city, however, were in the 1980s and 1990s, during Thailand's economic boom, with a rash of high-rise buildings and an invasion of the newly affluent from Bangkok wanting second homes. One of the good things to have come out of the recession of the late 1990s has been a curb on this development.

THE OLD CITY

The three-and-a-half square kilometres of old Chiang Mai within the walls contain thirty-three functioning *wat* (originally there may have been eighty-five). However, not all of these are of equal interest, mainly because their condition varies; as elsewhere in Lanna, restoration has sometimes been destructive.

We start with a central walking tour that takes in the three most important *wat* – Wat Phra Singh, Wat Chedi Luang and Wat Chiang Man – and others of interest nearby. The many noodle stalls and small restaurants offer opportunities for breaks. This is then followed by a

Sunrise over the north of the city, with the chedis of Wat Lok Moli and Wat Chiang Yuen.

Man riding a samlor with Wat Chai Sri Phum in the background.

description of sites near the edges of the city, following the walls in a clockwise direction, although this is too long a circuit to walk all at once.

Wat Phra Singh ***
'The Monastery of the Lion Buddha' is located to the west of the city centre, at the end of Phra Singh Road. Justifiably the city's most famous *wat,* it was founded in 1345, and contains two of the finest extant Lanna buildings in Thailand, as well as one of its most highly regarded Buddha images and a series of accomplished and naturalistic mural paintings. These latter give an intriguing glimpse of 19th century dress and customs.

A *chedi* was first built here in 1345 by King Pha Yu, seventh in the Mangrai dynasty, to enshrine the ashes of his father, King Kham Fu. A couple of years later, a *viharn* and other buildings were added, and the monastery was given the name Li Chiang Phra. It was not until 1925 that three urns – gold, silver and bronze – were found in the base of a small *chedi*, and it is assumed that these contained the royal ashes, although they subsequently disappeared.

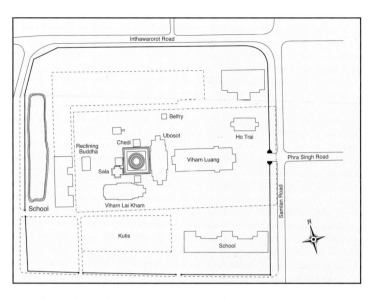

Map of Wat Phra Singh.

The *wat* acquired its current name in 1367, when the famous Phra Sihing Buddha was installed here. In the 18th century, however, it was abandoned and fell into disrepair, in common with much of the city, and it was not until Chiang Mai's resurrection under Chao Kawila at the turn of that century that the *chedi* was rebuilt and an *ubosot* added. Kawila's successor, Chao Thammalangka, was responsible for commissioning the famous murals in the Viharn Lai Kham. Finally, the *wat* was extensively renovated in the 1920s under the supervision of the monk Khru Ba Srivichai, who also added the large modern *viharn* that today dominates the approach from the east.

The Viharn Luang and Ho Trai

Known as the Viharn Luang, the building is of little architectural interest, having replaced in 1925 the original *viharn* which was built between 1385 and 1400. It houses a large seated Buddha facing east, and at the rear of the building –perhaps of greater interest – is the seated bronze Buddha known as the Phra Chao Thong Thip, which was given by two monks in Sipsongpanna to Chao Kawila in 1805 as his personal image.

The ho trai or scripture repository, is architecturally the finest of its kind in Lanna.

To the north and east of the Viharn Luang, however, is a magnificent *ho trai* – scripture repository – that is the finest example of this kind of structure in Lanna. Reputedly built in 1477 in the reign of King Tilokaraj, it was restored in 1867 and again in the 1920s. The small wooden building, with its three-tiered roof, sits on a high stuccoed brick base, accessed by a steep staircase on the east side. It is flanked by balustrades, which instead of the normal *naga-makara* combination, feature lions emerging from the jaws of the *makara*. These creatures are unusually well sculpted, with forelegs, hind legs and a neatly coiled tail. The magnificent gable is almost entirely covered with stucco, glass mosaic and gilded lacquer, including the arch-like *sum* design in diminishing tiers known as *sum khong*. The stucco reliefs around the whitewashed base are particularly fine. Standing *thewada* in various postures occupy the spaces between the windows on the north and south sides, while in the frieze below, various animals appear in ornamental panels. The stucco work on the south side is the most striking shortly after sunrise.

Viharn Lai Kham

Walk back to the front of the Viharn Luang and around its south side. Directly ahead, to the southwest of the

Principal Buddha image of the Viharn Luang, Wat Phra Singh.

Viharn Luang, is the *wat*'s main attraction: the small but exquisitely proportioned Viharn Lai Kham. It was originally built shortly after 1345, and renovated in the first decade of the 19th century. Facing east, its highly decorated, gilded lacquer façade catches the morning light dramatically ('*lai kham*' means 'gold-patterned').

With its low walls and sweeping roof-line, it is almost the archetypal Lanna monastic building. Note how the two tiers of tiled roof cover the *viharn*, to which the portico adds a third, lower tier. Each of these tiers is in two sections, and from the front elevation you can see both the gentle concave curve of each and the shallower angle of the lower section. The combined effect is a pronounced flaring, enhanced by the outer diagonals of the eave brackets. Two red-lacquered teak pillars flank the head of the *naga*-balustraded steps, and the gable within employs a typical Lanna design of rectangular panels; however, the elegant curves of the *kong khiu*, or 'eyebrow' pelmet below soften this rigidity.

Smaller *kong khiu* decorate the winged gables on either side, and the carved strip immediately above the pelmet features a Chinese-influenced cloud design. The eave-brackets, carved with a leafy *kanok* design, are in the triangular *hu chang* ('elephant ear') style.

Inside the Viharn

This *viharn* contains the Phra Sihing Buddha, which sits against the west wall. Unfortunately, the original head was stolen in 1922 and what you see is a replica on the original body. It is flanked by two smaller, though very similar, gilded bronze images. The other interior walls of the *viharn* are decorated with murals illustrating two non-canonical

Stucco thewada figures surrounding the ho trai.

The Viharn Lai Kham at sunrise.

The Phra Sihing Buddha.

jataka tales. On the north wall is the story of *Sang Thong* – the Golden Prince of the Conch Shell – while on the south wall is the story of *Phra Suwannahong*: the Golden Swan (or Goose). The originals were painted in the second decade of the 19th century, probably by a local artist Jek Seng, but restored, with some stylistic changes, in the 1920s. These changes in turn were largely removed in a recent restoration.

The chief attraction of these murals is their naturalism and the individuality of expression given to the characters, with the result that the many scenes in effect document contemporary life. These vignettes expressively capture the insouciance of Northern people, and the quality and vitality of the murals compare with those in Wat Buak Khrok Luang to the east of the city (*see page 106*) and in Wat Phumin, Nan (*see page 179*). The *viharn* also once housed a very fine wooden footprint of the Buddha, now in the National Museum (*page 99*).

The Ubosot

Next to the Viharn Lai Kham, immediately behind and at right-angles to the Viharn Luang, is the *ubosot*, built in 1806. Inside is an elaborate gilded *ku,* but this is difficult to see as the building is normally locked.

With porticos at each end, it has a full three-tiered roof, decorated

Early 19th century murals on the north wall of the Viharn Lai Kham, which include scenes from daily life in Lanna.

The Phra Sihing Buddha
This famous and revered image in gilded bronze, and seated in the *bhumisparsa* pose, is the most important 15th century iconic type in Lanna art. The original, now lost, appeared during the reign of King Tilokaraj, supposedly from Sri Lanka, and was identified at the time as a return to the purity of form that had been lost to the softness and sinuosity introduced at Sukhothai. It became the model for a number of others, including this image at Wat Phra Singh, and was for a time the palladium of the Lanna kingdom.

The name, whether in Thai as *Singh* or Pali as *Sihingh*, comes from the Sanskrit *simha*, meaning 'lion' and refers to the massive solidity and strength of the trunk, with broad shoulders, plump face and marked plasticity. The right hand rests on the knee, the thumb is curved, and the radiance above the head is in the form of a bulbous gem rather than a flame. During the Thai New Year *Songkran* festival in April, the image is taken in procession around Chiang Mai (below). Among other images of this type are three important ones in the Putthaisawan Chapel at Bangkok's National Museum, in Nakhon Si Thammarat, and in Wat Phra Singh, Chiang Rai.

with *cho fa* that are more than usually upright, and lower roof finials in the plain, rounded *tua ngao* style rather than *naga*. The entrance to the south portico is framed with ornate gilded stucco pilasters and a *naga-makara* arch enclosing a *dharmachakra* (Wheel of the Law), which has a circle of fantastic creatures, including a bat, at the bottom. Its gable is intricately carved on all surfaces, including the pillars and the projecting *pae* beams – originally with gold and glass mosaic – and repays close inspection. Note the many small animals, again many of them fantastic, both carved and in stucco. The 'elephant ear' eave brackets combine sinuous *naga* with floral motifs.

The Chedi

This lies to the west behind the ubusot, and is much enlarged since its original construction in 1345. Standing on a high square base with the forepart of an elephant projecting from the middle of each otherwise-

unadorned side, it has three diminishing circular plinths and is bell-shaped in the Lanna style. This means that the bell is diminished at the expense of the lower circular mouldings, some of which are indented.

Wat Prasat **

Immediately north of Wat Phra Singh, on the opposite side of Intharawot Road and west of Soi 3, is Wat Prasat, which retains a beautiful *viharn* in traditional Lanna style, built in 1823. Within the compound, behind frangipani trees, the *ubosot* and *viharn* are aligned in a row, both with a square-based *chedi* close to their western walls. The *ubosot*

Detail of gilded chakra above the entrance to the ubosot at Wat Phra Singh.

unfortunately has been renovated in concrete with no artistic merit, but in contrast the *viharn* has been very well preserved, with wooden walls and an intricately decorated façade in stucco on teak. Inside, the main feature of interest, something of a curiosity, is the entrance to a short tunnel in the west wall (where the altar would normally be) connecting to the *chedi*. The Buddha images flank this decorated entrance; the one on the right is bronze from 1590. There are also murals from the early 19th century.

Wat Sri Gerd

The elegant viharn at Wat Prasat, with the chedi of the ubosot at left.

Return to the main, east entrance of Wat Phra Singh, and walk east along Ratchadamnoen Road. Wat Sri Gerd is on the right, and contains

an important Buddha image showing U Thong influence, in *bhumisparsa,* and called the Phra Chao Khaeng Khom. The monastery pre-dates 1500, the date of a chronicle which mentions it.

Wat Phan Tao **

If you continue to the intersection with Pra Pokklao Road and turn right at the corner, you come to 'The Monastery of a Thousand Kilns', a title which probably refers to the casting of Buddha images for Wat Chedi Luang next door. Its only building of significance is its *viharn*, but this is striking, both in size and style; it is one of the few remaining all-wood monastery buildings in the city. In fact, it was re-assembled and converted from a royal residence – a *ho kham* ('gilded hall') known as the Chao Mahotra Prathet – used by Chao Mahawong, ruler of Chiang Mai from 1846 to 1854. Note, for example, the central Thai style of wall, made of panels, but the Lanna decorative carvings over the door and windows. These spectacular ornaments, gilded and inlaid with coloured glass, were carved separately and attached to the gable; the tall central panel over the pelmet features a magnificent peacock straddling a curled-up dog, which is the zodiacal animal for the year that Chao Mahawong was born. The dog also appears in the ornamental *sum* designs over the windows on either side. The 'eyebrow' pelmet is carved with deep relief lotus flowers, both opened and unopened.

The triple-tiered roof is much taller than a typical Lanna religious building, and has a unique style of *naga* bargeboard, the body decorated with flowers and the lower finials in the form of three-headed *nagas*. The roof ridge carries small *hong* (*hamsa*) birds, and the red-painted eave-brackets are in a leafy design worked to suggest the heads of birds known as *kanok hua nok*. There is no *ubosot*, and this *viharn* doubles for the purpose. The building was originally raised on piles, but now has a stronger masonry base. You can appreciate the dimensions of the hall even better from inside, where huge tall teak pillars, lacquered red, support the high roof.

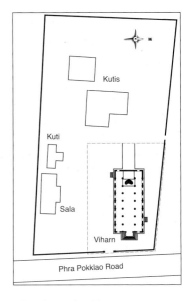

Plan of Wat Phan Tao.

The tall 19th century viharn at Wat Phan Tao, converted from a royal palace.

Above: Gilded nagas on the viharn roof at Wat Phan Tao.

Right: Also decorating the viharn is a gilded carving of a peacock studded with glass, situated over the door.

Wat Chedi Luang **

This is 'The Monastery of the Great Stupa', the city's largest religious monument and, by virtue of the location of the city pillar here, the most important. It is situated next to Wat Phan Tao, south along Pra Pokklao Road.

The present monastery is in fact made up of three earlier ones: the original Wat Chedi Luang, Wat Ho Tham and Wat Sukmin. Work began here at the end of the 14th century on the reliquary in which King Saen Muang Ma planned to enshrine the ashes of his father, Kü Na. The area was cleared and a ceremonial *bodhi* tree was erected with a silver trunk and leaves of gold. To this were added a gold and a silver Buddha, and the base of a reliquary was built around them. Since it did not contain relics of the Buddha, it was called a *ku luang* rather than a *chedi*, and it only came to have its present name in the reign of King Tilokaraj. For unexplained reasons, after ten years it was finished "only to eaves-height", according to the Chiang Mai Chronicle, and when Saen Muang Ma died, the building work continued to be supervised by his wife.

The construction of this great reliquary seems to have had more than its share of problems, and at some point it partly collapsed. It was finally completed in the mid-15th century under King Tilokaraj, who had it reinforced with laterite. It was now the kingdom's largest structure: about 82 metres high and 54 metres at the base.

Buddha Images and Viharn

In 1468 the Emerald Buddha, *Phra Kaeo Morakot*, was installed in its eastern niche. Four naga-balustraded staircases ascended the high base, which was surrounded, in Sinhalese style, by elephants (of which only one of the originals remains: on the south side, next to the staircase). In 1545, an earthquake toppled the upper 30 metres, leaving the ruins of the base and northern side until 1991 2, when it was subjected to an aggressive and somewhat imaginative restoration. The Emerald Buddha had been removed shortly after the great earthquake, when the Laotian King Setthathirat, who ruled Chiang Mai very briefly, took the image with him in 1551 when he returned to Luang Prabang on the death of his father. However, a copy of it was done in an almost black jade, and called the *Phra Yok* ('Jade Buddha'). This was installed in the restored eastern niche to commemorate the *chedi*'s 600th anniversary, although it is difficult to see because of the height of the niche.

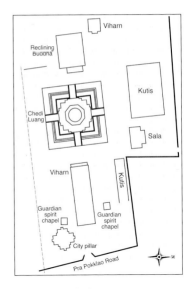

Plan of Wat Chedi Luang.

The large modern *viharn* facing the main entrance on Pra Pokklao Road was built in 1928 and renovated in 1999, and contains the large standing Buddha image Phra Chao Attarot ('Eighteen-cubit Buddha', one of many such in Thailand), cast in the late 14th century. On your left as you face the *viharn* from the main entrance is a small cruciform *mondop* housing the city pillar, known as the Sao Inthakin ('Indra's Pillar'), supposedly of stone and about 50 centimetres tall, but totally enclosed in an octagonal brick structure. This was moved here from its original site at Wat Sadeu Muang (*q.v.*) by Chao Kawila in 180, during the re-building of Chiang Mai. Three dipterocarp trees were also planted, the largest of which towers over the Sao Inthakin and is supposed to help protect the city for as long as it stands. Next to it is one of two small chapels housing the statues of the guardian spirits, *kumphan*, who reputedly carried the Sao Inthakin from the Tavatimsa heaven, the home of the gods presided over by Indra on Mount Meru. Its sister chapel is on the other side of the enclosure, across the main entrance, and both were installed by Chao Kawila in 1801.

The recently restored chedi; unusually, it does not contain any relics of the Buddha.

Dipterocarp tree and one of the two small chapels, Wat Chedi Luang.

Projecting elephant, an original figure on the base of the chedi.

Behind the *chedi*, on its west side, is an open-sided long pavilion housing a reclining Buddha. Behind this, and rather obscured, is a simple, attractive *viharn*. It is set in its own walled enclosure, with plain, whitewashed walls and some fine, boldly-carved panels on the east façade: that is to say, the pediment, the deep rectangular panel below and the two winged gables. The openwork designs, largely floral, are attached to a silver glazed background.

Wat Sadeu Muang
Return north along Pra Pokklao Road, passing Wat Phan Tao on your left and continuing across Ratchadamnoen Road. At the next intersection, to the left, are two brick *chedi* on either side of the small road: a 14th century octagonal one on the right, and a 15th-16th century circular one on the left that has been partly opened up to reveal an older brick *chedi* inside. These are all that remain of Wat Sadeu Muang ('The Monastery of the City Navel'), also known as Wat Inthakin. The city pillar was originally installed on this site, where reputedly King Mangrai saw the two hog-deer resisting a pack of wolves. This was the first auspicious sign instrumental in siting the city. However, for unrecorded reasons, Chao Kawila had the city pillar removed from here to Wat Chedi Luang.

Wat Duang Di **
If you return to Pra Pokklao Road, cross over and walk back down south for a few metres, you will find a small entrance which leads to this extremely attractive *wat*. Its name translates as 'The Good Luck Monastery', and it is set in a secluded enclosure of longan trees. The tall 19th century wooden *viharn*, more central Thai than Lanna in style, has beautifully carved pediments at the front and the rear, both completely covered with plant motifs, and the main east façade is similarly ornate. Its carvings extend to a rectangular panel below, winged gables and a finely carved pelmet which is scalloped rather than in the 'eyebrow' design. Below this, over the door, is an exceptional gilded carved wooden *sum* in the form of a triangular frame of diminishing intertwined *naga*; these enclose two mirror-image chains of *kanok* plant motifs worked to represent *naga* heads (*khankhot hua nak*). Inside the *viharn,* you can immediately see another non-Lanna feature of the building: the fact that there are no pillars, but instead, load-bearing walls which support heavy cross-beams.

Immediately next to the *viharn*, on its south side, is the much smaller *ubosot*, also very attractive. Note the strongly projecting moulding of the building's high pedestal. Differently coloured glass panels are set into the gilded decorations of its east gable. Close to both of these buildings, in the southeast corner of the enclosure, is a square single-storied *ho trai* with a three-tiered roof, one of the finest of its type in Lanna for the quality of its stucco decoration. It has recently been restored with great care, and – commendably – those areas where the stucco is missing have been left plain rather than attempting new decoration.

Behind the *viharn* to the west is the *chedi*, in three sections; the redented base is square, the plinths and three mouldings are octagonal, while the bell and spire are round. Half-seated elephants guard the corners of the terrace.

Wat Umong Maha Thera Chan *

Provided both gates are open at Wat Duang Di, as they usually are, you can walk in a couple of minutes due east from there to this *wat*, 'The Monastery of the Great Monk's Cave'. This means that you enter from the back of this small *wat*, so make your way through to the main east entrance on Ratchapakhinai Road. The small *viharn* is here, recently renovated but still with a certain charm. The 'eyebrow' pelmet carries a rather folksy *kala* guardian in its centre, created from leaf motifs. The pediment, which is divided into rectangular panels, has a central *kalasa* – the Brahmanic cornucopia – surround above and at the sides by standing *thewada*. The zodiacal animals, rabbit and horse, occupy lower panels.

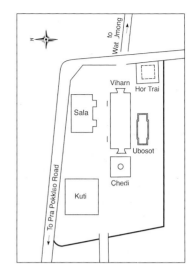

Plan of Wat Duang Di.

The ubosot at Wat Duang Di, its coloured glass panels reflecting in the sun.

The carved wooden sum over the viharn door, Wat Duang Di.

Stucco detail from the carefully restored ho trai, Wat Duang Di.

The unusual name of this *wat* derives from the small brick *chedi* on the south side of the *viharn*. In the 14th century the monastery was known as Wat Po Noi ('Monastery of the Little Bodhi Tree'), and in 1375 an important monk reputedly settled here and used the niche in the *chedi* for meditation: hence 'cave'. This story may be more legend than fact, but he is supposed to have remained here as abbot until 1402, at which point the *wat* was renamed in his honour. The small *ubosot*, although quite attractive from a distance, was restored in the early 1990s with little finesse. It therefore does not bear up to close examination, apart from the well-executed and supple dragons which flank the staircase, in place of the more usual *naga-makara* combination. Behind the *viharn* is the principal *chedi*.

Wat Lam Chang

Continue north up Ratchapakhinai Road, almost to the limit of the old city; on the right, just before Wiang Kaeo Road, is 'The Elephant Kraal Monastery', so named because King Mangrai's elephants were kept here. The *viharn* houses a collection of Buddha images from the city's abandoned *wat*, arranged in a row on the high altar. Note also that the *ho trai* is built above the *ubosot*.

Wat Chiang Man

Diagonally across the road from Wat Lam Chang is Wat Chiang Man ('The Monastery of the Fortified City'), the city's oldest. In keeping with Brahmanic and later Buddhist tradition, Mangrai built his palace in this northern sector, and founded this *wat* in 1297, the year after Chiang Mai was established.

The Chedi
A 19th century restoration of the 15th century original gilded *chedi* is its most striking feature: an amalgam of Lanna style – a very high redented square base supports an octagonal middle part and small bell – and Sinhalese via Sukhothai. This latter style can be seen in the foreparts of stuccoed elephants surrounding the base that give it the name Chedi Chang Lom ('Stupa Surrounded by Elephants'). Note that the octagonal form is created by the redenting at the corners; this stays the same width all the way up to the mouldings, at which point it has cut into the square so much that it produces eight equal sides. Contrast this with the *chedi* of Wat Boromathat Doi Suthep (page 101). Above the elephants on each side are three tall arched niches, and the lower corners of the gilded section carry stylised projecting *naga* heads.

The small viharn of Wat Umong Thera Chan still retains some of its original charm despite recent renovation.

The Viharn
In front of the *chedi*, to its east, is a large *viharn* which was restored in the 1920s as part of Khru Ba Srivichai's programme of works, with a deep portico at either end; the rear portico houses a large seated Buddha image facing the *chedi*. The east façade of the *viharn* is decorated with carved, gilded openwork designs set against a background of coloured glass mirrors. Note the intricately carved *kong khieu* pelmet with a deep-hanging central projection. On the winged gables, tiger heads form the centre of the design, while below each is a strip featuring a monkey pulling on a branch of the *khrue thao* vine; above, the floral lozenges are known as *pracham yam kam pu,* and the hanging floral projections below are know as *krachang*.

The Chedi Chang Lom at Wat Chiang Man, with its mixture of styles and superb restoration, is one of the most striking features of the wat.

Kala over the door of the main viharn, the design contrasting with the mirrored background.

Monkey carving on the winged gable of the main viharn.

Buddha Images

Inside, on the right side of the altar, is the city's oldest dated Buddha image. It stands in the position of holding an alms bowl, and the inscription on the pedestal – in both Pali and Tai Yuan – records that it was cast in 1465 and commissioned by two monks and a laywoman.

In the smaller *viharn* to the north, enshrined in the elaborate *ku*, are two of the city's most revered Buddha images: both of them small and locked behind bars. One is a gilded black stone tablet bas-relief standing Buddha in the *tribhanga* triple-flexion position, known as the Phra Sila Buddha: clearly Indian in origin, probably from between the 8th and 10th centuries. It shows the Buddha subduing the enraged elephant Nalagiri sent to destroy him, and according to one chronicle came from Bihar via Sri Lanka and Si Satchanalai. It is believed to have rain-making powers and is honoured at Songkran.

The second image is a small quartz carving, mainly clear but with some dark areas including the head, in the *bhumisparsa* pose, with

*The standing Buddha in the main
viharn dates from 1465.*

The ku of the small viharn.

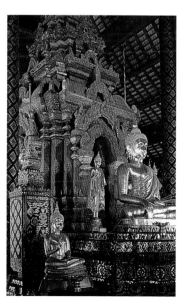

curled hair and *ushnisha* worked in gold. This, known as the Phra Sae
Tang Khamani, is reputed to have belonged to Queen Chamathewi of
Lamphun and taken from that city when it was captured by King
Mangrai and retained as his personal talisman. It is held to be able to
prevent disaster, despite its ineffectiveness during the razing of
Lamphun in 1281.

The other monastic buildings include a 19th century *ubosot* to the
south of the main *viharn* and an attractive wooden *ho trai* raised on a
whitewashed brick base. A *stele* in front of the *ubosot* installed in 1581
describes the founding of the city, with the exact date: Thursday, 12
April 1296 at around 4 am.

From Wat Chiang Man, one option is to continue northwards
outside the walls, for which see below: *North of the Old City*. Here,
however, we complete the description of *wat* inside the walls, and for
convenience these are described in the same order as you would see
them when walking in a clockwise direction.

Eyebrow pelmet on the ho trai, Wat Chiang Man.

Jaeng Sri Phum, one of the four corner bastions of the city wall.

Jaeng Sri Phum

This name means 'Glory-of-the-Land Bastion', and it is one of the four corners of the City Wall, which has since been pulled down. Jaeng Sri Phum lies at the northeast of the old city overlooking the moat, and, like the other three corners, has recently been sensitively rebuilt from 19th century photographs.

King Pha Yu had reinforced the original earthen ramparts of the city with brick in 1341, shortly after moving the capital from Chiang Rai for the last time, but it was Chao Kawila who added bastions like this at the turn of the 18th century; after two centuries of Burmese rule, he was determined to protect the city adequately. These added to the basic defensive structure of walls and an outer moat, fed by the Huai Kaeo stream rising on Doi Suthep. Excavation of the moat provided the earth for the ramparts. The cosmology of the city plan involved a magical relationship between the centre and cardinal points, important for the city's welfare and protection. This, the northeastern corner, was responsible for the city's glory; the others controlled the fortifications, inauspicious events, and longevity. The last complete restoration of the city wall before it was pulled down was around 1880.

Close to the Si Phum corner there were, for a short while in the 15th century, a gate and a bridge over the moat of the same name; these were built in 1465 for access to King Tilokaraj's palace. In 1517, however, the gate was walled up by his successor, King Muang Kaeo, as part of a rebuilding of the walls. He then moved the palace to Wat Pa Daeng, and no trace of either the gate or bridge remains.

Tha Phae Gate

Some 750 metres south of Jaeng Sri Phum, in the middle of the east city wall, is a modern reconstruction – based on an 1891 photograph – of an unknown gate. *Tha Phae* means 'raft landing', and refers to the river access at the end of the Tha Phae Road which runs east from here for a little over 1 kilometre. The original Tha Pae Gate was down near the river in the outer wall (*see under Kamphaeng Din below*) until it was dismantled early in the 20th century, and the gate here was called the Chiang Ruak Gate. Following the cosmological plan for the city, the cardinal directions were protected by guardian deities as follows:

Direction	Gate Guardian deity	Guardian function	Equivalent Brahmanic deity
East	Tha Phae Surakkhito	city's foundation	Indra
South	Chiang Mai Choeyaphumo	city's nobility	Yama
West	Suan Dok Surachato	city's followers	Varuna
North	Chang Phuak Khantharakhito	city's power	Kubera

MORE SITES OF INTEREST

Again, the following buildings and landmarks are listed by the order in which you would come across them when travelling on foot.

Wat Meuan Lan

This *wat* can be found a short distance up Ratchadamnoen Road, to the west of the gate and on the north side. It is a small *wat* with an interesting *ho trai* in Burmese-influenced style. Square in plan, its upper storey and diminishing rooves are in teak, on a stuccoed brick base.

Further south again is the **Jaeng Katam** guarding the southeast corner of the city. *Katam* means 'fish trap', for it was here that the water flowed out of the moat, and fish were caught.

Wat Pan Waen

Continue west along Bamrungburi Road that runs on the inside of the moat, passing the **Chiang Mai Gate**. Almost 500 metres beyond this, Bamrungburi Soi 3 on the right leads to Wat Pan Waen. The small *viharn* here is particularly notable for its finely decorated doors, with gilded male and female guardian figures. The *chedi* is strongly redented at the base to provide an octagonal plan for the plinths and mouldings above.

Wat Phra Chao Mangrai *

This *wat* is situated 300 metres north of Wat Pan Waen. Its modern cement *viharn* contains a standing Buddha, reputedly in King Mangrai's likeness. It had been intended for Wat Chiang Man, but the cart carrying it from Wiang Kum Kam (*see page 106*) broke down here, and as often in such cases, this was taken as an omen to be heeded. The ceremonial gate is elaborately decorated, with Indra's three-headed elephant in relief over the entrance and a spoked *dharmachakra* above. This is supported by two deer which recall the Deer Park at Sarnath where the Buddha gave his first sermon.

The moat and Jaeng Katam, which guards the south-east corner of the city.

Suan Prung Gate

Continue west from Chao Mangrai until you reach Samlan Road, and turn left – south – toward the Suan Prung Gate , which was added after the original four (it may be the one mentioned in the chronicles as having been built early in the 15th century by King Sam Fang Kaen. If so, it was intended as access for his mother from her palace to supervise the building of Wat Chedi Luang). Being in the inauspicious southwest part of the city, and following the Brahmanic tradition that south is the direction of the dead – who are guarded by Yama the supreme Judge – this was the gate for funeral processions.

Wat Phuak Hong *

A little before the gate, turn right into a small lane, Samlan Soi 7, at the end of which is 'The Monastery of the Flight of Swans'. This *wat* is notable for its pagoda-like *chedi,* which some believe shows Yunnanese influence: one of only three in the city. However, another interpretation is that this is simply a round version of the square-stepped pyramid of the Mon *chedi* at Wat Ku Kut near Lamphun, and so more originally Lanna. Built in the 16th or 17th century, its round structure has seven diminishing tiers, each capped with a projecting 'roof' and encircled by niches-fifty-two in all. Note the vase-like representations of *kalasa* set into the brickworks of the lowest tier.

The *viharn* in front of the *chedi* is a pleasantly typical Lanna building with two tiers of roof over the main structure and a third lower tier over the portico. The gable is divided into rectangular panels – on which are a naïvely carved tiger and ox facing each other – and the eave brackets are in the elephant-ear form with a sinuous *naga* backed by flowering plants, similar to those on the *ubosot* of Wat Phra Singh. The carved door carries two identical opposed figures, unusually in the form of the Hindu god Vishnu (with four arms and carrying the four attributes) standing on demon monkeys.

Overlooking the southwest corner of the moat, the **Jaeng Ku Ruang** ('urn') is in the most inauspicious part of the city. North from here, the **Suan Dok Gate** opens onto Suthep Road, which leads to Wat Suan Dok.

North again, the **Jaeng Hua Rin** at the northwest corner of the city is where the Huai Kaeo stream feeds the moat (*'hua rin'* means 'water source').

Wat Dab Phai

This is situated a short distance in towards the centre of the city, on the corner of Singharat Road and Soi 3. The carved gable of its *viharn* carries a *khrue thao* vine motif across the three sections: pediment, rectangular panel, and deeply curved *kong khieu* pelmet. The right side is a mirror image of the left, a symmetrical design which is a central

The ornate ceremonial gate of Wat Phra Chao Mangrai.

Thai influence. Note also the two tigers on the pediment. Within the portico, a gilded stucco *sum*, with twin rearing *naga* in the round and *hamsa* birds, frames the main entrance.

NORTH OF THE OLD CITY

The Chang Phuak Gate
This gate, whose name means 'White Elephant', is the city's northern entrance. Beyond it, however, there are still very many sites worth visiting, and so what follows is a description of the area north of here.

Wat Lok Moli *
This monastery is situated 400 metres west of the gate, on the right a short distance down Maninopparat Soi 2. It was founded by King Kü Na, late in the 14th century, although in fact the large *chedi*, which is all that remains, was built by King Chettharat in 1527-8. It has a very tall square base in diminishing storeys, and a small bell and spire on top. The upper levels of the base are multiply-redented, and the cubic section has niches on all four sides framed by double arches in stucco, with standing *thewada* in pairs at the corner. This is altogether one of the most imposing *chedi* in Chiang Mai.

The Khuang Chang Phuak
This is the 'White Elephant Terrace' which was built over an existing shrine in 1800 by Chao Kawila; it pays homage to two of King Saen Muang Ma's attendants who saved his life during his unsuccessful 1387 attack on Sukhothai. From Wat Lok Moli, return to the Chang Phuak Road, either along Maninopparat Road by the moat or by Chang Phuak Soi 2. Continuing north, on the right-hand side of the road just beyond the bus station, is a small traffic island with a whitewashed shrine containing statues of the foreparts of two elephants; this is Khuang Chang Phuak. The two elephants were called Prap Chakravala ('Lord World-Conqueror') and Prap Muang Mara Muang Yaksa ('Lord Conqueror of Demons and Devils').

Wat Ku Tao *
Continue north for 300 metres and turn right into Chang Phuak Soi 6. The *wat* is at the end of this road, after approximately 200 metres. One of its most notable features is the particularly unusual *chedi*, which is in the form of five diminishing spheres standing on a low redented square base. It may have been built in 1613 to enshrine the remains of the first Burmese ruler of Chiang Mai, Prince Saravadi (1578-1607), although this is by no means certain. Moulded niches, curved to fit the spherical surface of each tier, face the four cardinal directions, and a small spire tops the assembly. This is a design which is unique in Thailand, and may have been influenced by Yunnanese pagodas, with the five spheres representing the five Jinas ('conqeror' in Sanskrit, referring to the five historical and future Buddhas and to other groupings of five in the Buddhist world). Ceramic flowers in various colours cover most of the spheres in the Chinese style, and at least until the late 19th century it was known locally as the "Chinese pagoda".

Chedi Sri Phuak Hong; it is open to interpretation whether its architecture shows more Lanna or Yunnanese influence.

This impressive chedi is all that remains of Wat Lok Moli (previous page).

The unusual chedi of Wat Ku Tao is in the form of diminishing tiered spheres.

Chedi Prong

Back on Chang Phuak Road and 500 metres further north (almost 1 kilometre from Chang Phuak Gate and just after the concrete footbridge), turn left down the narrow Soi Chedi Prong. After 200 metres you reach the brick Chedi Prong , all that remains of an unrecorded *wat*. However, it is interesting for being the third of Chiang Mai's round pagoda-style *chedi*, after those at Wat Phuak Hong and Wat Rampoeng. The only difference is that here there are six rather than seven tiers with niches, but note that the lower two have more closely-packed niches to achieve the same number in total: fifty-two.

OTHER SITES TO VISIT

Back down towards the city moat, around the north-east corner, is **Wat Chiang Yeun**; it is near the corner of Sanam Kila Road and Maninopparat Road. The *wat* is notable for its massive *chedi* with a whitewashed square base and octagonal middle section, dotted with applied porcelain flowers similar to those at Wat Ku Tao. In contrast, the building near to the entrance on Sanam Kila Road is now nearly derelict: an octagonal pavilion in Chinese style, with a three-tiered roof.

From here, walk east along the moat and then turn left just before Jaeng Si Phumand. Here is the Burmese-style **Wat Pa Pao**, built in 1883 by Shans who had moved to Chiang Mai with British logging interests. Set peacefully among trees, including frangipani, the courtyard is surrounded by a low crenellated wall and contains a *chedi* and an *ubosot* topped with a multi-tiered *phyathat*, all in brick and cement. The more modern Shan *viharn* is nearby.

EAST OF THE OLD CITY

Wat Chai Sri Phum *

This *wat* is just around the north-east corner from Wat Pa Pao, and has been renovated to a high standard. The large *viharn* and adjacent *ubosot* both show evidence of central Thai influence: in the proportions, for instance, and in the image of Vishnu riding Garuda on the high pediment of the *viharn*. The two-storey *ho trai* with a double-tiered roof and projecting porches replaced a fine old original in the 1980s. In the far corner of the enclosure, next to the road that runs around the moat, stands the *chedi*; niches, painted red on the inside, contain standing Buddha images on all four sides of its high square base.

Wat Mahawan *

Continue south to Tha Phae Gate, and turn left, heading down towards the river. On the right, between Tha Phae Soi 5 and Soi 4, is Wat Mahawan, which combines both Lanna and Burmese features in a distinctive and lively manner. The buildings and trees are quite closely packed together, making it a little difficult in places to distinguish the main points, but the principal components are a Lanna-style *viharn* and

The massive chedi of Wat Chiang Yuen, north of the city moat.

The Burmese-style chedi and ubosot of Wat Pa Po.

ubosot on the east side, a Burmese *chedi*, a large *ho trai* and a highly unusual tall, square brick-built *viharn* on the west side. From the Tha Phae Road the *wat* can be seen very clearly because of its three stuccoed brick towers and similar gatehouse arranged along the low wall. Burmese *chinthe* with various accompanying figures face outward from these to the street, while from the central tower balustrades topped by lithe *makara* actually spill halfway out onto the sidewalk, flanking a false entrance.

The two main entrances are on either side of the northwest corner, right next to the Lanna-style *viharn*, built in 1865 and restored in 1957 (although the ornately carved and gilded doors are recent). The smaller *ubosot* is next to it on its south side. Behind the *viharn* is the elaborately stuccoed *chedi* in distinctly Burmese style, surrounded by rampant *chinthe* and frangipani trees. Immediately south of the *chedi* and *ubosot* is a fine large *ho trai* in teak on a white masonry lower floor, with an elaborate roof, a hipped tier below and a double-tiered gabled

The viharn (left) and ubosot (right) at Wat Chai Sri Phum, both showing central Thai architectural influence.

Map of Wat Mahawan

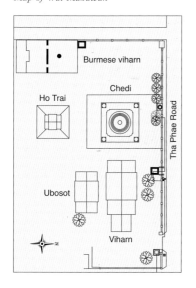

section above. It is now used as the abbot's residence.

Partly obscured by trees, by the west wall, is the tall Viharn Pra Chao To ('The Viharn of the Great Buddha') which, as its name suggests, houses a large Burmese-style seated Buddha image, and was built in the 19th century by a Burmese teak agent. The baroque entrance, with exuberant Burmese stucco motifs, is on the far side, immediately next to the wall, and the building is normally kept locked. Ask for permission to enter.

Wat Chetawan *

This *wat* is directly across Tha Phae Road from the east entrances of Wat Mahawan. It features Burmese architecture in the form of three bell-shaped *chedi* in a row, each characteristically flared at the base. The new, large *viharn* is an unfortunately grandiose concrete structure at odds with the intimate scale of the three *chedi*.

Wat Buppharam *

Continue towards the river. On the right, after Tha Phae Soi 3, is Wat Buppharam, where in March 1797 Chao Kawila began the ritual circumnambulation of the city to re-occupy it formally after two centuries of Burmese rule. Its architecture is a mixture of old – the attractive miniature Lanna *viharn* – and new. Unfortunately, the new architecture, seen in the excessive and overpowering *ho monthientham*, breaches every Lanna architectural canon. It is perhaps best ignored in favour of the small viharn, which faces north (a breach with tradition), and is almost filled with the large principal Buddha image, its flame disappearing from view up into the ceiling.

The Lanna-style viharn of Wat Mahawan, with the ubosot at left.

The Viharns

Although the *wat* was founded in 1497 and the smaller *viharn* first built three years later, most of what you see today dates from the late 19th century, including the restoration of this small *viharn*. However, the teak itself is obviously very old and may date back to the 17th century. Almost the entire façade, including the pillars of the portico, is decorated with stucco and coloured glass inlay. The pediment is divided into rectangular panels, in the typical style, and small stucco *thewada* stand in full relief. The two guardian beasts flanking the entrance are modern, and were carved by the same artist who made those for the *ubosot* at Wat Umong Maha Therachan.

A second larger *viharn* is to the right, also facing north, with recently carved and gilded doors. Behind it is a Burmese-style *chedi*.

Wat Saen Fang *

A little further east on the opposite side of the road, on the corner with Chiang Moi Tat Mai Road, is Wat Saen Fang, one of the most important in this part of the city. It was founded in the 14th century but, like Wat Buppharam, all the structures are later, and none earlier than the 19th century.

The entrance is impressive; marked by a tall, roofed gatehouse, its approach is flanked on either side by long undulating *naga-makara* balustrades, their bodies covered in green glazed scales. Along the approach, notice on the left side the *ho trai* in red-painted teak built in 1869, which unusually stands in a pond. On the right side, the tall building is the local community hall, the front and rear pediments decorated with blue and gold panels depicting various mythical animals.

Ahead, at right angles to where you are, and facing the elaborate east gatehouse, is the Lanna-style *viharn*. This has an impressively carved façade, and is interesting for having been converted from a *ho kham*, as was that of Wat Phan Tao *q.v.* In this case, the *ho kham* was the residence of Chao Kawilorot in the 1860s, and was re-assembled as a *viharn* by his successor Chao Inthanon in 1878, although the carved decorations are a more recent restoration. The gable is divided into rectangular panels, each containing a pair of opposing animals: elephants, horses, rabbits and so on. The winged gables show rather more central Thai influence, and are carved with a *khrue thao* vine motif. They feature opposed leaping figures of Hanuman, the monkey king, and mock window shutters carved with *thewada* armed with swords.

Stucco guardian figure at Wat Buppharam.

90

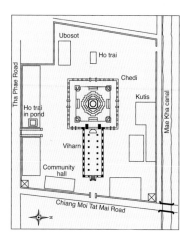

Map of Wat Saen Fang

Behind the viharn is the Burmese-style *chedi*, guarded by pairs of *chinthe* at each corner and surrounded by a recently built wall. This is whitewashed and boasts pillars enthusiastically decorated with glass mosaic. West again of the *chedi* are two buildings: a new *ho trai* (though in fairly traditional style) and the *ubosot*. The latter was built in 1910, and combines both Burmese and Lanna styles, with an ornate gabled upper tier over a hipped roof brick and concrete building. Rows of *kinnorn* parade down the ridges of the lower roof.

Ban Upayokin *
By the river, on Charoen Prathet Road is Ban Upayokin, built in 1877 in Lanna-European style, although it is now a restaurant. Square in plan, its two principal stories are surrounded by verandahs with carved balustrades and surmounted by an overhanging hipped roof. It has a gabled roof over the small third storey..

Elaborate Burmese-style chedi at Wat Saen Fang, guarded by Burmese chinthe.

Kinnorn figures on the roof ridge of the ubosost, Wat Saen Fang.

SOUTH OF THE OLD CITY

Kamphaeng Din

To the south and south-east of the old city, approximately a kilometre distant from the moat, are the remains of an earthen rampart: the Kamphaeng Din or 'earth wall'. This was the city's outer line of defence, and curves in a broad arc from the Thiphanet bastion close to Mahidol Road. The Khlong Mae Kha and other diverted streams form an adjacent narrow outer moat, but it is uncertain when these defences were first built. Enclosed between this and the city's main moat is the area where a number of Shan communities were forcibly re-settled at the beginning of the 19th century.

Wat Muang Mang

Close to the southeast corner of the main moat, two villages from what is now Burma – Muang Mang and Ban Khaem – were moved here in their entirety, and are remembered in the name of Wat Muang Mang. Its three large new buildings are of little interest in themselves, although one unusual feature of this monastery is that it has resident nuns, who live in a long *kuti* with its own walled enclosure.

Wat Nantaram *

In the immediate vicinity of this temple, west of Wat Muang Muang, live the descendants of the Tai Khün people, who were brought here from the area around Keng Tung. The meaning of 'lacquerware' for *khün* comes from the skills they brought with them.

To find the *wat*, follow Nantaram Road southward from Chiang Mai Gate for 800 m. Its slim round *chedi* on an indented square base is a *phra that* containing a relic, and so is completely covered with gilded copper sheets, and the three circular mouldings stand out prominently. Next to the *viharn* and set among trees is an attractive small *ubosot* with a four-tiered roof.

Ban Upayokin is one of the few surviving Lanna-European houses from the days of the teak boom.

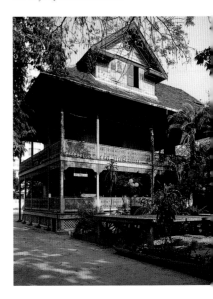

The Phra San Sae bronze Buddha head which can be seen in the National Museum.

The Phra Putthapatiha Buddha image in the ubosot of Wat Sri Suphan.

Wat Yang Kuang

Nearby, on Suriyawong Road, is the octagonal stepped *chedi* of Wat Yang Kuang, of unknown date. The magnificent large bronze head of the principal Buddha image here, the Phra San Sae, was taken by Prince Damrong to exhibit in the Bangkok National Museum, but it was returned in 1971 to Chiang Mai, where it is at the museum.

Wat Sri Suphan *

A short walk north of Wat Yang Kuang, along Wua Lai Road, is a concentration of silversmiths who came from a village called Ban Ngua Lai on the west bank of the Salween. They were captured in an 1800 Lanna attack on Burma led by General Kamoon: hence the name of the road, Wua Lai. However, Wat Sri Suphan pre-dates these events; indeed, it is one of the few *wat* with a foundation *stele*, inscribed in Phakkham, the ancient Lanna script, in 1509.

The temple can be reached from Wat Nantaram by taking Nantaram Soi 3 (the first left as you leave from the north gate along Nantaram Road) and following it across Wua Lai Road. It was founded in 1500 during the reign of King Muang Kaeo, with the *viharn* and *ho trai* added by Chao Kawila in 1860. The *viharn* and *chedi* were extensively and carefully renovated in 1998, retaining the original proportions. There are two important Buddha images: the one in the *viharn* commissioned by Chao Kawila, and the more beautiful Phra Putthapatiha image, reputedly with a high gold content, in the *ubosot*. The slight damage to the right foot and left leg are supposedly from a Japanese bullet (the city was occupied during World War II).

The Old Chiang Mai Cultural Centre **('Soonwattanatam')

This cultural quarter is one kilometre south of Wat Sri Suphan, down Wua Lai Road and just past the bridge over the khlong. Although best known for its *khantok* (a low round table) dinners, it also has a beautifully preserved Lanna teak house – the *Reuan Saw Hong* – which was built in 1870 and is very much worth seeing. Named for its owner, which is customary, it consists of two principal buildings and one smaller (the kitchen), side by side on a high platform. It is, therefore, a triple-gabled house, and the gable ends of the two main buildings are decorated with carved *kalae (see page 29),* signifying the prominent status of the owner.

WEST OF THE OLD CITY

The area west of Chiang Mai had considerable spiritual significance, being not only in the direction of the Amithaba Buddha, but also in that of the mountain Doi Suthep. This mountain is sacred to the original Lawa inhabitants as well as to the Tai *(see Wat Boromathat Doi Suthep on page 101).* As a result, some important religious centres were built here.

Wat Umong Suan Putthatham *

The first temple of significance to be built in this area was 'The Cave Monastery of the Buddha Garden', which can be reached by following Suthep Road west from Suan Dok Gate for 2 kilometres and turning left at Soi Wat Umong, where it is signposted. The remains of the *wat* are 1.1 kilometres along this small road.

In the tradition of forest monks who pursued their devotions away from the distractions of the city, Wat Umong was founded as a secluded site for meditation in the wooded area west of the city, just as in the Aranyik of Sukhothai. Possibly founded by King Mangrai, it was restored in 1371 by King Kü Na for the venerated monk Phra Sumana Thera Chan, whom the king had invited from Sukhothai and who had already spent a year at Wat Phra Yeun in Lamphun. Here he founded the first of two important forest sects in Chiang Mai (the second sect was founded some sixty years later, at the nearby Wat Pa Daeng).

There is now very little to see, but in a sense this is in keeping with the ascetic tradition of a forest *wat*. The path from the entrance leads past numerous *kuti* and a library. From the parking area, walk west to the staircase, which is guarded on either side by five-headed *naga* at the foot of the balustrades. Although these *naga* are new, one of the original ones is under a shelter on your left. The steps lead up to a large raised terrace on which stands the large Sukhothai-style *chedi*, very similar to that at Wat Nang Phaya in Si Satchanalai. Above the base edged with two rows of lotus petals are three circular moulding representing the Three Worlds, and above these are the bell, *harmika*, shaft and diminishing circular mouldings of the spire. Note the (now headless) lions at the lower corners of the *harmika* and the guardian faces above.

From the northeast corner of the terrace, a path leads a short distance to a striking sculpture of a starving Buddha: an uncommon ascetic image. Return to the corner of the terrace, where another path leads down to the west entrance of a set of tunnels and subterranean

The living room at Reuan Saw Hong, Lanna teak house in the Old Chiang Mai Cultural Centre.

Sukhothai-style chedi at Wat Umong.

Right: Emaciated Buddha figure, in the grounds of Wat Umong.

meditation cells that gave the *wat* its name. The walls originally carried murals of Buddha images and floral motifs, but these have now disappeared.

Wat Umong appears to have been abandoned in the late 15th century, but since 1948 it is once more a centre of Buddhist teaching which welcomes all who are interested in study and meditation. The forested grounds, which include a small lake teeming with fish and turtles, are a welcome relief from the noise of the city.

Wat Rampoeng

This is another forest-sect monastery that has become a meditation centre in modern times, and is located 1.5 kilometres further south along the same road. According to the Yonok Chronicle, it was founded in 1492 by King Yot Chiang Rai, and its most interesting feature is the round, stepped *chedi* showing the influence of Chinese pagodas. As at the smaller *chedi* of Wat Phuak Hong in the old city, the seven round tiers rise in diminishing size, each with a projecting round cap that curves gently up to the next tier, and each with niches containing seated Buddha images; again, there are fifty-two in total. The monastery now offers courses in Buddhist teaching.

Wat Pa Daeng *

Also nearby is 'The Monastery of the Deciduous Forest', which you can reach by taking the lane that runs along the north wall of Wat Umong's enclosure for 1 kilometre. In its time it was an important monastery for Chiang Mai, being the centre of the second main sect of Arannavasi 'forest-dwelling' monks to be founded near the city.

The *chedi* is a mixture of Haripunjaya and Sinhalese styles, and the history of the *wat* as a whole is similarly multicultural. In 1423 a group of twenty-five monks from Chiang Mai joined eight others from Cambodia on a pilgrimage to Sri Lanka, where they were ordained, and returned via Ayutthaya to establish a new sect here in 1430 under their abbot, Phra Yanna Kamphi. King Tilokaraj's mother apparently paid for the foundation, and in 1447 she and her husband were cremated here. A measure of the respect that the sect commanded was demonstrated in 1463, when King Trailok of Ayutthaya decided to abdicate and

become a monk, and twelve of Wat Pa Daeng's monks went south to ordain him. One of the most important of the northern chronicles, the Jinakalamali, was written here in 1516 by the monk Ratanapanna, and the *wat* was given a costly renovation around 1520.

The grounds were extensive, as at Wat Umong, although this has now been obscured by the surrounding houses. The *viharn* is at the head of a ninety four-step staircase, a fairly plain building with a triple-tiered roof and some excellent old stucco decoration on its gable and doors, featuring a variety of small mythical animals. Behind are three *chedi* in a row, the closest attached to the rear wall of the *viharn*. The *ubosot*, which was originally built in 1452 by King Tilokaraj, is 300 metres down the hill to the east; raised on two platforms, its unadorned walls support a hipped lower roof section and a small pitched tier above, with a *kala* clutching vines on the pediments at both ends. East of here, among houses, is a brick *chedi* with clear signs of Sukhothai influence; the circular mouldings and bell stand on diminishing square platforms, the uppermost of which has five niches set into each side, as at Wat Chang Lom in Si Satchanalai.

Seven-tier chedi at Wat Rampoeng, similar in style to the smaller one at Wat Phuak Hong.

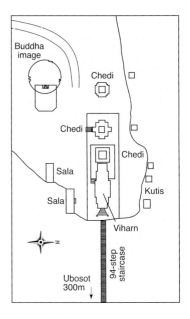

Plan of Wat Pa Daeng.

The viharn and two chedis at Wat Pa Daeng, a wat steeped in history and several cultural traditions.

The stucco decoration depicting mythical animals, from the viharn at Wat Pa Daeng. This figure is a hasadiling: a bird with the head of an elephant.

Wat Suan Dok *

Closer to the city, on Suthep Road and 1 kilometre west of Suan Dok Gate, is another temple built for the monk Sumana by King Kü Na, in 1371. 'The Flower Garden Monastery' was a *wiang*, or fortified settlement, built on the site of a former royal flower garden ('*suan dok*') to house a relic that the monk had found in Sukhothai following a vision. However, as the relic was about to be enshrined in the *chedi* it broke into two pieces. On the advice of the monk, one piece only was enshrined and the other was placed on the back of a white elephant which eventually found its way to what was to become Wat Doi Suthep *q.v.* A wall surrounds Wat Suan Dok, and on the other side of Suthep Road are the remains of the earthen rampart which originally surrounded the *wiang*.

The dominant feature of the *wat* is its tall *chedi* and the collection of whitewashed tombs of various styles and sizes. The *chedi* housing the relic dates from the 14th-century founding of the *wat*, and is more purely Sinhalese than most in Lanna; note the prominent bell, which does not flare at its base. In the enclosure next to it are the tombs containing the remains of several generations of the Chiang Mai royal family, collected here from their originally scattered locations around the city by Princess Dararatsami in 1909.

The large building east of the *chedi* is a *sala gan parian*, or preaching hall, and was built in 1932 by the ubiquitous Khru Ba Srivichai at the same time as his renovation of the chedi and *ubosot*. This is a central Thai type of building, not Lanna, and it contains two principal Buddha images back-to-back, one standing, the other seated in the *bhumisparsa* pose. In the *ubosot* is another Buddha, a 4.7 metre-tall seated bronze image, also in the *bhumisparsa* pose and cast during the reign of King Muang Kaeo in 1504. Known as Phra Chao Kao Tue, it was cast in nine segments and is distinctive in that, while the four fingers are equal in length as in the Sukhothai style, the robes are in a large sheet as in the Ayutthaya style.

Wat Chet Yot **

1.5 kilometres north-west of the moat is 'The Monastery of the Seven Spires', the modern popular name for what used to be Wat Potharam Maha Viharn ('The Monastery of the Sacred Tree and Great Viharn'). You can reach it by taking Huai Kaeo Road from the north-west corner of the city moat in the direction of the mountain for 1.2 kilometres; at the junction with the Super-Highway, turn right, and the temple is on the left after 900 metres.

Plan of Wat Suan Dok.

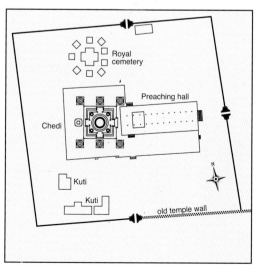

The tombs contain the once scattered remains of several members of the Chiang Mai royal family.

Head of the standing Buddha in the Sala Gan Parian.

History and Design

According to the Jinakalamali chronicle, King Tilokaraj planted a *bodhi* tree and established a monastery here in 1455, and in 1476 "had a great sanctuary constructed in this monastery", apparently to celebrate the 2000th anniversary of Buddhism. An indication of the status that the Lanna kingdom had reached by this time is the fact that in 1477 the Eighth World Buddhist Council was held here at Wat Chet Yot to revise the Tripitaka (the Pali canon of Theravada Buddhism). If the dates are correct, Tilokaraj's builders were faster than most. Strangely, however, none of the other chronicles mentions this temple.

In design, the principal structure is partially similar to the Mahabodhi

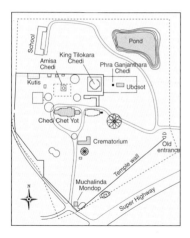

Plan of Wat Chet Yot.

The Viharn Maha Pho is the main structure of Wat Chet Yot, a loose interpretation of the Mahabodhi Temple in Bodh Gaya.

Temple, Bodhi Gaya, in the Indian state of Bihar: the place where Gautama attained enlightenment as the Buddha. The main laterite body is a redented rectangle in plan, with two stubby wings on each side near the front; on its flat roof stands the main pyramidal spire, offset to the rear, with four smaller versions at the corners and two small bell-shaped *chedi* at the front. However, the claim in the chronicles that the builders actually visited Bodhi Gaya and copied it outright is highly unlikely, given that the proportions are quite different from the original. The spires are much reduced, and the main spire the most, so that instead of a soaring pyramidal *shikara* on a low unobtrusive sanctuary (the original is over 55 metres high), we have here the inelegant effect of a solid main building with a group of stubby spires sitting on top. Moreover, the original sanctuary is square in plan, while this is very elongated.

Another suggestion is that the design was copied from the Mahabodhi temple in Pagan, and was built after King Alaungsithu had sent builders to India to repair the original, incidentally adding the corner spires. However, the Pagan version is different in other ways, narrowing much more at the top and lacking the *amalaka* (the round ribbed element of the finials). The decorations at Wat Chet Yot also differ considerably; on the spires, the bands of arch-like motifs become leaf motifs pierced by circular holes, and alternate with bands of Buddha's feet, while the walls of the building have two registers of seventy high-relief *thewada*. These are larger than life-size, in standing and floating seated postures, and, with their Sukhothai-influenced sculpting, are the finest element of the *chedi*. The redented angles at the rear corners have standing stucco *thewada* flanked by unusually curved columns reminiscent of Laotian *that* spires.

Other Features

A 16 metre-long barrel-vaulted tunnel (probably an imported Burmese building skill), penetrates the structure from the east. At the end of this is a large seated Buddha image, and from here two narrow staircases, now closed, lead up to the roof. Formerly, a *bodhi* tree grew up through the roof, in keeping with the monument's homage to Bodhi Gaya, but in 1910 it was uprooted to preserve the structure. At the west end of the building, there is a crypt containing another Buddha image.

To the north of here, in a line from east to west, are a simple *ubosot* with a small *chedi* containing the Phra Ganjanthara Buddha image, a large Lanna-style *chedi* built in 1487 to enshrine the ashes of King Tilokara, and the small octagonal Amisa Chedi. The *ubosot* has a well-carved wooden pediment with a continuous *khrue thao* vine design on vertically joined planks.

The National Museum **

First opened in 1973, the National Museum is located about 400 metres from Wat Chet Yot further along the Super-Highway. In front of the building are two pottery kilns: one from the 15th century excavated at Ban Pong Daeng in Chiang Rai province, and the other from the 14th or 15th centuries, excavated at Wang Nua in Lampang province. The museum houses a wide range of Lanna exhibits, from prehistoric artefacts to the howdah used by King Rama VII on his entry to Chiang Mai in 1926, the first visit to Lanna of a Siamese king.

Stucco thewada from the walls of the Viharn Maha Pho.

Probably the finest piece in the collection is an exquisitely decorated 2 metre by 1.24 metre wooden footprint of the Buddha. It is from the Viharn Lai Kham at Wat Phra Singh, and was made in 1794 in the *chakrawan* design that represents a map of the cosmos. The glass inlay central circle and surrounding rings represent Mount Meru, while the remainder is decorated with scenes worked in extremely detailed mother-of-pearl inlay. It contains, among other scenes, the hundred and eight important features of the cosmos known as *mangalalakkhana*, and the workmanship stands up to the very closest inspection.

Other notable exhibits are a 15th century Lanna-style bronze head – measuring 178 centimetres – from the Phra Saen Sae Buddha image, which itself is from Wat Yang Kuang in the south of the city. It shows possible Chinese influence in the heavy rounded lower features, and a large 19th century hanging banner from the Hot district depicting a standing Buddha and disciple. There are also two wooden *prasat*-style *busabok* (reliquaries in the form of aerial chariots), a *panjarop* (stand for hanging a gong in the form of a beast that combines five different animals) and several scripture cabinets and chests decorated in various styles.

Another museum of interest, though much smaller, is at the **Tribal Research Institute** on the campus of Chiang Mai University, further up Huai Kaeo Road from the Super-Highway intersection, on the left. It has hill-tribe artefacts and a library.

Right: part of a 19th century banner from Hot, Chiang Mai.

Below: exquisitely decorated wooden footprint of the Buddha, dating from 1794.

Below right: Silver thread coat that belonged to one of the rulers of Chiang Mai.

MOUNTAIN *WAT*

The 1601-metre Doi Suthep and its neighbouring peak Doi Pui (1685 metres) have long been held sacred, and are considered the home of the city's guardian spirits Pu Sae and Ya Sae. Doi Suthep was a factor in the location of Chiang Mai, just as the hills west of Sakhothai and Si Satchanali were in siting these ancient capitals. It is Doi Suthep that we shall explore next.

Wat Phra Boromathat Doi Suthep ***

About half-way up Doi Suthep, on a spur overlooking the city, is the highly venerated Wat Phra Boromathat Doi Suthep. It owes its existence to an accident that occurred during the enshrining of a relic in 1371 at Wat Suan Dok (*q.v*). The relic, brought from Sukhothai by the monk Sumana, split in two. It was considered inauspicious to enshrine both pieces at Wat Suan Dok, and the problem of what to do with the second half was solved by placing it in a reliquary on the back of a white elephant. According to legend, the elephant was allowed to wander, which it did in the direction of the mountain. It stopped just three times in its three-day journey, twice on lower hilltops (the first was later named Doi Chang Non: 'Hill of the Sleeping Elephant'), and finally on the level top of a spur where there was a hermit known as Wasuthep. Here it trumpeted three times, turned in a circle three times, knelt down and died. After these auspicious signs there was no doubt that this was the site to enshrine the broken relic, and for this purpose a 7-metre *chedi* was built. At the very end of the 15th century or in the early 16th century the chedi was enlarged to its present octagonal form, which is 16 metres high and 12 metres in diameter at the base.

Manuscript chest, also on display at the National Museum.

To reach the *wat*, follow Huai Kaeo Road out of the city to its end, where the mountain road, built in 1935 entirely by the voluntary efforts of Khru Ba Srivichai's followers, winds up the eastern slopes. At the Km. 14 marker you reach the turning and parking area, with the expected assortment of food and souvenir stalls associated with a heavily visited site. A long and steep staircase, flanked by undulating *naga-makara* balustrades covered in glazed ceramic scales, leads up to the *wat*: two hundred steps from head to tail. Alternatively – though of course without the physically rewarding climb! – you can take the recent funicular, provided that it is in working order (it was broken in 1998 but may since have been repaired). At the top of the staircase, built in the mid-16th century by the ruler Phra Mekuti, two fierce green *yak* guardians stand

Plan of Wat Doi Suthep.

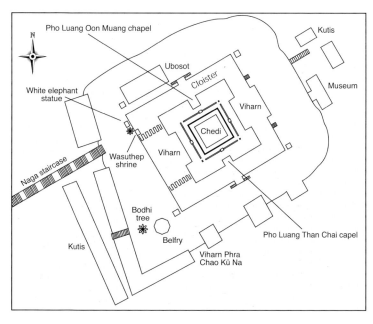

Yaksha guardian at the top of the steps, leading to the terrace at Wat Doi Suthep.

Statue of the hermit Wasuthep, who was living on the site when it was founded.

in small chapels on either side, protecting the entrance to the terrace.

Through this gateway, you face the walled enclosure rising above, but before climbing the next set of stairs to enter it, there are several points of interest on the surrounding terrace itself.

Important features

Directly ahead, on the right of an ancient jack-fruit tree, is a small shrine containing an image of the hermit Wasuthep, who was living on the site in the early 14th century at the time when the white elephant delivered the famous relic. The tiger-stripe cloth draped around his body symbolises the tiger skin traditionally worn by hermits in India and beyond. From here, circumnambulate the terrace in the usual clockwise direction. On the other side of the jack-fruit tree is a statue of the founding elephant, the portable reliquary strapped to its back; a number of people's ashes are enshrined in the plinth below. Next is the *ubosot* of the *wat*, a modern building of little intrinsic interest, other than a statue of Mae Thorani, the Earth Goddess, on the outer back wall. She is in the characteristic pose of wringing out her hair to release a flood of water that will drown the army of Mara that is attacking the Buddha.

Rounding the corner of this building, walk along the side wall of the enclosure and the rows of bells hanging from poles. These are rung in sequence by the faithful, and their sound, each with a slightly different pitch, permeates the *wat* throughout the day. Two narrow staircases run up the wall, leading to small doors that enter the two small shrines of the enclosure, but which are kept closed. At the end, turn right again. Three larger bells hang here, and the small building at the end of the terrace is the small museum. On its other side, the views over the city and the Ping Valley can be spectacular if the weather is clear, although modern pollution makes this less common than before.

From this position, it can be noted that the orientation of the *wat* is not exactly to the cardinal points; the longer axis is in fact from south-southwest to north-northeast, and this corner is east-northeast. Continue around, passing more rows of bells along the wall and the new Viharn Phra Chao Kü Na, named after the king responsible for bringing the relic from Sukhothai. It was built in 1999 to a high standard of wood-carving, and in authentic Lanna proportions. Just beyond, in the corner, is a new bell-tower, octagonal in plan and with a giant bronze gong set into a circular hole in one wall. Behind this is a sacred *bodhi* tree, grown from a sapling brought from India in 1943, and now surrounded by Buddha images and others.

You are now back near the top of the staircase. On either side of a tableau depicting Khru Ba Srivichai and his followers from a 1935 photograph, two staircases lead up to the terrace. Both are guarded by pairs of statues: the one on the left by white-faced *thewada* wielding swords, and the one on the right by a blue and a green elephant-head Ganesh, the son of Shiva and bringer of wealth and good fortune.

The Cloister

The sacred enclosure opposite owes its present form to building and renovation undertaken by Chao Kawila at the beginning of the 19th century. The *phra rabieng* or cloister is lined with a variety of Buddha images against modern murals and is interrupted on each side by buildings containing different Buddha images. The largest of these is next to you as you enter, and is called the Sala Khru Ba Srivichai in honour of the monk who made the *wat* accessible in the 1930s. It was built in 1806, and contains murals illustrating the founding of the *wat*. The enclosure is distinctly cramped because of the lack of building space on the brow of the hill, and the press of visitors, particularly in the early morning, can be overwhelming. Due to its importance and proximity to Chiang Mai, this is hardly ever a peaceful *wat*, although lunchtime usually has the fewest visitors.

White elephant statue in the gardens at Wat Doi Suthep; this is the animal responsible for the wat's foundation.

Blue elephant-head Ganesh guarding the staircase to the terrace.

THE PING VALLEY · 105

The Chedi

In the centre, offset slightly to the north, is the *chedi*, sheathed entirely in gilded copper plates and surrounded by a railing, painted bright red with gilded tips. Because this is a *phra that*, containing an important relic, the purpose of the railing is to maintain its sanctity. Traditionally, the faithful (but not women) may circumnambulate on auspicious days inside the railing, but in a recent restoration a low wall has been built around this, so that anyone may make the ritual circumnambulation, clockwise and often holding a lotus flower between the hands. At the corners are massive Burmese-style filigreed *chat* (sacred parasols), their gilded pillars in imitation of bamboo. The stone blocks at the base of these *chat* are decorated with bas-relief panels depicting the three-headed elephant Erawan on the two outer faces, and *singh* on the inner faces.

The *chedi*'s design, with its repoussée sheets in diamond-shaped cut-outs on each face, and on the the strongly indented base, repays close attention. The corners of the high base are so deeply redented as to make the plan octagonal, which the mouldings above follow as they taper without any curve to the relatively small relic chamber. The gilded and lacquered copper *chat* on the very top was raised in 1788-9 by Chao Kawila in celebration of the defeat of a Burmese attack. At the corners are gilded metal lotus plants emerging from red and gold jars.

The Viharns

If you walk clockwise around the enclosure, the first building you come to, in the middle of the west side, is a small chapel where the majority of worshippers stop to pray, both towards the *chedi* and in the opposite direction to the Buddha image known as the Pho Luang Oon Muang. On the far side of the roofed area is a plaque sitting on the ground carrying bas-relief images of the twelve zodiacal animals, now almost unrecognisable from the repeated applications of gold and coins. Worshippers add gold leaf to the animal of their birth year.

Continue round to the north side across the polished granite surface of the enclosure. The *viharn* here contains a Buddha image known as the Phra Purahatsabodhi Boromathat, the 'Thursday Buddha', worshipped by those born on that day, and murals illustrating the Vessantara Jataka. Like the slightly larger *viharn* on the opposite side by the entrance, it was built in 1806. Finally, on the east side of the *chedi* is a second small chapel containing the Pho Luang Than Chai Buddha image, and another plaque of zodiacal animals.

Wat Buak Khrok Luang **

This wat is a short drive to the east of Chiang Mai on the way to the villages of Bo Sang and San Kamphaeng (well known and best forgotten for their tourist-inspired craft industries). Take Route 1006 out of the city, ignoring as much as possible the emporia selling over-priced souvenirs, and immediately before the Km. 4 marker, turn right

Opposite page: the chedi and sacred enclosure at Wat Doi Suthep.

People praying in the west chapel of the chedi.

Zodiacal animal encrusted with gold, east side of the chedi.

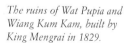

Mural in the viharn at Wat Buak Khrok Luang showing Chinese building a house.

down a lane signposted to Ban Suan restaurant. After 300 metres you reach the *wat* on the right. The chief attraction of the simple and attractive Lanna village *viharn*, built in 1837, is its murals, which are not much later in period than those in Wat Phra Singh's Viharn Lai Kham. They have the same informality and individuality of expression in depicting the *jataka* tales in a Lanna context. Note also the scene showing Chinese men assembling the framework of a building. The large Buddha image is Laotian in inspiration and rustic in execution.

Wiang Kum Kam *

At Saraphi, just south of the city and on the east bank of the river is the site of this fortified settlement which preceded Chiang Mai when King Mangrai decided to move his capital to this part of the valley. Having captured Haripunjaya (now Lamphun) in 1281, Mangrai founded this settlement some 15 kilometres to the north in 1286. He fortified it with a palisade and a moat on four sides, channeling the Ping River for this purpose (at this time it flowed east before turning south, so that the *wiang* was located on the west bank). Wiang Kum Kam remained Mangrai's capital for only ten years until he founded Chiang Mai in 1296; then, in the 16th century when the river changed course, it was largely buried. One of the first things to be established was the market, followed by religious buildings.

Excavations in the 1980s revealed a dozen former temples that can now be visited easily by following the connecting lanes. Take the Om Muang highway (Route 1141) from the airport east, and just after it crosses the river, turn right (south) onto Koh Klang Road (Route 1008), from where the sites are signposted. Alternatively, take the old Chiang Mai-Lamphun Road Route (106) south from the Nawarat Bridge, and at Ban Nong Hoi take the right fork, which is Koh Klang Road (Route 1008). Again, continue across the Om Muang highway as above. Most of the excavated monuments have been restored to the bases of their *chedis* and *viharns*; the principal sites are Wat That Khao, Wat That Pupia, Wat That Ikang and Wat That Noi.

The ruins of Wat Pupia and Wiang Kum Kam, built by King Mengrai in 1829.

Wat Chedi Liam **

At the western end of the historical park, close to the river, is 'The Monastery of the Square Chedi'. The *chedi* was one of the first structures in the new settlement, and was built in 1288-9 with the name of Ku Kham. Mangrai clearly held the Mon civilisation which he had captured at Haripunjaya in high regard, because the *chedi* he built here is a copy of the famous Mahapol Chedi at Wat Ku Kut (*q.v*). It was restored in 1908 with Burmese additions. Square in plan, it rises in five stepped tiers to form a slender pyramid, with three niches on each of the four sides containing standing Buddhas; the second and third tiers have *makara*-framed arches, the other three floral designs. The Buddha images, though, are not the same. With Burmese-style faces, they differ slightly from tier to tier, as follows. *1st row:* right hand raised in a version of the *abhaya pose*, robe covering both

Wat Chedi Liam, built by King Mangrai in the late Dvaravati style.

shoulders; *2nd row:* both hands at the sides, robe covering left shoulder; *3rd row:* right hand raised, robe covering left shoulder; *4th and 5th rows:* both hands at the sides, robe covering both shoulders. In addition, the spire is not Mon in style, but has the four-sided sinuous curve of a Laotian *that*, and is topped with a Burmese *hti*. The four corners of its base are guarded by lions in the Burmese *chinthe* style.

There are a few other functioning *wat* in this area, including **Wat Si Bun Ruang** with a restored *viharn* and **Wat Chang Kham**. The latter was built on the grounds of the ruins of Wat Kan Thom; it has a *viharn* which was added in 1987 and a spirit house in which the spirit of King Mangrai is held to reside.

Wat Thon Kwain **

Route 108, which leads past the airport and southwest from Chiang Mai, is the road to Chom Thong, the Mae Cham Valley and ultimately across the western hills to Mae Sariang. Just past the Km. 10 marker at Ban Muang Kung turn right onto Route 1269. About 100 metres after the road crosses the canal, turn left (south) down a lane, and after 200 metres you will reach Wat Thon Kwain, also known as Wat Inthrawat. This lovely rural *wat*, built in 1858, has thankfully so far been spared any 'improvement' while at the same time being well maintained.

It is widely regarded as a near-perfect example of a Lanna rural temple. Its peaceful setting, with a clear view east past sugar palms and across rice fields, and the high standard of the wood carving that decorates the *viharn*, makes it in every way a delight to visit.

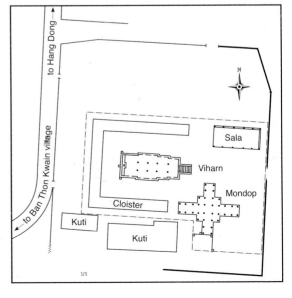

The viharn at Wat Thon Kwain in its unspoiled rural setting.

Detail of the eyebrow pelmet on the viharn.

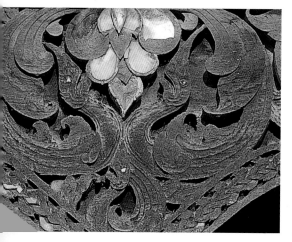

The bargeboards, with intricate fretwork on the undersides, have delicately carved *makara* disgorging the rearing *naga* finials. The gable area inside the two octagonal pillars is divided into several tiers. The scalloped pelmet immediately over the door has a looping *khrue thao* vine design containing *naga* heads, and in the narrow strip above you can see the very Chinese *mek lai* floating cloud motif. The rectangular panels above this contain circular sunflowers in coloured glass mosaic. The eave-brackets are of the triangular *hu chang* type, and feature the half-human half-bird *kinnorn*.

In the corner of the enclosure is an open-sided, four-gabled *mondop* with a low roof, built as a resting place for the procession of the Wat Phra That Si Chom Thong relics on their way to Chiang Mai. The *cho fa* roof-ridge finials are of the *pak nok kaeo* ('parrot's beak') type, and are fitted with a concrete body, feathers and legs to make them look as if they are perched. In the centre of the roof is a metal umbrella of state finial: a Laotian or Tai Lü influence. Stucco *makara* disgorge each other down the sloping ridges.

An alternative approach to this *wat*, if you have been visiting Wat Suan Dok or Wat Umong Suan Putthatham, is to follow the canalside Chonprathan Road south from Huai Kaeo Road or from Suthep Road. 10 kilometres past the Suthep Road intersection you reach the intersection with Route 1269. Turn right here and continue as above.

THE LOWER VALLEY

South from Chiang Mai, the Ping River flows on to its confluence with the Chao Phraya River at Nakhon Sawan, some 20 kilometres downstream. Below the town of Hot, the valley narrows, and for this reason has never developed into an important route, even though it connects Lanna to Siam. Indeed, for boats travelling from the central plains there were sixteen cataracts on the river before Chiang Mai was reached, and the journey from Bangkok took several weeks. The area south of Hot is sparsely populated as far as the plains. However, the valley immediately below Chiang Mai has a long history of settlement, most significantly by the Mon, in and around what is now Lamphun.

Map of Lamphun, as far west as Wat Ku Kut.

THE HISTORY OF LAMPHUN

This small, quiet town, too close to Chiang Mai to develop its own tourist infrastructure, contains two very important *wat* and a number of others, dating back to around the 10th century. Before King Mangrai forcibly annexed it, Haripunjaya (Haripunchai in Thai), as both town and kingdom were then called, was the most northerly outpost of the Dvaravati civilisation, and its last stronghold. According to the Chamadevivamsa and Jinakalamali chronicles, which embraced tradition as well as historical fact and may not be wholly accurate on this point, a hermit, Vasudeva, founded the town in 661, and on his request the Mon ruler of Lopburi in the central plains sent his daughter Chamathewi to rule. Because of various dating problems associated with the chronicles, it is now generally held that the founding was at the beginning of the ninth century.

Having subdued the local Lawa tribes, the Mon ruled this area without challenge until at least the 11th century, when they came into conflict with the

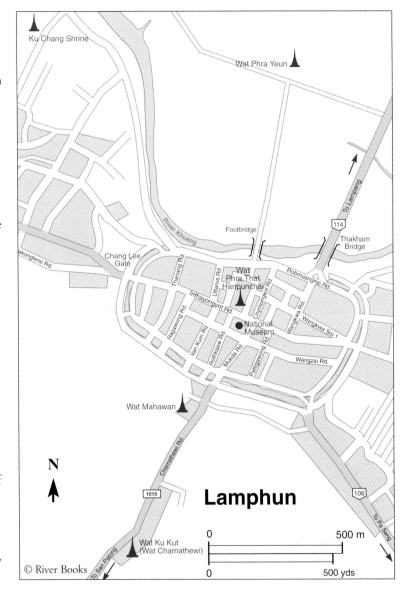

Khmers who had, by 1025 at the latest, taken over Lopburi. The chronicles describe two wars between Haripunjaya and Lopburi about a century apart, but with many embellishments that may be more legendary than factual. After the first war, the town apparently suffered a cholera epidemic around 1050, and the population reportedly emigrated to the Mon area of lower Burma (around Pegu) for six years. The second war with Lopburi involved Haripunjaya's King Adityaraja, who came to power around 1150. He supposedly attacked Lopburi but was forced to flee back to Haripunjaya, where the Khmer troops laid siege. They returned twice to attack the town, but without result.

Since these accounts may be partly imaginary, it is not known whether or not Khmer hegemony prevailed at this distance from the capital at Angkor. The lack of evidence from the Khmer side, and lack of archaeological remains, suggest that it was weak or non-existent. In any case, by the mid-13th century Khmer power in the central plains weakened and Thai rebellions took place at Si Satchanalai, Sukhothai and elsewhere. Haripunjaya's independence, however, ended definitively in 1281 when it was seized by the Tai King Mangrai.

Rule from the North

Traders from Haripunjaya regularly visited the Kok valley in the north, and Mangrai, who had made his capital at Chiang Rai in 1262, began to hear reports of Haripunjaya's wealth and considered launching a military offensive. His generals, however, were less confident and advised against it. An official in Mangrai's administration called Ai Fa thought it could be managed "by stratagems and ruses of one sort or another", and Mangrai agreed to this very Tai approach to problems of this kind. Under the pretence of banishment, Ai Fa went to Haripunjaya and gained the confidence of the Mon king, Yi Ba. He became a judge and a close adviser, and over seven years managed to isolate the king from the people, deviously representing him as an oppressor. By the time Mangrai had arrived with his troops, the Haripunjaya population were so alienated that the city fell with little resistance, marking the end of the Mon kingdom.

Mon settlements such as Lamphun, Lampang and Phrae were typically oval in plan, and this can still be seen in the form of the moat and the roads flanking it on either side. An interesting embellishment on this is the reference in at least two of the chronicles to the planning of the city by two legendary ascetics, Sudorasi and Sukkadandarasi, who chose the shape of a sea-shell for its outline. This feature was known and discussed by King Mangrai and his friends when he founded Chiang Mai, although the actual shape of Lamphun conforms to a shell only in the vaguest way.

Wat Phra That Haripunchai ***

Located in the centre of the town, this is the largest *wat* and certainly one of the most important in Lanna. The most usual access is from Inthayongyot Road, from where a gate on the east side allows vehicles to enter the outer enclosure. In fact, the main entrance is on the east from a small road running by the River Khuang, a tributary of the Ping, and this a more rewarding approach; in any case the description, as for most *wat*,

Mon terracotta Buddha head from Wat Mahawan, at the National Museum.

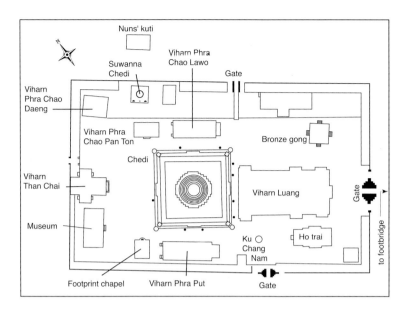

Plan of Wat Phra That Haripunchai.

begins here. Because of Wat Phra That Haripunchai's size and importance, it is surrounded by an outer enclosure for various secular activities: a school to the north, and on your left as you enter, a car park. The actual *putthawat* – the sacred enclosure – is within the cloistered walls guarded by the two large *singh* guardians ahead of you, painted brown with white trim. The modern building on your right within its own small enclosure is the *ubosot*, located outside the *putthawat* for extra seclusion.

Wat Haripunchai was the principal *wat* of the early Mon settlement, and reputedly founded by King Adityaraja to enshrine a relic of the Buddha that he had discovered in an urn buried in the garden of his palace. This was shortly after his accession around 1150, although none of the present buildings was built earlier than the 15th century.

The Viharn Luang

As you enter through the elaborately stuccoed gatehouse, ahead of you is the large Viharn Luang, rebuilt in 1925 after the earlier building had collapsed during an earthquake in 1915. It contains the bronze Phra Chao Thong Thip Buddha, flanked by two other large images. As its name indicated, this is the principal *viharn* of the *wat*, and according to Boisselier, The Buddhas "Combined the Pala-Sena tradition of attire and and attitude with an aesthetic derived from the Dvaravati school ..... but in 1964

Wat Haripunchai, with its 46-metre gold-encrusted chedi.

*Above: cleaning the temple lion
guardian at the east gate.*

*Right: Buddhas in Viharn Luang, the
main viharn*

*Below: ninteenth century ho trai, or
library.*

they were excessively restored and unfortunately defaced
.... one still may see that the neck wrinkles were
emphatically marked in concentric lines and that the large
curls of hair were surmounted by an undeveloped *ushnisha*
ending in a large, smooth conical ornament."

The Ho Trai
To the left of the Viharn Luang is a very fine 19th century
raised *ho trai*, restored in the 1920s. Like that at Wat Phra
Singh, it is an elegant wooden triple-roofed building,
rather like a miniature, vertically-elongated *viharn*, on a
high masonry base and facing west. Note the carving of the
guardian *kala* face on the pediments at each end, and the
completely carved walls. This entire structure stands on a
raised platform, reached by steps guarded by two small
Chinese lions. Between the *ho trai* and the south cloister
wall of the enclosure is a well with an old stone kneeling
elephant, possibly Mon. From here, walk across to the
opposite side of the Viharn Luang, where a huge bronze
gong hangs in a raised open pavilion. This was cast in 1860
at Wat Phra Singh in Chiang Mai and is claimed to be the
world's largest (although in fact it is smaller than that at
the Mahamuni Pagoda in Mandalay).

The Chedi

Behind the Viharn Luang, in the middle of the enclosure, is the spectacular Phra Maha That Chedi, dedicated to the Year of the Cock and rising to 46 metres. The Jinakalamali chronicle records that the original reliquary, just four metres high, had four pillars, was open on its four sides and was sheathed in gold supplied by the king's wife. In the early 13th century a *chedi* twice the height was built around it, and in 1448 the *chedi* that you now see was built over all this on the

Kala on the east gable of the ho-trai.

instructions of King Tilokaraj. The final additions were the four *chat* (parasols) at the corners and the nine-tier one on the summit,

Bronze gong in its open pavilion.

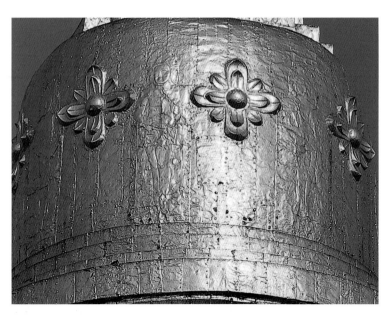

Repoussée Buddha images, just visible under the gold on the chedi, Wat Haripunchai.

reputedly weighing 68 kilos of gold, all installed by Chao Kawila at the beginning of the 19th century. The entire structure, with its redented square base and three prominent circular mouldings below the relic chamber, is covered in gilded copper plates known as *chang-go* and is surrounded by gilded railings. Four small chapels, each with miniature multi-tiered roofs, stand in the middle of each side, containing Buddha images.

This *phra that* is one of the most perfect examples of a 15th century Lanna *chedi*, with every important element clearly defined. The base is pure Lanna – square, redented at the corners, and indented vertically – and distinctive triangular projections decorate the top of each corner. Above this rises the type example of a Sukhothai-modified Sinhalese round *stupa:* three diminishing plinths, topped with three circular mouldings representing the Three Worlds. The bell, square *harmika*, shaft and diminishing circular mouldings taper to the finial. The bell is decorated with relief flowers, and in between these, just visible under the latest application of gold in 1980, are larger-than-lifesize walking Buddha images in repoussée on bronze sheets. These were attached in 1447 when the *chedi* in its present form was built; however, according to inscriptions they date from around 1330 and may have been on the underlying *chedi*. Their sinuous walking pose is in the Sukhothai style, and for this reason may possibly date from the later part of the 14th century.

Other features

Surrounding the main *chedi* are a number of other buildings, principally *viharn*, named after the various Buddha images that they house. If you stand by the *ho trai* looking towards the *chedi*, the oldest and most attractive of these is facing you; this is the Viharn Phra Put. As you walk towards it, you pass the Ku Chang Nam, a drum-like red stone topped with diminishing rings. It is a symbolic model of Mount Meru, built over a former well. Immediately behind the Viharn Phra Put, you will find a small open pavilion which contains the Phra Putthabat Si Roi: a set of four footprints of the Buddha, one inside the other. Beyond this, in the south-west corner, is an ostentatious new building that houses the *wat* museum.

Continue around the north side of the *chedi*. On the left, before the gate leading out to Inthayongyot Road, is the Viharn Than Chai, containing a standing Buddha image flanked by six others. On the other side of the gate is the Viharn Phra Chao Daeng, and directly to the east of this is the slim brick Suwanna Chedi. This rises in diminishing square tiers – each lined with niches containing standing

The Viharn Phra Put at Wat Haripunchai.

The Suwanna Chedi is a copy of the Mahapol Chedi at Wat Ku Kut.

images of the Buddha – and is a 1418 copy of the Mahapol Chedi at Wat Ku Kut, the most famous of all the Mon Haripunchai monuments. Finally, between this and the main *chedi* are two other *viharn*: the Viharn Phra Chao Pan Ton and the Viharn Phra Chao Lawo.

This completes the inventory of the inner enclosure, although outside through the north gate, by the school playground, are two other buildings of passing interest. One is the small Viharn Saenkachai, which contains a gilded image of Saenkachai (Kaccadana in Pali). He was a scholar and disciple of the Buddha, usually rendered as a fat-bodied gnome-like figure and generally believed nowadays to impart good luck. The other is an old but undated brick *chedi* called the Chedi Chiang Yan, featuring a tall square base with projecting niches on all four sides, a slim bell and spire, and four small spires at the corners. In style it is similar to the four-corner *chedi* at the heart of Wat Mahathat in Sukhothai.

Gilded image of Saenkachai - whose image is believed to impart good luck - in the viharn of the same name.

The National Museum **

On Inthayongyot Road, opposite the rear entrance to Wat Haripunchai, is the National Museum, which has a small but good collection, including Mon sculptures, most in stucco and terracotta, but including a fine head, torso, feet and hands of a bronze Buddha image. The facial features and the animated expressions of many of these pieces are distinctive. Also of note is a fine howdah which includes its original canopy, elegantly curved in lacquered bamboo.

Howdah in gilded wood, in the National Museum.

Mon bronze Buddha torso and head, in the National Museum.

Wat Phra Yeun *

Across the Khuang River by footbridge from the main east entrance of Wat Haripunchai, and one kilometre down the lane, is 'The Monastery of the Standing Buddha', set among trees. An alternative approach by car is to take Route 114 in the direction of Lampang and, having crossed the river to the southeast of the footbridge, turn left after one kilometre.

It was built in 1370 by King Kü Na for the monk Sumana (whom he had persuaded to move from Sukhothai), on a site that already had an 8.5-metre standing Buddha, supposedly from the 11th century. Kü Na added three more large standing Buddha images, and then had a *mondop* built to house them all, even though the revered monk stayed only for a couple of years before moving on to Wat Umong in Chiang Mai. Between 1900 and 1907 the original *mondop* was replaced by the present *chedi*, which is in the form of a square, stepped Burmese temple in late-Pagan style. Its redented corners and large projecting niches each contain a standing Buddha image smaller than the original statues. The bell-shaped *chedi* on the summit is relatively small, topped with a *hti* and surrounded by four smaller versions. The entire structure stands on a high square terraced base with staircase. At its base on the north side, a grey sandstone *stele* – the oldest in the Ping Valley, inscribed around 1371 – records the 14th century building work in Thai and Pali scripts, and refers to King Mangrai, who had died some 55 or 60 years previously.

Ku Chang

In the north-west part of town is Ku Chang, or 'Elephant Shrine'. It is locally believed to be the burial site of Queen Chamathewi's famous elephant, which helped save Haripunchai in a battle with the Lawa by crushing the attacking commander at the northern city gate. In front of two ruined brick *chedi* a number of carved elephants have been installed. Although it is probably not worth the effort of visiting except for model elephant enthusiasts, you can reach it from the east entrance of Wat Haripunchai by following the road along the river for 1.8 kilometres and turning down the lane on the left for 200 metres.

After Wat Haripunchai, Lamphun's other famous *chedi* is that at Wat Ku Kut, a kilometre out of town to the west. From the east entrance of Wat Haripunchai drive south, and continue around the curving road that follows the canal and traces the outline of the original oval city walls.

Wat Mahawan

On the west side of town, Route 1015 heads west in the direction of San Patong. Almost immediately, you pass Wat Mahawan on your right. Despite the stunningly garish *viharn*, it is worth a brief stop to look at the *ho trai*. Although only 60 years old, this is an attractive and substantial two-storied building, cruciform in plan and with two roof tiers along each axis: possibly a central Thai influence. The gable

This chedi replaced Wat Phra Yeun's original mondop.

Standing Buddha on the east side of the chedi.

design features intertwined *naga* among lotus flowers, with a single elephant head in the centre, all gilded. The elegant bell-tower is from the same period.

Wat Ku Kut **

A kilometre west of Lamphun on this road on the left-hand side, you come to the stylistically and historically important Wat Ku Kut (also known as Wat Chamathewi). According to legend, Queen Chamathewi ordered an archer to fire an arrow north, and where it landed determined the site of the temple, although given its distance from town even an English longbowman would have fallen far short.

The gable of the ho trai, Wat Mahawan.

Plan of Wat Ku Kut.

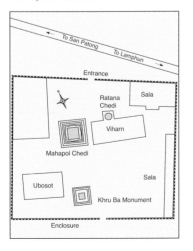

The importance of this site is that it contains one of the last surviving examples of Dvaravati architecture, the Mahapol Chedi, also called the Suwan Chang Kot Chedi. This is a slender 21-metre five-tiered pyramid on a square plan, a style known as *ratana cetiya* ('jewel monument'): brick and laterite with stucco decoration. Its date is uncertain, but the legendary origins of the 7th or 8th century can be discounted. According to a Mon inscription from the beginning of the early 13th century, it was rebuilt by King Adityaraja as Mahabalachetiya ('Great Power Chedi') in about 1150, but the present structure dates from a 1218 restoration, following an earthquake. It has been copied a number of times elsewhere in Lanna, as in the grounds of Wat Haripunchai; also, the seven-tiered Satmahal Prasada in Polonnaruwa, the 11th and 12th century capital of Sri Lanka, is quite similar. This latter may have been built by Mon monks, copying either the Mahapol Chedi or other examples, long since ruined, in Mon centres further south. Archaeological evidence at Nakhon Pathom suggests that this style of *chedi* might have been quite common among the Mon.

Three niches on each side of each tier contain standing Buddha images in stucco cast from molds, with the broad foreheads typical of Mon sculpture and which are evident at the museum in town. The left hand of each hangs down and the right hand, where not broken off, is raised in *abhaya*. The hem of the robe shows clearly as a ridge across the ankles, but the legs show through so as to make the robe seem transparent, a device to convey the golden glow of the Buddha's skin. In style, they show clear continuity with the Dvaravati tradition of the Mon to the south, although the way in which the robes are drawn back from the forearm possibly shows a Pala-Sena influence, maybe from Pagan. From the 15-metre square base, the proportionate reduction of everything, statues included, gives the illusion of even greater height, but the finial above the fifth tier is broken.

Left: the stepped Mahapol Chedi of Wat Ku Kut, with Buddhas in niches.

Above: Dvaravati Buddha in niche.

On the left of the enclosure from the entrance, next to the modern *viharn*, is the smaller Ratana Chedi ('Gem Chedi'), also Mon, 11.5 metres tall and made of brick with stucco decoration. Thought to have been built at the beginning of the 13th century by King Sabbasiddhi, it is octagonal up to the bell-shaped relic chamber and, with its 4.4-metre base, is quite slender in proportion. Each of the eight faces of the tall principal tier has a terracotta standing Buddha image in a niche, with both hands raised in *abhaya*. Above this are three reductions, the topmost tier with small curved triangular niches, and even further above is the relic chamber, whose finial is missing.

The *ubosot*, usually ignored in the attention given to the Mon *chedi*, is certainly worth looking at for its well-carved gable. This is the east-

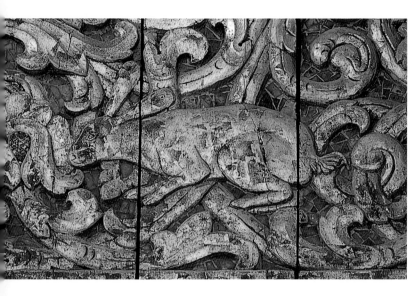

Gilded rabbit, detail from the ubosot gable at Wat Ku Kut.

facing building on the south-west side of the grounds, set among trees and in its own walled enclosure. Its tall proportions identify central Thai influence, but the gable carving is distinctly Lanna, featuring zodiacal animals set among openwork vines, all gilded. An old *stele* stands in front of the doorway.

HEADING SOUTH FROM LAMPHUN

Take Route 106 and head in a south-westerly direction. This takes you through the small town of Pa Sang, which was established by Chao Kawila after the defeat of the Burmese in the late 18th century. Before the devastated and deserted Chiang Mai was made habitable again, Kawila and the royal court lived here, between 1775 and 1797. The area is known for cotton weaving, for its Mon population, and also for its Tai Lü settlements.

Wat Pa Sang Ngam
Its name translates as 'The Beautiful Pa Sang Monastery'; it is located in the centre of town and is worth a brief stop *en route,* especially for its attractive 19th century *ho trai*. This is a two-storey plastered brick structure with signs of European influence in its arches, pillars and mouldings.

Wat Chang Khao Noi Neua *
A further 2 kilometres south on Route 106 on the right is 'The Northern Monastery of the Small Rice-threshing Basket'. The gilded *chedi* just inside the gate is its most immediately striking feature. Gilded copper sheets cover it entirely, and its redented and indented base is a miniature version of the one at Wat Haripunchai, including the triangular corner projections. Its position in front of the *viharn* rather than behind it is unusual, but the *wat* of this area have a number of idiosyncracies. Inside the *viharn,* two rows of seven lacquered and gilded teak pillars make a narrow aisle leading to the Buddha image, and the hanging cloth *tung* banners from the roof beams are a clue that this is a Tai Lü *wat*. A smaller gable on the left of the main building fronts a long hall joined to the *viharn* roof at the gutter.

Wat Chang Khao Noi Tai
'The Southern Monastery of the Small Rice-threshing Basket' is another 2 kilometres south from its sister monastery. Recent modernisation of the buildings in the enclosure on the left side of the road make this less interesting, but an unusual feature is the siting of

the *ubosot* and a Burmese-style *chedi* on the opposite side of the road. Note that the *bai sema* surrounding the *ubosot* demarcating the sacred area are natural stones rather than carved slabs: a local characteristic. The Burmese-style *chedi* is in a sunken courtyard, surrounded by a wall, and has more than the usual profusion of stucco figures, including a number of animated *chinthe* and various *thewada*.

The gilded chedi at Wat Chang Khao Noi Neua, its base copied from the one at Wat Phra That Haripunchai.

Wat Pa Tan

A rash of modern reconstruction has reduced the number of formerly interesting *wat* along this road, although Wat Pa Tan ('The Sugar Palm Forest Monastery'), 3 kilometres further south, has a Burmese-style *chedi* similar to that at Wat Chang Khao Noi Tai.

Wat San Kamphaeng

After another kilometre (8 kilometres from Pa Sang), turn right at the village of Ban Makok. A lane winds through the largely traditional village, with a sprinkling of pleasant old teak houses, before emerging into rice fields. At almost 2 kilometres from the main road, on the right-hand side, Wat San Kamphaeng is set among the fields. While this, too, has been the victim of some garish re-building, it has two curiosities tucked away on the east side of the laterite-walled enclosure. These are two small square ponds next to each other, one containing a dilapidated wooden *ho trai* standing in the water on pillars, the other containing a *bot nam*: an ubosot surrounded by water. Windowless, and built of unfaced laterite blocks, this is idiosyncratic rather than attractive. As elsewhere, the *bai sema* are rough stones.

Gilded lion on the ubosot at Wat Chang Khao Noi Tai.

Wat Phra Putthabat Tak Pha

Continuing south, at the Km. 136 marker is a road to the left leading to the hill-top *chedi* of Wat Phra Putthabat Tak Pha 2 kilometres away. A *viharn* contains a footprint of the Buddha, while the former abbot Khru Ba Phroma Jakko, who died in 1984, is commemorated in a *kuti*.

FURTHER AFIELD

Wat Ban Pang is 51 kilometres south of here on Route 106, and, being at the birthplace of Khru Ba Srivichai, contains memorabilia of the famous monk. However, it is probably not worth the journey for itself.

Further to the west, Route 108 from Chiang Mai follows the lower Ping River down towards the Bhumipol Dam. After 44 kilometres you pass, on your left, an isolated hill on top of which is **Wat Phra That Doi Noi**, with a *chedi* and fine views of the surrounding valley all around.

Wat Phra That Sri Chom Thong **

The town of Chom Thong is 15 kilometres further on from Wat Phra That Doi Noi. While the town has little in itself to offer, its wat is one of the oldest and most famous in Lanna, and worth the drive. Because the enclosure is on a low hill that falls away sharply on the east side, with room only for a narrow staircase, the main entrance is at the rear from the main road, through a white-and-gold archway. Dominating the enclosure is the exceptionally attractive *chedi*, covered in gilded copper plates and built in 1452. It features a high square redented base which is also strongly indented in two stages. The upper part, circular in plan, continues the same diminishing profile, through three prominently ribbed mouldings, diminutive bell, *harmika*, ribbed spire and *hti*.

Wat Sri Chom Thong's importance derives from its sacred relic of the *wat*, which is believed to be a fragment from the right cranium of the Buddha and is called Thakhinamoli. According to legend it emerged in 1499 after centuries in a cave under the hill, and its late arrival explains why it is kept in the *viharn* rather than the *chedi*, which had already been built. There are, in fact, two *viharn*, joined together and immediately to the east of the *chedi*, facing out over the valley of the Ping.

The principal *viharn* was rebuilt in 1818 on the site of the original, which was constructed in 1517 on the command of King Muang Kaeo

Guardian figure at the entrance to the viharn at Wat Chom Thong.

Right: Plan of Wat Phra That Sri Chom Thong.

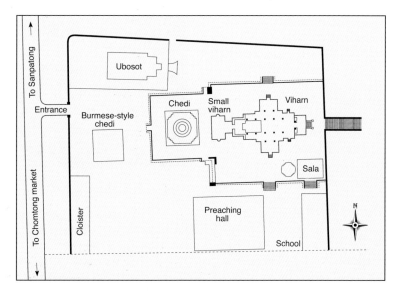

The distinctive, high chedi of Wat Phra That Sri Chom Thong, with its three exaggerated mouldings representing the three worlds.

Guardian and lion.

Buddha images and inscribed stones behind the ku in the viharn.

Poles supporting the bodhi tree at Wat Chom Thong.

Map of Mae Chaem valley

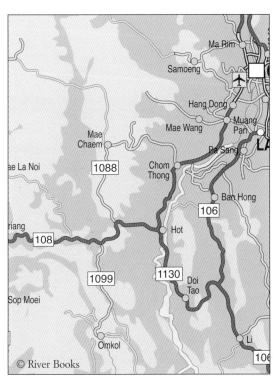

© River Books

of Chiang Mai, and has a triple-tiered roof and two extensions at the sides that give it essentially a cruciform floor plan. At the transept is the gilded stucco *ku* containing the relic in its crystal and gold urn, also built in 1517. Behind the *ku*, a door connects to the much smaller Viharn Noi, built at right angles so that it faces south, and squeezed between the main *viharn* and the *chedi*. This contains a monk's bed from the early 16th century donated by King Muang Kaeo.

The complex of *chedi* and *viharn* occupy a raised terrace, guarded by lions in different styles. Also within the enclosure are a tall *ubosot* in central Thai style, a smaller Burmese *chedi,* a large, old *bodhi* tree and an active meditation centre founded by the present abbot.

THE MAE CHAEM VALLEY

To the west of Chom Thong rises Thailand's highest mountain, Doi Inthanon (2565 metres), and behind this is the isolated valley of the Mae Chaem River, a tributary of the Ping. Because of geological uplift, the lower reaches have cut a deep gorge, the Ob Luang, making access difficult. It is only recently that sealed roads have made it easier to drive in and out, and the valley has retained a considerable and so far unspoilt charm. Leave Chom Thong on the road back to Chiang Mai, and 1.5 kilometres north of town turn left onto Route 1009 towards Doi Inthanon. Higher up, where this road turns north towards the summit, a smaller road, Route 1192, turns left towards Mae Chaem, signposted 22 kilometres away.

This narrow road winds its way down through forested hills, and after 20 kilometres makes a long right-hand bend round the spur of a hill. At the end of this bend, look out for a sharp left turn onto Route 1088, in the direction of Hot.

Wat Pa Daet **

After 1 kilometre, take the second of two lanes to the right and you are almost immediately in the grounds of Wat Pa Daet As its name implies, this was a forest *wat*, set apart from the villages, and it is still surrounded by ricefields.

The enclosure contains the *viharn*, a *ho trai* and *sala*, while the new *ubosot* is outside, surrounded by a small moat. The *viharn* was built in 1877 and carefully restored in the 1980s. Note the quirky conflation of Burmese *chinthe* and *naga-makara* balustrade, in which the lions emerge from the *makara* mouths, as at Wat Phra Singh's library in Chiang Mai and a number of other *wat* in the Mae Chaem Valley. The pediment is divided into three rectangular panels, into which are attached separately carved figures: the one on top is a *thewada* emerging from a lotus flower, and the two below are mythical lions. The long panel below is a mixture of the floating cloud design and *khankhot hua nak*: the heads of *nagas* worked from leaves. Inside, on the upper wall panels, are murals dating from the 19th

The carefully restored viharn of Wat Pa Daet.

The Karen

The most numerous of Thailand's hill-tribes, and the longest settled (since the 18th century) are the Karen. Because their original homeland, at least within historical times was in eastern Burma, they naturally settled in the west of Lanna — not just in Mae Hong Son province, but also in the hills west of the Ping valley, particularly around Doi Inthanon. There are two divisions of the tribe in Lanna, Sgaw and Pwo, identifiable in their homespun dress. Sgaw women generally stick to red or pink stitching, while the Pwo decorate their dress more elaborately. 'Karen' is the English name for this tribe; the Thai is 'Kariang' or 'Yang', but they themselves do not have a term for the entire tribal group. Among the hill-tribes, the Karen have the strongest weaving reputation, and use a simple back-strap loom and a single-warp technique to make strong geometric designs, usually in red and white — both banded and checquerboard. The tunic is very simple: two rectangular panels, stitched together with openings for the neck and arms. The women pictured here are from the Pwo sub-group.

century. Note the scenes showing the birth of the Buddha in the centre, which include an old local way of giving birth, with the woman hanging onto the branches of a tree while assisted by the mid-wife.

Mural showing the birth of the Buddha in a local interpretation.

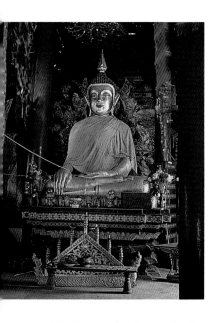

Buddha image in the viharn at Wat Pa Daet.

Right; One of few surviving bot nam, Wat Puttha En.

Rectangular panels decorate the gable end of the viharn at Wat Puttha En.

Wat Yang Luang *

Back on Route 1088, turn left and immediately left again down another lane that leads, after 1 kilometre, to Wat Yang Luang, which was founded in 1483. The *viharn*, with its elegantly curved roof-lines, houses a principal Buddha in *bhumisparsa* and an ancient *ku*.

Wat Puttha En *

From these two *wat* return to Route 1192 and continue the 2.5 kilometres into the town of Mae Chaem. At the T-junction in front of the municipal offices, turn left, then right to cross the bridge over the Mae Chaem River. Then turn right and follow the river. After almost 2 kilometres you will see **Wat Phrao Num** on your right, and about 600 metres beyond this, on the left where the road bends to the right, Wat Puttha En. Built in 1868, it has one of the country's few surviving *bot nam* ('water chapel'): an *ubosot* on piles in the middle of a lotus pond. This is on your right as soon as you enter the gate. Note the arrangement of the *naga* running the length of each side also just above the surface of the water, with heads at both ends; this is, of

Buddha image in the local primitive style at Wat Kong Kan.

course, a water serpent. The *viharn* at the head of the staircase has a crude but attractive gable, decorated with coloured rectangles and lozenges with glass inlay. Behind are the newly renovated *chedi* and a *ho trai* raised on pillars, painted red with gold decorations.

Wat Kong Kan *
4.5 kilometres further north along this same road is Wat Kong Kan; though dilapidated, the *viharn* has considerable rustic charm, and also contains a large Buddha image, the Phra Ong Yai, which is in local primitive style with large eyes. In the same way as Wat Pa Daet, the entrance is flanked with *makara* disgorging lions rather than *naga*.

Returning to Mae Chaem, if instead of turning left to cross the bridge you continue straight on, you reach the weaving village of Ban Thong Fai after 1 kilometre. On looms under the houses, local women weave *tin chok* – the decorated hem of the traditional Thai dress – and *sabai* – scarves – in the distinctive patterns of the Mae Chaem. An alternative way in or out of the valley is on Route 1088 from Hot, 68 kilometres distant; this can be combined with the Doi Inthanon road to make a 154-kilometre circuit.

Tin chock, the decorated hem of the traditional Thai dress, woven at Ban Thong Fai.

THE UPPER VALLEY

North of Chiang Mai, the upper valley of the Ping contains some very attractive scenery, but little of art interest. Nevertheless, now that the road across the mountains from Fang to Chiang Rai has been finished and sealed, this makes a pleasant way to reach the north of Lanna. The alternative, which is rather more direct, is to drive north-east from Chiang Mai on Route 118, leaving the valley and the province by crossing the watershed and descending to Chiang Rai *via* Mae Khachan, Wiang Pa Pao and Mae Suai. For the upper Valley, however, take the Chang Phuak Road north and continue. As Route 107 it leads north to the town of Fang.

Wat Po Thong Charoen, set among ricefields near Doi Saket.

Wat Ta Kham

At the small market town of Mae Malai, 36 kilometres north of Chiang Mai, turn left onto Route 1095, the road to Pai, for a short detour. At the Km. 9 marker, turn left into a lane that winds through fields for 1 kilometre before reaching this attractive and unspoiled village *wat*. The *viharn*, unusually for such a small community, has a four-tiered roof,

The unspoiled four-tiered viharn at Wat Ta Kham.

the topmost carrying a central finial of a *hongse* and gilded umbrella. There is also the addition of an entrance in the south side with a portico that has a two-tiered roof. The main portico at the east end is open, with four gold-on-red teak pillars, but the approach to it is from the sides rather than the front. Inside are the remains of naïve murals.

Return to the main highway at Mae Malai or, if you are heading for Pai and Mae Hong Son (*see pages 224 and 225*) continue west up into the hills on Route 1095. North from Mae Malai, the main valley road passes through the district town of Mae Taeng after just 4 kilometres and then, 14 kilometres further on enters the narrow gorge where the Ping River descends sharply from the upper valley floor around Chiang Dao. Once through this you are among striking limestone scenery, with the summit of Doi Chiang Dao (2175 metres) visible on the left.

Chiang Dao

The 'Chiang Dao Cave' is located on the eastern slopes of the mountain, 5 kilometres west of the main road; you need to turn at the Km. 72 marker, 2 kilometres north of the small market town of Chiang Dao. The limestone passages that wind deep under the mountain were used by *reussi* (hermits), and contain a number of Burmese-style Buddha images and offerings of various kinds left by local Shan. The first cavern is lit by daylight from an opening in the roof; steps lead down to a dark cavern containing more statues.

Chiang Dao itself has a curious history. It began in the 18th century as a place of banishment for people who were believed to be possessed by evil spirits known as *phi pop*. There were other similar settlements in Lanna, and it is an indication of the level of superstition that ran through its communities that a town could be so populated. The hapless exiles were more often than not suffering from malaria or else, through their behaviour, stood out from society in some unacceptable way. Today, the town retains a number of two-storey teak buildings along the main street.

Mural in the viharn at Wat Ta Kham.

PHRAO AND THE LANNA COUNTRYSIDE

East of Chiang Dao, across the limestone hills and ridges that now comprise the Sri Lanna National Park, is the tributary valley of the Ngat River, of which the small town of Phrao is the principal settlement. You can reach this from Chiang Dao by way of a small road that passes through pleasant landscape, though not much else.

Route 1150 leaves the main highway to the right at the Km. 83 marker, 13 kilometres north of Chiang Dao. The drive is 32 kilometres to Phrao, from where Route 1001 leads south to Chiang Mai (94 kilometres). This is typical Lanna countryside, sufficiently out of the way to be largely undeveloped, so there is little of architectural interest. Phrao itself was built as a *wiang* (a fortified settlement), and has two circular earthen ramparts on its two hills, connected by two short parallel ramparts. It is now a small market town, also frequented by hill-tribes.

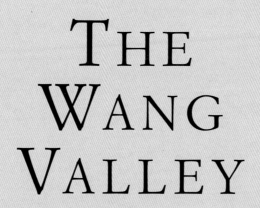

THE WANG VALLEY

To the east of Chiang Mai, across a range of forested hills, lies the Wang Valley. Its main town and provincial capital, Lampang, preserves more of its long history than does Chiang Mai, and the surrounding countryside is dotted with ancient monasteries, including the jewel of Lanna, Wat Phra That Lampang Luang.

Harvest time in the upper valley; winnowing rice into a traditional large basket

The second most important Lanna valley draining south into the Chao Phraya basin is that of the Wang River, to the east of the Ping, even though it is only 335 kilometres long. Access to the Central Plains is in fact much easier up this valley, and it carries Route 1 up from Tak to the principal town, Lampang, as well as the railway line from Bangkok. The main road that connects the two valleys is Route 11 from Chiang Mai to Lampang (108 kilometres), crossing the watershed south of the peak Doi Khun Tan.

LAMPANG

Map of the central part of the Wang Valley.

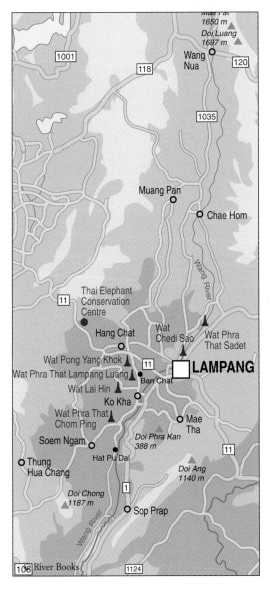

The town was originally a Mon settlement, as can be seen from the slightly skewed oval plan of its walls. Called Khelang Nakhon and later Lakhon, it was a part of the Haripunchai kingdom, ruled from what is now Lamphun and reputedly founded by one of the twin sons of Queen Chamathewi. The original centre was north of the river, around the location of Wat Phra Kaeo Don Tao, but this later spread to the south side.

The town was protected not only by its walls but by four strategically sited *wiang*: fortified settlements, of which Lampang Luang to the south-west and a site next to Wat Phra That Sadet to the north-east can be identified. Nevertheless, it fell to King Mangrai's troops at the end of 1296 after a decisive battle near Chiang Mai. When Haripunchai fell in 1281, the Mon King Yi Ba retreated to Khelang Nakhon, which was ruled by his son, and the two prepared over the years an attack on the Tai forces. In the event, the Chiang Mai army proved victorious under Mangrai's son, who was subsequently given the name Chai Songkhram ('Victorious in War'), and Khelang Nakhon became a part of the kingdom of Lanna.

However, it too fell under Burmese suzerainty from the middle of the 16th century until, in 1774, Prince Kawila of Lampang joined Phraya Chaban of Chiang Mai and, with Siamese help, defeated the Burmese army and ended the two centuries of Lanna's suppression. Kawila went on to rule Chiang Mai for the Siamese in 1781. Lampang's location, with its reasonably direct access to the Central Plains, ensured its role as a trading centre, and this was consolidated by the extension of the railway from Bangkok to here in 1916, and to Chiang Mai in 1919.

During the 19th century Lampang became, as did Chiang Mai, an important centre for teak, with at least 4,000 elephants regularly working in the area. Because this industry was controlled by the British, they naturally brought many Burmese to work with them, with the result that Lampang now has a number of fine Burmese temples, although the town's population today has little interest in them, and some are deteriorating through lack of funding.

While Chiang Mai has the greatest concentration of *wat* in Lanna, it has also inevitably been the focus of

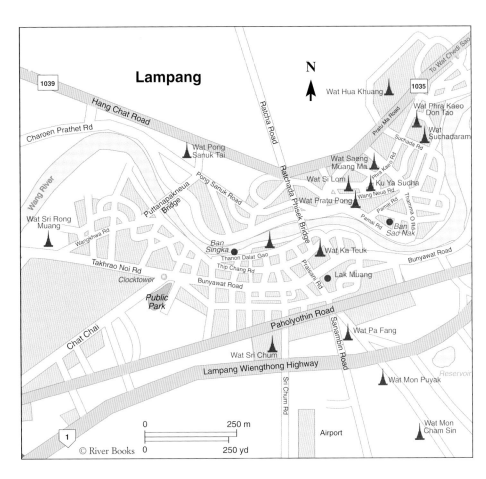

The city of Lampang.

development, with the result that it has been subject not only to increasing Central Thai influences but also cosmopolitan growth. In this respect, Lampang has so far been largely passed by, and because of this the town has both fine, well-preserved *wat* and a reasonably traditional urban setting with some lovely old teak houses and pleasant river views. It is also a short drive from what is generally considered to be the most beautiful and traditional of all Lanna *wat*, Wat Phra That Lampang Luang *(see page 146)*. In all, the town can justifiably lay claim to being the leading centre of Lanna culture.

THE OLD CITY

The city fortifications at their greatest extent enclosed a roughly oval area curving from the north-west to the south-east, bisected by the Wang River. Within these old city limits, the newer market and commercial districts are south of the river, while the original settlement is to the north, with now a quiet, village-like residential district and Lampang's principal *wat*. There were city gates: two north and two south of the river. The north-east Pratu Ma ('Horse Gate') led to the upper valley, while the Pratu Chiang Mai on the west led across the hills to the Lanna capital. South of the river, the Pratu Hua Wiang led east, and the Pratu Chiang Rai south-west towards Tak.

Old Market Road (Thanon Talat Gao), Lampang.

One important building that has been removed to Ancient City near Bangkok is the **Prince of Lampang's Palace**, a large and spacious *ho kham* raised on teak pillars. This is one of many traditional structures from around the country which have been collected and preserved (including a Shan *wat* from Ngao) in natural settings, and it is well worth a half-day visit from Bangkok.

We start in the oldest part of Lampang, north of the river. Because the original street pattern followed the bends of the river, the several *wat* were not oriented exactly to face east. Instead, those close to the river face towards the water, which means between south and east, while a few others, in the western part of town, took the other alternative – between north and north-east. The street layout is rather disorienting at first, and most of the directions given here are from the starting point of Lampang's oldest bridge, which is distinctive and easy enough to find. For no good reason, Lampang's highway department uses non-standard and inconsistent spelling of street names in English, which adds to the confusion.

Wat Phra Kaeo Don Tao ***

The city's principal *wat* lies close to the river in the east, and was supposedly founded by the first Mon ruler of Lampang. To reach it from the centre of town, cross the river by the Ratchada Phisek Bridge and turn right at the first set of traffic lights onto Phra Kaeo Road. This turns sharp left after less than 100 metres, and then forks right after another 100 metres. Continue for 1 kilometre, and you will find the large *wat* enclosure on your right.

A local legend asserts that around the year 500, while the area suffered a famine, a monk descended from heaven and a pious local woman, Mae ('mother') Suchada, offered him an unusually shaped water-melon. Inside was a large green gem, which turned miraculously into a Buddha image with help from the god Indra. Thus the temple acquired its name: 'The Monastery of the Emerald Buddha on the Water Jar Knoll'. However, the joint efforts of Mae Suchada and the monk were altogether too close for local propriety, and carnal relations were suspected. The then king had the woman put to death, while the monk escaped. Naturally, another famine struck the area as a result of this poor judgement. The Buddha image that caused so much trouble is now at Wat Phra That Lampang Luang.

This legend apart, the *wat* did for 32 years actually enshrine the Emerald Buddha, Phra Kaeo Morakot, that is now in the Grand Palace, Bangkok. Two years after the image was discovered in Chiang Rai's Wat Phra Kaeo in 1434, it was taken by elephant towards Chiang Mai, where it was to have been installed. However, the animal repeatedly turned towards Lampang and, this being taken as an omen, the sacred statue was allowed to remain here until 1468, when King Tilokaraj finally had it removed to Wat Phra Singh in Chiang Mai. The statue, incidentally, is not of emerald, but probably green jasper, although, as the palladium of the Thai kingdom, it has never been subjected to an examination.

The monastic buildings are on a terrace reached by steps to the left. The approach to these steps has been somewhat defaced by an

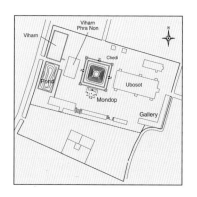

Plan of Wat Phra Kaeo Don Tao, including Wat Suchadaram

The tall gilded chedi, and next to it the Burmese-roofed open-sided mondop of Wat Don Tao.

Interior of the Burmese style mondop, with coffered ceiling and encrusted decoration.

Detail of the pyatthat, tiered spire of the mondop.

This European style cherub is a detail from the mondop's beautifully decorated ceiling.

To-scale statue of the elephant which brought the emerald Buddha to Lampang instead of Chiang Mai.

elaborate shrine to a famous monk from Wat Rakhang in Bangkok, Phra Puthha Jan To, even though he has nothing to do with this monastery. The shrine was erected by Bangkok followers. It is joined on the right by shrines to the local hero, Thippachak, who liberated Wat Lampang Luang, and to Mae Suchada and her monk.

Dominating the monastic enclosure as you walk up to the terrace is the Chedi Phra Boromathat, 50 metres tall and reputedly containing a hair of the Buddha. It has a large bell and upper section, all covered in gilded copper sheets, and a square base. In front from where you stand at the top of the steps, is a beautiful *mondop* in the style of a Burmese *pyatthat*, commissioned in 1909 by the governor of Lampang, Bunwat Wongmanit. The coffered ceiling is elaborately decorated with glass inlay in Burmese style, but with the curious addition of small gilded *cherubim,* which are evidence of some European influence. The principal Buddha image is in Burmese Mandalay style.

Northwest of the *chedi* is the Viharn Phra Non which dates from 1926 and, as its name indicates, houses a reclining Buddha. In front of this is a *sao hongse* – a tall pillar bearing the Brahmanic sacred goose – which is a Mon legacy. On the opposite side of the *chedi* is an *ubosot* built in 1924 to central Thai dimensions, and across from this is a modern *sala,* housing the Phra Chao Thong Thip Buddha which was cast in 1957. On the north side of the enclosure is a life-size statue of the recalcitrant white elephant responsible for bringing the Emerald Buddha here.

Wat Suchadaram **

Within the same outer enclosure as Wat Phra Kaeo Don Tao, in the southeast corner, is Wat Suchadaram, named after the Chao Mae Suchada of legend. In addition to a substantial *chedi* with circular mouldings, bell and spire on a square base, all raised on a stepped terrace, it comprises two very attractive and pleasantly situated buildings: the large Viharn Lai Kham in front of the *chedi*, and a smaller *ubosot* beside it. Their proportions, with sweeping, curved multi-tiered rooves reaching low towards the ground, betray an almost Laotian shape, and in fact they were built by Chiang Saen artisans who moved here in 1804 when their city, recently recaptured from the Burmese, was razed as a 'scorched earth' defensive move.

The larger *viharn* has a triple-tiered roof with unusual finials. The *cho fa* rise vertically from the gables and are backed with a decorative fin, and there is a central roof ridge finial. The lower roof finials are in the plain *tua ngao* style rather than *naga*. The gable is decorated in a combination of geometric and floral motifs, both carved and in stucco, with coloured glass inlay. Note in particular the stucco-ornamented octagonal teak pillars. Two Burmese *chinthe* guard the door. The *ubosot*, next to an old frangipani tree, stands on a raised terrace.

Burmese chinthe flank the entrance to the viharn of Wat Suchadaram, with its almost Laotian roof-line.

The ubosot's triple-tiered roof complements those of the viharn, above.

Wat Hua Khuang *

Northwest of the Wat Phra Kaeo Don Tao and Wat Suchadaram compound is 'The Monastery North of the Plaza'; the name refers to the original city centre, which was on this side of the river. To reach it, turn right out of Wat Phra Kaeo and continue north for 300 metres up Phra Kaeo Road to the junction with Pratu Ma Road. Turn left here, and the *wat* is 100 metres down the road on your right. Its *viharn* was built by the same Chiang Saen artisans responsible for the buildings at Wat Suchadaram, and has manuscripts concerning casting techniques for Buddha images.

The viharn of Wat Hua Khuang.

Wat Saeng Muang Ma.

The third of the *wat* built by the Chiang Saen deportees is also nearby. Continue southwest along Pratu Ma Road for 500 metres beyond Wat Hua Khuang and turn left onto Thamma O Road. On the right-hand side 200 metres further on, close by the junction with Phra Kaeo Road, is Wat Saeng Muang Ma. This *wat* is actually the most important in all Lampang for ritual practice, and has the local reputation of having been founded by Queen Chamathewi. The *viharn* has a striking gable, in painted and gilded wood inlaid with coloured glass, with a fierce guardian figure in the centre derived from a *kala*, flanked by monkey warriors. Inexplicably, a large part of this is obscured by a new portico.

Detail of kala figure decorating the gable at Wat Saeng Muang Ma.

The figure of a yak guards the tree shine at Wat Si Lom.

Wat Si Lom

From Wat Saeng Muang Ma, turn into Phra Kaeo Road heading south-west back into the centre of town. On the way, after 400 metres, you pass Wat Si Lom, with a revered tree shrine guarded by the statues of two ferocious *yak*, one seated on the wall, the other standing.

Ku Ya Sudha *

Just beyond here, Phra Kaeo Road joins Pratu Ma Road, and almost immediately you will find Wang Neua Road on your left. 500 metres along here, on the left of the road, is a substantial brick gate house with fine stucco decoration that includes standing *thewada*. The *wat*'s name means 'Grandmother Sudha's Grotto', and it was the entrance to the enclosure of a 15th century *wat* that must have been an impressive size, judging from this remaining gate.

Ban Sao Nak *

A short distance east along Wang Neua Road, take the lane to the right, and then first left, and you will see Ban Sao Nak ('The Many-Pillared House') on your right. It was built in 1896 for a Burmese family and is notable for the 116 teak pillars that support it. From 1964 to 1974 it was extensively restored, and concrete plinths were installed under each pillar to prevent further sinking under the considerable weight of the structure.

Wat Pratu Pong *

From Ban Sao Nak, continue a short way east to Tamma O Road, turn right towards the river and just before the bridge turn right onto Pamai Road, which follows the river bank. Another 500 metres along here, on the right, is 'The Marsh Gate Monastery'. Over the entrance to the *viharn* is a stucco relief of a grimacing *kala* grasping the writhing coils of two *naga* with massive

The remaining gate entrance to a former 15th century wat, Ku Ya Sudha.

arms, its tongue protruding. The doors below are carved in a Laotian style featuring opposed *thewada* with swords raised, standing on fantastic lions. The treatment of these creatures and the floating clouds below betrays Chinese influence. The eave brackets of the building are in the form of a leaping Hanuman.

Right: stucco relief over the entrance to the viharn at Wat Pratu Bong.

Above: Laotian style doors at the viharn entrance.

Wat Pong Sanuk Tai **

Continuing west along Pamai Road will take you back to the northern end of the Ratchada Phisek Bridge. At the traffic lights where you originally turned to go to Wat Phra Kaeo, take the opposite direction, west along Pong Sanuk Road. After 500 metres you come to Wat Pong Sanuk Tai ('The Monastery of the Southern Fun Marsh' - yes, really!) on the right. This highly distinctive late-18th century *wat* combines Lanna and Burmese styles on a mound built up to represent Mount Meru, home of the gods. Steps approach three of the four sides of the walled terrace, with a stuccoed gate at the top of the main southeast

The chedi and mondop at the unusually named Wat Pong Sanuk Tai.

staircase. In the centre of the terrace is a Lanna-style *chedi* sheathed in gilded copper sheets with *chat* at each corner in the Burmese style.

Next to it is an unusual *mondop* that blends Burmese and Lanna elements, although the workmanship is disputed and could be that of craftsmen from either Keng Tung in Burma (formerly part of Lanna) or Phayao. Square in plan, with three tiers of roof, topped with a spire and *hti*, its open-sided structure is supported by 28 teak pillars, the bases of most of which have been replaced with cement. Large gabled porches project on each side to give a cruciform base, and the intervals known as *kho song* below the two upper roof tiers are treated as false storeys, with decorated walls and windows. The corners of the second level have carved wooden figures of half-human half-bird *kinnorn*, while the top level have *hongse* with raised wings.

In the centre of the *mondop* is a cage with four Buddha images, sitting with their backs against a realistic model of a *bodhi* tree. The northwest side of the terrace is occupied by a *viharn* housing an 11-metre reclining Buddha.

Wat Ka Teuk

Across the Ratchada Phisek Bridge bridge to the southern part of the old city, this *wat* lies directly ahead at the intersection with Thip Chang Road. The older and smaller of its two *viharn* is in the traditional low Lanna style, with the front open-sided and a three-tiered roof, but with no *naga* balustrade.

Wat Pong Sanuk Tai's open-sided mondop is a mixture of Burmese and Lanna architectural styles.

Carved wooden hongse bird supporting the eave of the upper roof.

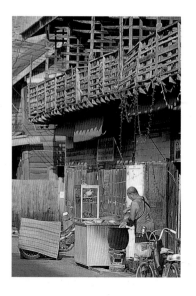

Another view of Old Market Road.

The 'Twenty-Chedi Monastery', much of which has been extensively restored.

OTHER LOCAL FEATURES

Running parallel to Thip Chang Road but next to the river, west from the bridge, is one of Lampang's oldest and best-preserved streets, **Thanon Talat Gao *** ('Old Market Road'). Most of the shops and houses date from the 19th century and are a mixture of Chinese, Burmese and European styles. At its western end, on the north side, is a fine example of a substantial Lanna house, complete with carved *kalae* crossed-beam roof decorations, called **Ban Singka ***. Close to the market area, on the corner of Praisani and Bunyawat Roads, is the **City Pillar**, the *lak muang*, unusually a group of three tall wooden posts between 2.5 and 4 metres in height.

OUTSIDE THE OLD WALLS

Wat Chedi Sao
On the north side of the city, 1.5 kilometres past Pratu Ma on Route 1035 and at the end of a lane to the left, is 'The Twenty-Chedi Monastery', so-called because of its field of whitewashed *chedi*, all with Burmese-style upper parts on redented and indented Lanna-style bases. Heavy renovation of the *chedi* as well as the buildings reduces its interest, but there is a small museum with various artefacts, including a small golden Buddha image discovered in a neighbouring field by a farmer who was ploughing, and in the process decapitated it.

Wat Pa Fang **

On the south side of the city are several Shan monasteries, some of which are highly individual. Wat Pa Fang is located 400 metres south on Sanambin Road from its intersection with Phaholyothin Road, on the way to the airport on the left. The monastery has an impressive interior, with huge round teak pillars lacquered red below and gilded above, and two principal Mandalay-style Buddha images. The *chedi* is Burmese in its flaring shape, but unusually is octagonal in plan including the large gilded bell and spire. This octagonal theme is carried through to the base, where triple-roofed porticos protected by *chinthe* project from each of eight niches containing Buddha images in white Mandalay marble.

The substantial *ubosot* is in whitewashed brick and concrete, with a complex multi-tiered roof which makes effective use of the corrugated iron so loved by the builders of Burmese monasteries. It takes the form of a lower hipped roof, on top of which is a gabled superstructure with three small roof tiers of its own and two-tiered extensions on each of its four sides. The stylised *cho fa* on the roof ridges are a Lanna addition, but the panelled decoration of the upper part is typically Shan, with redented rectangular outlines enclosing a single flower motif. The upper parts of the pillars to the portico are encrusted in a typically ornate Burmese stucco and glass decoration.

The interior of Wat Pa Fang; note the teak pillars with their mixture of gilt and red lacquer.

The chedi and Burmese pyatthat of Wat Sri Chum.

Wat Sri Chum

This is another Burmese-style monastery, and is nearby on Sri Chum Road directly west Of Wat Pa Fang. The monastery and adjacent *chedi* share the same walled enclosure and have an attractive setting among palm trees; however, the new *ubosot* opposite is sadly no replacement for the original, which was built by carpenters brought from Mandalay and burned down in 1992. The *ubosot*, which was built in 1900, is in the style of a *mondop* surmounted by not one but five *pyatthat*, arranged in a Meru-like quincunx. Its floor plan is a redented square, and 28 pillars support the projecting eaves. The more recent *chedi*, built in 1949, with its tall redented square base, is more Lanna than Burmese; its relief cement decorations are painted green and yellow, and the rabbit plaques on the *harmika* signify the year of its construction.

Wat Mon Cham Sin

The *wat* boasts more past glory than present; it currently has three Burmese-style *chedi,* but the drastic renovation, and the abandonment of the old Shan Viharn Charod, now unfortunately make it hardly worth the visit. However, for the truly dedicated, it can be reached by following either of the above roads south to their junction with the dual carriageway Route 1, then turning left. At the next traffic lights turn right onto the signposted Uttaradit Road. After 200 metres turn right onto an unmade road that runs alongside a small canal. After another 200 metres you come to a small crossroads. The bridge on your left leads up the hill to the three *chedi* of Wat Mon Cham Sin.

Mandalay-style Buddha image in the viharn at Wat Mon Puyak.

Wat Mon Puyak

Turn right back down towards Route 1, and near the end on your right is Wat Mon Puyak, another Shan monastery with an interesting variety of styles. The multi-tiered roof has an ornately decorated ceiling and, like the tall brick *ubosot*, is aligned north-south. In contrast, the Burmese-style *chedi* and brick *viharn* stand on a high terrace aligned northwest-southeast. The *ubosot*, cruciform, whitewashed with a green roof, is strongly influenced by British Burmese architecture, while the *viharn* in front of the *chedi* combines both colonial and Chinese elements. Inside this building, three central pillars support the roof ridge, and

there is a large seated Mandalay-style Buddha image. The upper parts of the walls have 19th century murals, some of them well-executed, but partly spoiled by whitewash streaks.

Wat Si Rong Muang

This is yet another Burmese monastery, and is found on the west side of town, 500 metres west of the clock tower ('*ho naligar*') on Takhrao Road. It has an imposing and complex multi-functional building with several two-and three-tiered gabled superstructures rising above the interlocking hipped roofs of the lower tier. Again, corrugated iron is the material of choice, painted red, with fretwork bargeboards painted an unfortunate shade of yellow. The interior is one of the most sumptuous in Lanna, with encrustations of gilt, coloured glass and mirror mosaic on most surfaces, including the pillars.

The extremely imposing interior of the Burmese monastery, Wat Si Rong Muang.

THE LOWER VALLEY

Below Lampang, the River Wang, 335 kilometres long, flows south and slightly east towards its confluence with the Ping River just north of the town of Tak. Route 1, which eventually reaches Bangkok, follows the valley, heading southeast out of town. About 20 kilometres downriver is the most important concentration of traditional Lanna religious architecture in the North. In Ko Kha district, just north of the small town of the same name, are three ancient and well-maintained *wat* and the site of a former *wiang*: a fortified, originally Mon, settlement that symbolically guarded Lampang, together with three other *wiang*.

A young elephant being cared for at the Elephant Hospital in the lower valley receives its morning shower.

Bullet hole in one of the railings from the shooting of a Burmese commander.

Wat Phra That Lampang Luang ***

Drive south from Lampang on Route 1 in the direction of Nakhon Sawan and Tak, and take the signposted exit into the town of Ko Kha, 14.5 kilometres from Lampang's clock tower. Continue through the town, following the signpost to Hang Chat, across the bridge over the Wang River, and at the T-junction just ahead turn right. Continue north for 3 kilometres, making sure to take the turning to the left after 2 kilometres rather than follow the short by-pass, until you see the walls and tall ornamented gate of a large *wat* on the left of the road. This is the magnificent Wat Phra That Lampang Luang, elevated and surrounded by a high brick wall.

The monastic complex is itself a *wiang*, and indeed has seen battles. As a result of an incident in which a so-called Man of Merit (*phu mi bun*) possessed of special powers was pursued and killed by Burmese troops near here, a Burmese garrison was established in the enclosure in 1729-30. A local man with a reputation as a fighter and a vagabond, Thippachak, was given the task of re-taking the *wat* in 1732, with apparently 300 men. The raid began with Thippachak and a small group climbing through a water conduit in the rear wall and shooting dead the Burmese commander Tao Maha Yot (the bullet-hole remains in one of the bronze railings of the balustrade that surrounds the *chedi*).

The main entrance is a *naga*-balustraded staircase leading up to the stuccoed gateway in the centre of the east wall. However, this is not always open, and certainly not in the early morning, which is probably the most attractive time of the day to visit. The usual approach is from the corner of the parking area in front of the *wat*. From here, walk up towards the small doorway in the south wall known as the Sri Lanka gate. On the way you pass two sacred *bodhi* trees, their branches propped up by clusters of decorated forked poles placed by worshippers.

Within the walled enclosure is a remarkable collection of buildings, including an enormous principal *viharn*, an elegant gilded *chedi*, three

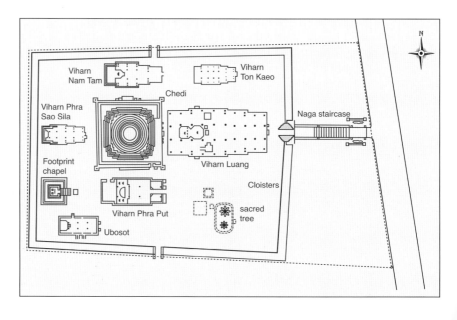

Plan of Wat Phra That Lampang Luang.

The chedi, principal viharn and stuccoed main gate.

smaller *viharn* of which one is probably the oldest extant wooden religious structure in Thailand, a chapel containing a footprint of the Buddha, and a small *ubosot*. Some of these are of the first order architecturally, and have been carefully preserved with almost complete authenticity, right down to the unpaved sandy floor of the enclosure. The importance of Wat Phra That Lampang Luang ('The Great Relic Monastery of Lampang') derives from the belief that the Buddha himself once visited here and donated a tuft of his hair, now enshrined in the *chedi*.

Buddha Images and Viharns

On either side, cloisters (*phra rabieng*) line the outer walls. Immediately ahead of you is the Viharn Phra Put, possibly dating back to the 13th century and rebuilt in 1802 with beautiful coloured glass inlay work covering the entire façade in rectangular panels. The central panels have floral designs, while those on the winged gables have the Chinese-style diagonal cross-weave pattern known as *prachae chin*, derived from woven bamboo matting. Below these on either side, tiny guardian *Rahu* figures devour the sun, their arms linked into a writhing mass of *naga* serpent bodies. Naïve gilded *thewada* and lotus flowers grace the wooden shutters, while the entrance is surrounded by a sumptuous three-tiered stucco *sum* arch.

Rahu figure worked in local glass inlay, over the door of the Viharn Phra Put.

Inside, flanked by thick teak pillars intricately decorated in gold on black and red lacquer, is a 5.25 metre-tall gilded brick Buddha image in *bhumisparsa*. Directly in front of the portico are two free-

Buddha image in the Viharn Phra Put.

Opposite page: the chedi and one of its guardians, Kampakan.

Below: the chedi is covered with these 'chang-go' diamond shape plates, and is distinctively Lanna in style.

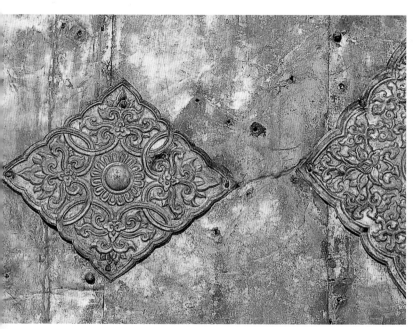

standing teak poles surmounted by the Brahmanic sacred goose. This type of pole, known as a *sao hongse* ('sacred goose post') and found in some other sites in Thailand, including the Grand Palace in Bangkok, is of Mon origin. In front of the *viharn* is another *sao hongse*, next to a low belfry and an ancient *kachao* tree, or Indian elm (*Holoptelea integriflora Plach*) which by legend was planted at the time of the Buddha's visit two and a half thousand years ago.

The Chedi

Next to the Viharn Phra Put, slightly north and east of the centre of the enclosure, is the magnificent *chedi*, covered in gilded copper sheets known as *chang-go*, to which are attached repoussée gilded sheets in diamond shapes and decorated with floral designs. Its original date of construction is not known (although it was reputedly just 3.5 metres high to begin with), but it was enlarged in 1449, and again in 1496 to its present size and shape: 45 metres high and 24 metres at the base. Its design is quintessentially Lanna, with a high redented square base above which the prominent circular mouldings, bell and spire taper smoothly to

the finial. Note the votive offerings placed on the pillars of the surrounding balustrade, including models of oxen; the *chedi* is dedicated to those born in the Year of the Ox. Four massive gilded parasols stand at the corners.

The Viharn Luang

In front of the *chedi*, which is to say the east, and almost entirely filling the distance between it and the east wall, is the principal *viharn* of the *wat*, the Viharn Luang. This is undoubtedly the most exceptional large wooden structure of its type in Lanna, built in 1476 at the same time as the walls. Despite its size, it is gracefully proportioned, with the three sections of each of its three roof tiers flaring outwards in a curve over the open sides. In the centre of the pediment is a full relief wooden figure of a standing *thewada* in prayer over a wooden goat, the significance of the latter being the birth year of the donor who last rebuilt the *viharn*. The background to these figures is a gold painting depicting *thewada* being born from flowers, a theme continued in the carvings on either side of the entrance below; one suggested explanation is that this is an invocation to be reborn in heaven. Below, carved monks' fans, water bowls and spittoons flank the seal of the monastic governor of Lampang, Phra Thamma Chinda Nayok, in 1923, the date of a recent restoration.

Detail from the entrance to the viharn, which repeats the theme in the painting of thewada being born from flowers.

The *viharn* houses, at its western end, a spectacular gilded, stuccoed brick *ku* enshrining the *wat*'s principal Buddha image. This is the largest in the province: the bronze Phra Chao Lan Thong, cast in 1563 in the *bhumisparsa* pose. The *ku* is strongly redented at the corners all the way up through its seven diminishing tiers, and the predominant motifs are the *naga*, which rear up as corner finials and emerge from the jaws of *makara* as arches at each tier. A narrow vertical opening at the base reveals the Buddha image.

On the left is a superb, decorated *thammat* (pulpit) and on the right is an ornate *sattaphan* (candle holder). Behind the *ku* are five Buddha images, one seated and the others standing, on a raised altar, and several inscribed *stele*. A wooden ceiling covers the central aisle, with six carved wooden figures in Burmese style set in roundels between the entrance and the *ku*, in order: a goat, *kinnorn*, lion, *Rahu*, rabbit and peacock. Faded murals on the upper side walls depict the *jataka* with Tai, Chinese and Burmese figures and buildings. The only slightly jarring notes in the *viharn* are the replacement of the outer set of the original 46 teak pillars with concrete and the tiles on the floor, part of an 1830 renovation.

From the east entrance of the Viharn Luang, turn to see the fine stucco decoration of the late-15th century gateway at the main entrance to the enclosure. On each side, each of the seven arches on its diminishing tiers is different; the lowest features the intertwined tails of *naga* which, in the fashion of Chinese dragons, have wings and feet. Above the door, both inside and outside, is a gilded stucco *dharmachakra*: the Wheel of the Law.

The interior of the Viharn Luang, with its gilded ku, and pulpit on the left.

Left: ceiling roundel in the viharn Luang.

Above: mural in the Viharn Luang depicting one of the jataka tales.

Left: intertwined nagas in stucco on the side of the main gate.

Above: interior of the Viharn Nam Tam.

Top right: detail of a figure on one of the Viharn Nam Tam's eave brackets.

Bottom right: the remains of murals dating from the early 16th century, on the north wall of the Viharn Nam Tam.

The Viharn Ton Kaeo

North of the Viharn Luang is the much smaller Viharn Ton Kaeo, one of two *viharn* against the north wall of the enclosure. This open-sided building of unknown date, rebuilt in 1967, has an undecorated façade and barge boards in the form of *naga* bodies with curves and loops, in central Thai style.

The Viharn Nam Tam

In line with the Viharn Ton Kaeo, behind, is the open-sided Viharn Nam Tam, dating from the early 16th century and believed to be the oldest extant wooden religious building in the country. Note the intricately carved eave-brackets in the *nakkhatan* design, with *naga* that unusually have the feet and features of a Chinese dragon, similar to those on the main gateway. At its west end is a Buddha image in *bhumisparsa*, flanked, as at the rear of the Viharn Luang, with four standing images. This *viharn* also contains the remains of murals of the same date, the clearest being on the north wall close to the Buddha image; with confidently executed black outlines, they display a cartoon-like vitality, particularly in the faces of the women.

Continue walking west towards the rear of the enclosure. At the north-east and north-west corners are two seated statues draped in red

The 'Footprint of the Buddha' chapel, which also functions as a camera obscura.

cloth of Kumpakan, a guardian *yak*; these, like the two smaller standing figures at the entrance to the balustrade surrounding the *chedi*, protect the *chedi*.

The Viharn Phra Sao Sila

Directly behind the *chedi* is yet another *viharn*, called the Viharn Phra Sao Sila; the original was, according to legend, built by Queen Chamathewi's father in 657 to enshrine a stone image, the Phra Nak Pok. The carved, gilded decoration of the façade includes two standing wooden statues of *thewada* similar to that on the pediment of the Viharn Luang. Several metres south of this is a square, raised *Ho Phra Putthabat* ('Footprint-of-the-Buddha Chapel'), open only to men, that functions as a *camera obscura* when the door is closed, thanks to a small hole in the lintel. This feature is a local fad initiated by the one at Wat Phra That Chom Ping *(see page 157)*. In the southwest corner of the enclosure is the *ubosot*, dating from 1476 and rebuilt in 1924.

As you leave the *wat* by the doorway in the south wall, turn right. The monks' quarters (*kuti*) are west of the wall, together with a simple, sturdy scripture repository on a whitewashed masonry base called the Ho Phra Tam, and two museums. One of these, the Kuti Phra Kaeo, contains a small revered Buddha image in green jasper, the Phra Kaeo

Gilded wooden thewada figure on the façade of the Viharn Phra Sao Sila.

Monks entering the ubosot, which was originally built in 1476.

154

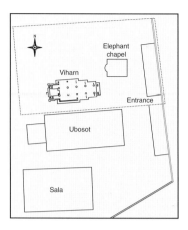

Plan of Wat Pong Yang Khok.

Extremely attractive yet simple interior of the viharn at Wat Pong Yang Khok.

The outside, though more austere, is nevertheless elegant.

Don Tao, securely locked behind two sets of steel grilles. According to one belief, this image was carved from the same stone as the Emerald Buddha (Phra Kaeo Morakot), and was formerly enshrined at Wat Phra Kaeo Don Tao in Lampang, where it had caused the trouble involving Mae Suchada (*see page 134*).

Wat Pong Yang Khok **

Apart from Wat Phra That Lampang Luang, there are two other *wat* of importance in the area. Continuing north along the same road, turn right after 7.5 kilometres, just before the Km. 11 marker, and carry on a further 100 metres down the lane; it is signposted.

This charming and historic country *wat* is largely unspoiled, set in a small walled enclosure among the fields. The *ubosot* is relatively recent, as is the open *sala* next to it, and neither are of great interest, but on the north side of the *ubosot* is a wonderfully preserved old, open-sided Lanna-style *viharn*. Known as the Viharn Phra Mae Chao Chamathewi ('The Queen Chamathewi Viharn'), it is in the truly traditional style that has all but disappeared in the North, and compares closely with the Viharn Nam Tam at Wat Phra That Lampang Luang down the road: minuscule proportions, very low eaves and a cool, dark interior. The exterior is extremely plain, in blackened unpainted teak. Gable decoration is limited to a thin floral strip over the door and three rosettes in the rectangular panels of the pediment, with more floral designs on the winged gables. The eave brackets are in the form of openwork *naga*, and the *naga* bargeboards are plain. The tiled roof is three-tiered including the portico.

By contrast, the interior is beautifully decorated in a simple, traditional style, the designs for the most part stencilled in gold on black and red lacquer. These cover the two rows of round teak pillars, the roof beams, the upper side-wall panels and the rear wall. Note the repeated motif of the *kalasa* (the Indic cornucopia) along the sides below the eaves, the frieze of Buddhas on the rear side walls and below them the representations of *bodhi* trees with birds. The principal

Buddha image is enshrined in an elaborate stucco *ku* at the west end, featuring *naga* with their tails intertwined around a *kala* face. Two other seated Buddha images are against the painted back wall. This *viharn* and its decorations date from the 17th century.

Various legends attach to this monastery, one being that the Mon Queen Chamathewi founded it in 690 as a result of a journey she made from Haripunchai (Lamphun) to Lampang, visiting King Ananta Yos. She brought a miniature golden umbrella to offer to Wat Phra That Lampang Luang a few kilometres down the road, but it was at this spot that the elephant carrying the offering dropped to its knees and raised its trunk in an attitude of respect. The Queen ordered a stop for the night, during which lightning bolts issued from a nearby anthill. This was sufficient for her to found a monastery. The only reasonable certainty, however, is that the viharn standing now was built between 1732 and 1759 by the local ruler Phraya Sulao Reuchai Songkhram. Although the main entrance nowadays is at the south-west corner, the original main gate on the east side, directly opposite the viharn, has above it a statue of the kneeling elephant statue, while just inside the gate, close to the front of the viharn, is a chapel dedicated to the elephant.

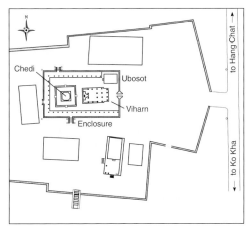

Plan of Wat Hai Lin.

Wat Lai Hin **

Return south along Route 1034 in the direction of Ko Kha, and 1.4 kilometres after passing Wat Phra That Lampang Luang, turn right (west). 6 kilometres down this road, on the left side just after the school, is 'The Monastery of the Standing Elephant with the Stone Shoulder' (Wat Lai Hin Kaew Chang Yuan, to give it its full name), built in 1683 by a prince and his craftsmen from Keng Tung in what is

Woman lighting candles at Wat Lai Hin, a miniature wat with a history full of legend.

now Burma, some 350 kilometres north. The site acquired its sacred status when an elephant reputedly carrying a relic of the Buddha (from India no less!) stopped here. As we've seen, the whims of important elephants were taken seriously in Lanna, and their various pauses, whether from tiredness or wilfulness, caused a number of temples to be built. This was one of Lanna's unspoiled treasures, made all the more exquisite by its tiny size (the *putthawat* measures only 33 metres by 20 metres on the outside wall of the cloister which surrounds the enclosure).

The entrance is a marvellous stuccoed gate, decorated in naïve style with *kinnorn*, *naga*, *singh* and *hongse* birds, some of them in glazed ceramic, with the arch immediately over the small doorway carrying a rustic stucco representation of the Buddha's Great Departure, and small *thewada* supporting the hooves of the horse. The gate is normally locked, but the monks will open it on request. Inside, there is barely enough space for the *viharn*, *chedi* and *ubosot*, even though all are on a miniature scale.

The *viharn* is open-sided in the traditional Lanna style except at the rear, which has plastered brick walls, and is so small that you can easily touch the gable. This is decorated in stucco on wood, and arranged in rectangular panels featuring floral designs, *singh* and other animals, with standing *thewada*. The curving and ridged *naga* barge boards betray a slight central Thai influence, but the proportions and roof-line are very much Lanna, with three roof tiers including that of the portico.

Inside, the available wooden surfaces are decorated in gilt on black and red lacquer, and the figures on the interior winged gables appear to be identical in style to the murals in the Viharn Nam Tam at Wat Phra That Lampang Luang. The Buddha image sits against the rear wall, with

Top: close-up of the gate depicting the Buddha's "Great Departure", with thewada supporting the hooves of the horse.

Above: an idiosyncratic ceramic creature on the gate.

The viharn interior at Wat Hai Lin.

a *thammat* on the left side. The original teak pillars of the principal *viharn* have been replaced by concrete ones, but this only marginally detracts from the appeal of this elegantly proportioned building. Behind it, an elegant *chedi* features a strongly indented high base. In the north-east corner, next to the front of the *viharn*, is a small open-sided *ubosot* facing west, and next to this is a statue of an early abbot of the *wat* who, according to legend, forbade major repair work on the buildings, saying that he would return to do this as necessary. Two small shrines flank the entrance, one containing models of elephants and other animals, the other an earthen receptacle for offerings in the form of a symbolic coconut.

The camera obscura image of the chedi at Wat Phra Chom Ping (left) and, on the right, the real view of it.

Wat Phra That Chom Ping

Return to the main road, Route 1034, and turn right towards Ko Kha. After 1.6 kilometres, the road back to Lampang is on the left, but if you drive straight on, following the river downstream to the south, you will reach this *wat* after 13 kilometres. Although the *chedi* contains a relic, the *wat* is of little architectural interest, as all the buildings have been recently reconstructed. Nevertheless, it contains a curiosity in the *ubosot* in the far right of the enclosure. At some time in the past, a knot of wood in one of the shutters fell out, and the hole is exactly the right size for the darkened interior of the building to function as a *camera obscura*. A caretaker is at hand to prop up a white sheet on a frame in front of the hole, and on this is projected an inverted image of the *chedi*.

Elephants

The Asian elephant, easily tamed unlike its African cousin, has long been an intimate part of the culture, economy and religion of Thailand. Over the centuries, elephants have won battles for the Thais, hauled the country's teak logs and entered its mythology, while the so-called 'white' elephants have actually lent the authority of kingship to its rulers. Until the 1920s the national flag was a white elephant on a red background; to early Western visitors the country's epithet was "Land of the White Elephant". At one stage it was estimated that more than 20,000 elephants were employed in transport alone; this, however, was when 90% of Thailand was still forest.

Today, when Thailand's forest covers only 20 percent of the land, there are probably no more than 3,800 elephants, with another 1,350 roaming free in the national parks. Deforestation has put elephants out of work, except for illegal logging, where the elephants involved are subject to overwork and mistreatment.

One of the king's elephants in its residence, being bathed.

Dr. Preecha Phongkum, attached to the Elephant Hospital, prepares to inject a tusker suffering from an abscess.

The principal viharn and gilded chedi at Wat Phra That Sadet.

Thai Elephant Conservation Centre **

On the road to Chiang Mai (Route 11, which can be taken from Route 1 on the way to Bangkok just outside Lampang, or by following the old Chiang Mai road Route 1093 through the village of Hang Chat) can be found the Thai Elephant Sanctuary; it is just before the pass, on the right. Another approach is from Wat Phra That Lampang Luang and Wat Pong Yang Khok, continuing north along Route 1034 for 5 kilometres past the latter until the junction with Route 11 at Thung Kwian; turn left here.

Formerly the Young Elephant Training Centre, it is operated by the Forest Industry Organisation, a state enterprise, and since the logging ban of 1989 its primary function is the care of now-unemployed elephants. In an effort to be self-sustaining, it actively encourages paying visitors, who can watch demonstrations of the animals' logging skills: a tourist show, certainly, but in a good cause. There is also a museum. In an adjacent area towards the hills, six of the King's White Elephants are cared for in pleasant surroundings, having been moved here from the grounds of Chitrlada Palace in Bangkok in 1986. Another four are in Sakon Nakhon, with only the most senior animal remaining in Bangkok. Each of these revered animals has its own newly constructed building and attendants, and although this area is not open to the public, the elephants can sometimes be seen in the Elephant Conservation Centre.

Elephant Hospital *

Closer to the Lampang road and run independently, is the Elephant Hospital *(Rongpayaban Chang)* operated by Friends of the Asian Elephant. The number of animals present varies, but many are the victims of road accidents, needing treatment and rehabilitation. Visitors and contributions are welcome.

THE UPPER VALLEY

North-east of Lampang, Route 1 follows the river for a short distance before crossing the hills that separate the Wang Valley from that of the Yom. The site of a *wiang*, an old fortified settlement, lies 16 kilometres out of town; this was an outlying defence for Lampang in much the same way as was Lampang Luang in the Ko Kha district *(q.v.)*. This latter is approximately the same distance from the city to the southwest. Associated with it is the following old but much-restored *wat*.

Wat Phra That Sadet

This *wat* reputedly dates from the earliest Mon times. From Lampang, take Route 1 in the direction of Ngao and Phayao, and just past the Km. 617 marker (the distance is from Bangkok) turn left; the *wat* is 1.5 kilometres ahead.

Of the two *viharn*, the principal one, in front of the *chedi*, is modern but open-sided, facing south-east. It houses, inside a *ku*, an important and elegant Buddha image, 4.5 metres tall and in the Sukhothai-style walking position. The history of this statue is that it was discovered broken in pieces in an abandoned *wat* near Chiang Kham, northeast of Phayao, at the end of the last century, and was moved first to Nan and then re-assembled here in 1934. The *chedi* behind is Lanna in style, enlarged to its present size in 1449, bell-shaped on a redented square base and covered in gilded copper. Next to it is a second, smaller *viharn* called the Viharn Phra Put, built in the local style with thick walls pierced by vertical slits and small cross-shaped openings instead of windows.

Wat Chae Son Luang *

The main road following the Wang River valley north is Route 1035, which leaves Lampang from the Pratu Ma Gate, just past Wat Phra Kaeo Don Tao. First, though, it crosses low hills before rejoining the valley at the head of the small Kiu Lom reservoir. Shortly after this, at 58 kilometres from Lampang, it passes the village of Chae Hom. A further 8 kilometres north of the village, Route 1252 on the left goes to Chae Son National Park. Take this, and after 6 kilometres, turn left to the village of Muang Pan; Wat Chae Son Luang is on the right-hand side after 2 kilometres.

The primitive Lanna style of the *ubosot* repays a close look; there are very few such buildings left in the North and it displays many local idiosyncracies. The roof has a single tier, although it has upper and lower sections, and projects right out over the portico. The eave brackets, in the elephant ear form, are unusual in that the loops of the *naga* bodies are carved in the style of Chinese clouds, while the lower roof finials have lost their *naga* form and loop right back. The *bai sema* demarcating the sacred area are elaborate and topped with *chedi*-like spires. Note the naïve *Rahu* over the doorway, flanked by tigers. The *viharn* is more traditional, but the *chedi* is quite elaborate for a village *wat*, with its upper parts, including a slim, tall bell, sheathed in copper sheets.

From here, Route 1157 goes back to Lampang, running parallel to Route 1035. Return to the intersection with Route 1035, turn left and continue north in the direction of Wang Nua and the head of the valley.

Wat Sop Li *

After 500 metres the road bends sharply to the left, and on the right is a road leading to the village of Ban Sop Li. Just over 1 kilometre further on is Wat Sop Li, the Lanna-style *viharn* of which was accurately restored in the 1980s by the Lampang Heritage Preservation Group, so that it retains, for instance, a shingled roof. Instead of windows it has a row of small cross-shaped openings in a local style.

Walking Buddha figure at Wat Phra That Sadet.

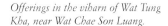

Offerings in the viharn of Wat Tung Kha, near Wat Chae Son Luang.

THE YOM VALLEY

East again from Lampang is the Yom river and the town of Phrae, little visited because of its remoteness, but with a particular flavour to its art and culture. This is rural Lanna at its most local and most individual, with few tourists and a firm sense of continuity with the past.

The hill-top monastery of Wat Phra That Cho Hae, south of Phrae.

162

The Yom River, which eventually joins the Chao Phraya in the Central Plains at Nakhon Sawan, lies east of the Wang Valley, flowing in the same direction from north to south for 555 kilometres. The main stretch of the valley is in upland Lanna, ranging from north to south between two arms of the Phi Pan Nam range of hills.

This is teak country, famously so in the 19th century when the extensive forests, which included the prized golden teak variety, attracted British and Burmese interests. Even today, despite the unbridled plundering of this rich national resource that finally led to the 1989 ban on logging, the hills are covered with stands of teak. Recently, small plantations of seedlings have been started, hopefully the beginning of a new, sustainable approach to the business. Less heartening, though, is the profusion of new houses using excessive amounts of the timber, and in particular thick, undressed tree trunks. Often, this is a scheme for investing in illegally cut timber while avoiding prosecution (because the logs are part of a building).

The capital, Phrae, is the only settlement of any significance. However, because the valley has never been a main route to the north, it remains relatively undeveloped, quiet and with few tourists. From the point of view of its Lanna culture, this makes it rewarding to visit, particularly the lanes and houses of the old city of the capital.

Map of the central part of the Yom Valley.

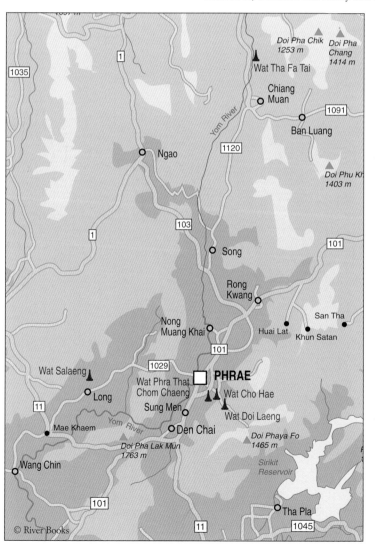

PHRAE

Phrae has a long history, dating back to the end of the first millenium, when it was founded by the Mon and was a part of the Haripunjaya kingdom. As with the other two Mon cities of Lanna – – Lamphun and Lampang – it was given an approximately oval plan, with earthen ramparts, walls and a surrounding moat, which can still be seen today in a fairly well-preserved state. The moat is fed by a stream, the Huai Mae Khaem, that flows into the Yom River from the east, and the old town abuts this confluence with the stream forming the northern boundary. As in the old days, four gates at roughly the cardinal points give access to the city: to the north the Pratu Sri Chum, the east the Pratu Mai, the south the Pratu Chai, and the west the Pratu Man.

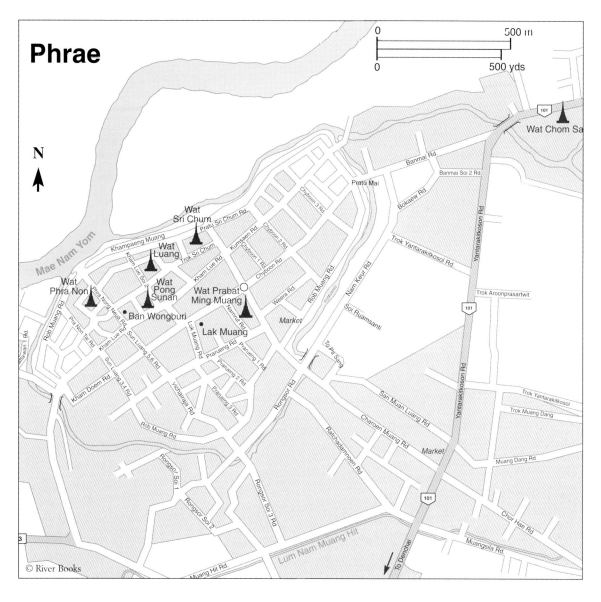

Map of the city.

Phrae fell under the rule of Chiang Mai during the reign of King Tilokaraj in 1443 as part of his expedition to capture Nan. While he was besieging that city, his mother took a part of the Chiang Mai army to capture Phrae. According to the Chiang Mai Chronicle, this was done simply by a demonstration of a new cannon, which a Vietnamese artillery expert among the queen mother's troops used with great accuracy to split the trunk of a sugar-palm close to the city gate. On seeing this, the Phrae ruler surrendered. The Phrae version of events understandably involves more destruction – many palm trees and part of the walls – but both agree that not a single life was lost. Like Lampang, Phrae became a centre of the teak industry in the 19th century, evident not only in the number of fine teak houses, but also in the Burmese *wat* built for Shan teak merchants who settled here.

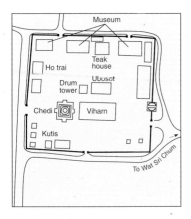

Above: Wat Luang dates back to the founding of the city itself.

Above right: the viharn-ubosot, Wat Luang.

THE OLD CITY

Wat Luang**

The most important of the city's *wat* are grouped together in the northwest part of town, and the earliest of all is Wat Luang ('The Great Monastery'). According to the chronicles, it was built at the same time as the city – in 829 – by Phor Khun Luang Pol. To find it, drive north from the central roundabout (unmissable because of its tall structure of diminishing rings) for a hundred metres and turn left down the small lane named Trok Sri Chum; the *wat* is a further two hundred metres down here.

The Viharn-Ubosot
On entering the *wat*, the first thing which faces you is the large combined *viharn-ubosot*, which was built in 1872. Its most immediately noticeable feature is the laterite bricks which have been used to wall up the open parts of the tall portico: an unattractive addition but perhaps understandable in view of the theft of an important gold Buddha image, the Phra Chao Saen Thong. This was supposedly stolen by Shans in 1902, when they also destroyed part of the *chedi* in an attempted coup led by one Paka Mong. The uprising was eventually put down after some fighting.

Aside from this, the gable carvings are of a high standard; the pediment, with a background carved in circular intertwined floral motifs, features a standing *thewada* on a lotus above *Rahu*, flanked by

Row of thewada decorating the gable.

Elephant on the portico gable.

figures of the monkey hero of the Ramayana, Hanuman. Below is a strip of twelve standing *thewada*, and a curved pelmet with lions and plant motifs. The roof ridge finials are striking; instead of the usual abstract *cho fa*, they are all in the form of large, full-bodied *hongse*.

Inside the building is the Phra Chao Saen Luang Buddha image, in *bhumisparsa mudra*, a bronze replacement for the original gold. The *sala* tree (*Saraca indica*) right in front of the building, identifiable during the hot season by its flowers which grow straight out of the trunk, is the species under which the Buddha is reputed to have been born.

The Phra Chao Saen Luang Buddha image.

The Ubosot and Ho Trai

Next to the *viharn-ubosot*, on its north side, is a smaller, older *ubosot*, its attractive small portico decorated with a carved gilded pediment featuring an elephant. Behind this is a brightly painted *ho trai* in the local style; all in wood and raised on pillars, its capitals carry carved and coloured *yak* guardians. Close by, behind the *viharn-ubosot*, is the Phra That Luang Chai Chang Kham ('The Great Relic Chedi Supported by Elephants'), rebuilt to its present form in 1336. Distinctively, it has a diminishing series of seven octagonal plinths, then a small octagonal bell, redented square *harmika*, circular rings and spire. The lowest octagonal plinth has four standing Buddha images in niches at the cardinal points, and the foreparts of four elephants emerging from the intermediate sides. There are gilded filigree *chat* at each of the four corners of the terrace in the Burmese style.

Wat Luang's octagonal chedi, whose present form dates back to 1336.

Two of the subsidiary buildings in the enclosure are extremely unusual in design. On the far west side of the enclosure is an old two-storied *ho trai* , built over a well, which you can still see in the ground floor. Its roof structure is unique, with two lower hipped tiers surmounted by a triple-tiered pitched roof. Note the rare central roof-ridge finial in the shape of a lotus-bud post. It is in the middle of a delicately carved *sum* arch design, framed by *naga*. On the north side of the compound is a new building containing the museum: the only

one in the city. Inside, there are some interesting Buddha images in the local style, and also a model *viharn*. Next to this is a small 19th century teak house in the local Phrae style. Raised on piles, it comprises two small-roofed buildings separated by a narrow walkway, but note that the *toen* (the verandah used as a living area) occupies the whole of one building, and faces inwards. The slightly larger building which faces you contains the bedroom. At the top of the stairs is a roofed shelf, very typical of the Lanna region, with jars of drinking water for guests.

Top: the rare design of the converted ho trai at Wat Luang.

Above: the living area of the 19th century local Phrae house in the grounds of Wat Luang.

Wat Phong Sunan *

This temple is a short walk south of Wat Luang, and can be reached by turning left out of the rear, west entrance of Wat Luang onto Kham Lue Soi 2 and walking down to the corner of Kham Lue Road. The large composite *viharn-ubosot* shows central Thai influence, not only in its tall proportions, but also in the undulating *naga* bargeboards. The gable is intricately carved in the style of Wat Luang, with a pediment in *khrue thao* vine motif, winged gables featuring monkeys fighting, and a large rectangular panel in the centre with five false windows. Below this are the heads of the twelve zodiacal animals in a row, treated in bas-relief, each peering out of a small niche.

The exterior of Ban Wongburi, a colonial style mansion.

Ban Wongburi **

Immediately west of Wat Phong Sunan, along Kham Lue Road, is the exceptionally well-preserved mansion of the former *chao muang*, Ban Wongburi. It was built between 1906 and 1909 by the daughter of Phraya Wongburi, former governer of Phrae. Its Colonial Gingerbread style, executed by Chinese craftsmen from Canton, reflects the influence of British teak merchants. It still has its original paintwork of white and pink.

Wat Phra Non *

If you walk north up Phra Nong Neua Road for 100 metres, you come to Wat Phra Non ('The Monastery of the Reclining Buddha') on the left. The Buddha image referred to is enshrined in the smaller building in the southwest of the enclosure next to the *chedi*. Built in the 18th century, this structure is a classic example of Phrae religious architecture, and one of the *wat*'s most striking features. The interior is illuminated not by windows, but by what are called *chong lom* ('wind gaps') – vertical slits between square-sectioned balusters set into the thick whitewashed walls – and by a continuous row of small cross-shaped openings above. This design, essentially a means of dealing with the summer heat, is an alternative solution to the more familiar open-sided buildings of Lanna, and is repeated in several *wat* throughout the Yom valley, as well as spreading a little into the neighbouring Wang and Nan valleys. The roof, also distinctive, is in two tiers. Hipped below, and

The chapel with 'wind gap' walls containing the reclining Buddha at Wat Phra Non.

Carvings from the winged gable at Wat Phra Non.

pitched above with an elegant curve, it is no doubt influenced by the Tai Lü, whose purest monastic buildings can be seen in the upper Nan valley.

The principal building is a combined *viharn* and *ubosot*, with a fine carved wooden gable and an open-sided two-tiered portico in front. Next door is a *ho trai* in the local style similar to that at Wat Luang, decorated in gold stencil on black lacquered wood. The *chedi* is similar to that of Wat Luang: diminishing octagonal plinths rising to a small octagonal bell, although the different levels are less obviously separated.

Wat Sri Chum *

Two blocks to the east of Wat Luang, and next to the city's northern gate, the Pratu Sri Chum, lies Wat Sri Chum. Facing onto the principal thoroughfare, Charoen Muang Road, it is slightly neglected, its main features being the brick *chedi* and a tall standing Buddha image. This latter is housed in the *viharn* on the left as you enter, almost filling its interior, and standing in the Phrae style locally known as "calling for rains": both arms, rendered very long, pointing straight down at the sides. The gable of the building is carved with a large central *garuda* surrounded by an openwork design of sunflowers and birds against plain wooden boards.

Next to this stands another building: also a *viharn*, but with a more colourful and exuberant decoration in bright paint and glass mosaic, and an unusual arrangement of three staircases leading up to three doorways. The principal Buddha image here is a copy of the elegant

The position of the Buddha's arms is known locally as 'calling for rains'.

Right: Also part of the viharn, horse detail from the design on the gable.

Chinnarat Buddha at Phitsanulok, one of several here and in Nan that are evidence of a persisting local fascination with Sukhothai style. The building on the far right is a small and fairly plain *ubosot*.

Finally, behind all these three structures is a tall 16th century brick *chedi* on a two-storeyed redented square base and a *ho trai* raised on pillars, as elsewhere in Phrae. Murals of the *Vessantara Jataka* are painted on the exterior of its wooden walls, an unusual variation which is probably a Lao influence.

Wat Phra Bat Ming Muang *

This temple is located a little further south along Charoen Muang Road, just after the roundabout. The enclosure is large, but crowded with all kinds of buildings, including a modern tower block which, in a triumph of thoughtless city planning, dwarfs the otherwise attractive *ho trai*. The principal monastic building in the south of the compound is a combined *viharn* and *ubosot*, while next to it is a *mondop* containing the Buddha footprint that gives the *wat* its name, but both buildings are modern and of little interest.

Gold stencilled animals on the ceiling of the Viharn Ming Muang.

In the northern part, however, right on the corner facing the roundabout, is the 18th century Viharn Ming Muang. The pediment on its portico has an unusual local treatment of *Rahu* about to swallow the Sun at the top, and the rectangular panel below features flowers, coiled *naga* at either side, and two large rats. Inside is a seated Buddha image with some Lao features such as the pointed 'bat' ears, and, in front, a small image of the pot-bellied Saenkacha. The ceiling is especially attractive, with gold stencilled animals, including flying bats, on black lacquer.

Lak Muang

Finally, also in this area of the city, is the Phrae city pillar, or Lak Muang. Located 200 metres to the west along Kham Doem Road, on the south side of the road, it is a single gilded wooden pillar similar to those of Lampang, and housed in a small, tall ornate chapel.

DOMESTIC ARCHITECTURE

As we have already seen, the old city is noted for its traditional teak houses in varying styles, of which Ban Wongburi (above) is just one. Moreover, because Phrae has remained something of a backwater amid Thailand's recent development, it is the best urban setting in Lanna in which to see old domestic architecture.

Ban Sang Mai *

On Muang Hit Road, 300 metres to the west of the junction with Ratchadamnoen Road, is a house named Ban Sang Mai, built in 1970. Its architecture is an eclectic mixture of different Lanna styles – Tai

Carved panel on the pediment at Ban Sang Mai.

Yuan, Burmese and Tai Lü – and is worth visiting for this highly individual design which is yet so typical of the region. Although a private residence and not open to the public, Ban Sang Mai can be clearly seen from the road, and is a wonderful example of varied domestic architecture. The basic structure borrows from a Shan *viharn*, with a triple-tiered roof over the entrance porch, and stairs leading up to a two-storey building with four tiers of roof, all shingled. However, the finials and gables are the sort you might expect on religious buildings, including a battle scene from the Ramayana on the west gable. The *kalae* are Tai Yuan, but multiple, and the eave decorations are in the Tai Lü water-drop design, known as *paen nam yoi*.

Ban Wirat *

On Vichairaja Road is the recently and carefully restored Ban Wirat. This was originally the palace of the local ruler Chao Nankan Seansiribhand, built in 1889 in the wooden Gingerbread style similar to Ban Wongburi.

Ban Fai *

This is a large open-sided restaurant situated to the south-west of the city along Yantarakitkosol Road, in the direction of Den Chai. Ban Fai's owner has collected several old Lanna buildings, notably a *ruen kalae (see page 29)* and an old general store, which have been carefully restored and furnished, and are well worth visiting. In contrast, however, the well-publicised and immodestly-

Ban Fai general store.

The recently restored Ban Wirat, in gingerbread style.

named **Ban Prathap Jai** ('Impressive House') is unfortunately no more than a conglomeration of teak wood designed for commercial tourism, built in 1972, and has nothing to do with northern domestic living, although it does feature 130 teak pillars.

OUTSIDE THE WALLS

Wat Chom Sawan **

North-east of the old city is one of the finest Burmese *wat* in the North. Leave the old city through the Pratu Mai ('New Gate') on Ban Mai Road, which is Route 101 in the direction of Nan. After 500 metres on the right-hand side of the road is Wat Chom Savan ('The Monastery of the Highest Heaven'). Built between 1910 and 1912, it stands alone in a large grassy enclosure, and is one of the purest surviving Shan monasteries in Lanna. On the left as you enter, among trees just before the north-facing entrance, is a Burmese-style *chedi*, slightly distressed but surrounded on its base by twelve small *stupas*. A roofed niche on its west side contains a Buddha image.

The pride of Wat Chom Sawan, however, is its multi-functional complex of interlocking wooden buildings with a mixture of roof shapes. The structure faces north and is raised on pillars, and as you enter through either of the roofed staircases, you can immediately see

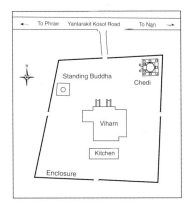

Plan of Wat Chom Sawan.

The interlocking wooden monastery buildings of Wat Chom Sawan.

The interior of Wat Chom Sawan with Buddha images.

Ornate roof and gable at the same monastery.

the different Shan style of monastery and Buddhist place of worship. The different floor levels demarcate the various areas of use. Where you stand, having just stepped up from the terrace, is the general area for the laity to pray. On the left is the daytime living area for the monks, and on the right the kitchen.

Ahead of you, the floor rises in two levels to the centre of the building; the first of these levels is reserved for monks at ceremonies, and the highest is the most sacred, for the Buddha images. On the left, a corridor runs to the back of the building, where there is a bedroom for the monks directly behind the Buddha images, and bathrooms on the left. It passes, on the left side, an area raised to the highest level and connected to a room; these are the abbot's quarters. Set in the floor in front of you are two small security hatches. At night, the building is locked, and if the temple dogs begin barking, the monks can peer down from these hatches to see if there is an intruder.

There are several Buddha images. The principal one, which is actually quite small, is seated in the *abhaya mudra*, but the most unusual is in the locked glass cabinet to the left, in Mandalay style. This follows a rare Burmese tradition of being made of gilded bamboo and is called Luang Phor San (*san* means 'bamboo wickerwork'). In another cabinet outside the abbot's room on the left are more religious artefacts, including a set of scriptures, the *Tripitaka*, painted on wafer-thin sheets of ivory.

The roofing of Shan monasteries is endlessly varied, and here is a particularly fine example. From a distance the different designs seem haphazard, but in relation to the interior spaces they make perfect sense. The main roof superstructure in the centre is over the altar, and the high ceiling with open windows in the upper walls keeps the lower part of the interior cool. The smaller superstructure on the east side is directly over the abbot's quarters, and is false-storeyed; the tall empty space inside carries heat up and away from the living area. Sadly, with few Shans left in the area, this *wat* receives few donations, and cannot afford full maintenance.

THE UPPER VALLEY

The head of the valley lies north of Phrae, a 150 kilometre drive to the village of Pong, which is 80 kilometres east of the town of Phayao. There is, however, little of architectural interest.

Wat Chong Kham *

The village of Ngao in the western hills, administratively in the Lampang province but physically in a small tributary valley of the Yom, lies 96 kilometres north of Phrae (31 kilometres north-east along Route 101, then 65 kilometres north-west along Route 103). Wat Chong Kham, a fine old Burmese *wat,* was formerly here, but it was in danger of falling into ruin until, in 1981, it was moved and re-assembled at Muang Boran (Ancient City) near Bangkok at Samut Prakhan, where it can now be seen.

Wat Tha Fa Tai *

This small rural temple is found near the head of the Yom Valley, 12 kilometres north of the village of Chiang Muan. It was built in 1769, and serves a Tai Lü community. Although very simple, the *viharn* is carefully maintained in a traditional style, and still retains a wooden shingle roof, the eaves of which are supported by brightly painted eave-brackets in the form of *naga.* Inside, hanging *tung* banners, locally woven, indicate the *wat*'s Tai Lü origins. On one side of the Buddha image is a fine *thammat* (pulpit), which remains here despite regular approaches by Bangkok antique dealers. Although too far to merit a special trip, the *wat* lies *en route* between Phayao and Nan on the east side of Route 1091.

Wat Chong Kham has now been transferred to Muang Boran.

The traditional viharn of Wat Tha Fa Tai.

THE LOWER VALLEY

South of Phrae, the river winds its way down towards the plains and the ancient twin cities of Sri Satchanalai and Sukhothai, and on the way passes several rural *wat* of interest.

This chedi is the focal point for an annual festival which takes place in February or March.

Wat Phra That Cho Hae *

Closest to the town, on a hill 9 kilometres to the south-east, is 'The Monastery of the Relic Wrapped in Satin Cloth', so-called because of the annual festival held in February or March at which the *chedi* is swathed in a special, finely woven Tai Lü cloth. This celebrates the tradition of a local personage, Khun Lua Ai Kom, who wrapped a hair of the Buddha in a scarf. The *wat* was restored in 1336 by King Lithai of Sukhothai when he was Viceroy to the North. To reach it, take Charoen Muang Road from the centre of town; this becomes Cho Hae Road and is signposted to the *wat* all the way. The sacred enclosure is on a hill visible for a few kilometres across the rice fields and small villages that surround it, and no fewer than five staircases – all flanked by *naga-makara* balustrades – lead up to it. The *viharn*, which like many others in the Yom and Nan valleys, is not aligned in the traditional easterly direction of Buddhism, faces north-northeast. The axis of the *wat*, which includes the *chedi* and its cloisters, is in line with this. The building is exceptionally tall, and also cruciform, restored in 1924 by Khru Ba Srivichai with rather garish decoration.

Behind it, crowded into its own cloistered enclosure, is the 33 metre-tall octagonal *chedi* in the Chiang Saen style believed to contain a hair of the Buddha sent by King Ashoka from India in the 3rd century B.C. Covered with gilded copper plates, it owes its present size and shape to the 1924 restoration and, as the name of the *wat* implies, it is wrapped in cloths, including one printed with the twelve zodiacal animals. Behind and outside this enclosure, near the south-west corner, is a shrine containing the Phra

Chao Than Chai Buddha, which has a regular stream of worshippers making offerings, including women wanting to have children. Finally, at the foot of the oldest and principal staircase, which faces the town of Phrae to the west-northwest, is a small reclining Buddha image in a new chapel.

Wat Phra That Chom Chaeng

Close by to Wat Phra That Cho Hae are two more relic-containing *chedi*. From where the road from Phrae enters the grounds of Wat Cho Hae, turn south-west to the signposted Wat Phra That Chom Chaeng, one and a half kilometres away, and one of the oldest *wat* in the valley, with a 29-metre *chedi*. It was thoroughly restored in 1992, a fact which, together with the addition of various crude statues that include a monolithic and not particularly attractive standing Buddha image, has eroded any atmosphere of antiquity. In the same way as its more famous neighbour, the *viharn* faces north-northeast.

Wat Phra That Doi Laeng

The other *phra that* is on the summit of a hill 3 kilometres east of Wat Cho Hae. It is in fact nothing more than a small *chedi* with a monk's residence, and has recently been thoroughly and excessively modernised, so it may not be worth the drive other than for the view on a clear day. To reach it, drive east from the foot of Wat Cho Hae for 1 kilometre into the village of Ban Mai. Ask the villagers for the turning, and continue another 2 kilometres up the hill.

The somewhat neglected ubosot at Wat Salaeng.

The viharn at Wat Salaeng, which has been recently restored.

Wat Salaeng *

Route 1023, the most direct way to Lampang, runs west from Phrae, over some low hills with teak forest, and rejoins the valley at the village of Long. Halfway between the Km. 40 and 41 markers, turn right and pass through Ban Chom Khwan village for 2 kilometres until you come to Wat Salaeng. This temple contains two buildings of particular note, both by the far entrance to the enclosure. One is a recently restored *viharn* facing southeast, quite plain and in the Phrae style of thick whitewashed walls with *chong lom* instead of windows. Secondly, close by among trees, is an old, small open-sided *ubosot* in Lanna style, raised on a platform. Unfortunately, it is not cared for, and shows signs of approaching dereliction. Behind is the *chedi*, called Phra That Kha-um Kham and believed to contain a relic of the Buddha brought by the Mon ruler of Lamphun, Queen Chamathewi.

THE NAN VALLEY

Isolated in the far east of Lanna, the Nan valley maintained its independence more strongly than any of the other principalities; it was incorporated into Siam only in 1931. Its rural individuality is evident even today, in the quiet life of its capital, Nan, and in the influence of the Tai Lü people who have migrated here from Yunnan at different periods of history, most recently in the early 1950s.

The village of Ban Khun Nam Nan, close to the headwaters of the Nan River

Historically one of the most remote areas of Lanna – and indeed of Thailand – the valley of the Nan River and its mountainous surroundings abut Laos on the north and east. The river rises close to the north-eastern border and flows south for 627 kilometres – the longest river in Lanna – towards Phitsanulok in the plains, where it joins the Ping and Yom to form the Chao Phraya. The principal town is Nan, 200 kilometres due east of Chiang Mai but 350 kilometres by road, and is separated from the Phrae Valley by the Phi Pan Nam range. Because of the valley's remoteness it has been able to maintain a greater measure of independence than the other valley states of Lanna, although not always without a struggle.

The first small independent kingdom was created around the city of Muang Pua (also known as Varanagara) in the late 13th century, in the upper Valley some 70 kilometres north of the present city of Nan. It was ruled by the Phukha dynasty, related to the founders of Vientiane, although it soon became a dependency of Sukhothai. With the grain of the land in this part of Lanna running north-south, communications across the valleys were difficult, and the Nan valley was more easily reached from – and so influenced by – Sukhothai than Chiang Mai. Sukhothai connections are more evident here in the art and architecture than anywhere else in Lanna, and the ways in which this influence, moving up the valley from the south, met the Lao and Tai Lü cultures spreading down from the north, give Nan much of its distinctive character.

The capital was moved to the area of present-day Nan in the middle of the 14th century, and during the 15th century, as Sukhothai's star waned and Chiang Mai's was in the ascendancy, Nan came under pressure to become a vassal *muang* of Chiang Mai. The seal was set on Nan's fate in 1443 when its ruler Kaen Thao devised a more than usually devious plot to capture Phayao – a plot that ultimately backfired. He asked King Tilokaraj to send troops to help him defend Nan against a fictitious Vietnamese army, and Tilokaraj duly despatched the Phayao army with its ruler. Kaen Thao managed to send the Phayao troops to harvest rice and had the Phayao ruler murdered. Incensed, Tilokaraj sent his own army to Nan, although it took until 1449 before he was able to capture it and make it a part of his Lanna kingdom.

After the death of the last ruler of the Phukha dynasty in 1461, Nan was ruled by princes sent from Chiang Mai, and this practice continued during the period of Burmese control of Lanna,

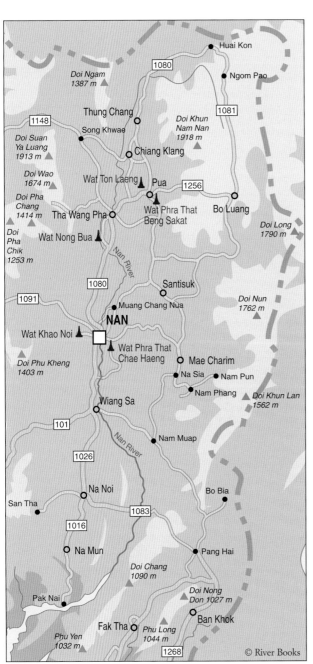

Map of the central and northern part of the valley.

© River Books

beginning in the mid-16th century. Nan rebelled against Burmese domination many times between 1597 and 1707, but without success, and in 1714 a Burmese prince, Cha Fa Meow Sa, was finally sent to rule the valley. The price that Nan ultimately had to pay for its freedom from the Burmese was to accept the suzerainty of Siam in 1788. Even so, it maintained a considerable degree of independence until 1931, when it was the last Lanna principality to be brought under direct Siamese rule.

One of the effects of the valley's proximity to Laos has been the influx at different times of Tai Lü peoples, originally from Sipsong-panna (Xishuangbanna in Chinese) in Yunnan, and these have significantly contributed to the Nan culture, in weaving, mural painting and architecture. The Nan Chronicle mentions a major population raid in 1812, recording that the ruler, Chao Suman "brought with him 6,000 prisoners from Muang La, Muang Pong, Chiang Kaeng and Muang Luang Pu Ka". Another less beneficial effect of Nan's location has been border disputes and related problems. As a result of the Paknam incident in which French gunboats were sent up the Chao Phraya River toward Bangkok, Nan lost a large territory to the east in the treaty between Siam and the French in 1893. More land was lost to the French, and so to Laos, in 1903. Most recently, the highlands of the north and east were under the control of the Communist Party of Thailand from 1968 until its final defeat by the Thai Army in 1983.

NAN

The town of Nan, while lacking the traditional domestic architecture of, say, the old parts of Lampang and Phrae, has several fine *wat*, and a quiet, almost sleepy, small-town atmosphere. Like most old Lanna towns, it no longer has its city wall, which is a pity because it is described by Reginald Le May as being, in about 1914, "high and built of red brick, and being newer, is in a better state of preservation than those of the other towns in the north". Le May also considered the town to be beautiful, which some might take exception to today.

Wat Phumin ***
It is almost worth making the journey to Nan for Wat Phumin alone. Certainly the city's finest *wat*, it is highly unusual in style and located on Pha Kong Road just south of the junction with Suriyaphong Road, on the west side.

Founded in 1596 by the ruler of Nan, Chao Chetabutprohmin, it owes its present form to the thorough renovation in the reign of Chao Anantaworaritthidej that took from 1867 to 1875, and was celebrated with two weeks of religious ceremonies and the firing of rockets. Architecturally, it is cruciform, with the main axis north-south, and the cross shape is treated as if the ends of two buildings, complete with three-tiered rooves in upper and lower sections, had been compacted into one another, giving quite an intricate appearance to the roof. As with many *wat* in both the Nan and Yom valleys, the *viharn* and *ubosot* are combined in this one building.

There are entrances on each of the four sides, but those on the north and south have longer approaches, flanked by massive *naga* balustrades.

Plan of Wat Phumin.

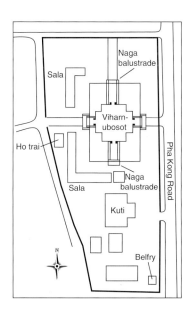

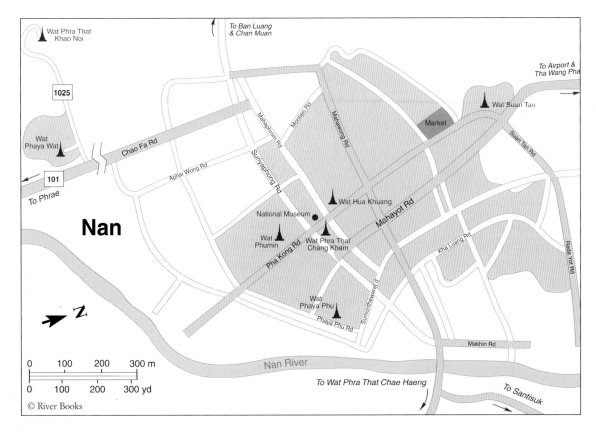

Map of the city of Nan.

Here, too, the treatment is striking because it is achieved with two parallel *nagas* which give the impression of undulating right through the building, their rearing heads on the north side and their coiled tails on the south. Each entrance is surmounted by an elaborate redented *mondop* (underlining the importance of the *wat* as a foundation of the Nan royal dynasty) and has elaborately carved doors; the motifs are Lanna-style forest scenes on the south and west, flowers on the north, and *sieo kang* demon guardians in the Chinese manner on the east.

The interior of the *wat* is just as remarkable. The structure of the roof demands substantial support, and there are twelve teak pillars supporting the tie-beams: eight at the outer corners and four at the inner corners. These are all decorated in gold on red and black lacquer, with a circle of elephants on each of the outer pillars, and *thewada* on the inner. The coffered ceiling is decorated with a closely patterned chequerboard of star-like gilded flowers, *kuek puang*. In the centre, following the cruciform theme, are four identical gilded Buddha images in *bhumisparsa*, back to back on a square altar, the gilded centrepiece of which rises above them to be topped with a lotus flower finial. The 'bat' ears and ridged nose coming to a sharp point show a distinct Lao influence. Next to this altar on the east side is a magnificent *thammat* (pulpit).

The murals on the interior walls repay a long look. Painted not long after the renovation of the building in the late 19th century, they depict two of the *jataka* tales – the *Khattana Kumara Jataka* on the north wall and the *Nimi Jataka* on the west – as well as scenes from the Life of the

The viharn-ubosot of Wat Phumin, Nan's finest wat.

Mondop style decoration over the south door of the building.

The Buddha in sumptuous surroundings; note the intricately decorated ceiling and pillars.

Close-up of the quadruple Buddha.

Buddha, all rendered in an individualistic and informal style not dissimilar to those in Wat Phra Singh in Chiang Mai. Here, however, the setting is the culture and daily life of the Tai Lü people. The two most famous scenes are on a larger scale than most of the murals: a man whispering in the ear of a woman (on the south side of the west door), and the figure flanking the south door, presumed to be the ruler Chao Anantaworaritthidej. The placing of full size painted figures on either side of this main entrance is a Chinese influence, another indication of Tai Lü origins. The inclusion of scenes with Westerners, including some in a paddle steamer, probably refers to the arrival of the French, to whom the area east of the Nan Valley was ceded in 1893. This suggests that at least some of the painting was completed in the 1890s.

National Museum *

Wat Phumin is one of a small cluster of sites in the centre of Nan, all within easy strolling distance of each other. Directly to the north, across Suriyaphong Road, is the National Museum. It is housed in the former palace, the *ho kham*, of the local ruler Phra Chao Suriyaphong Pharitdej, and was built in 1903. The entrance is on Pha Kong Road.

As well as historical and ethnographic displays, there are a number of Buddha images illustrating features of the local style. The museum's prize exhibit is a curious 'black' elephant tusk from the late 17th century weighing 18 kilos and measuring 94 centimetres, rather

In a scene from the Khattana Kumara, the mother of a miraculously born boy points out the footprint of a white elephant instrumental in his conception.

The arrival of the French: Europeans with paddle steamer.

Tattooed man whispering to woman, one of two famous scenes.

strangely mounted in the arms of a brightly painted carved wooden *garuda*.

Wat Ming Muang

Some 200 metres west along Suriyaphong Road from here, on the south side, is the city pillar, or *lak muang*, worth stoppiing to see for its unusual form. Standing in a small open-sided pavilion directly ahead of the main east entrance to Wat Ming Muang, it is a Shiva *linga* with four faces at the top: a so-called *mukha linga* and an ineresting example of how an animistic belief has absorbed a quite alien Brahmanic symbolism. The modern *viharn* behind, completely covered in Rococo cement reliefs, is in stunningly bad taste.

Wat Hua Khuang *

North of the museum grounds, on the corner of Pha Kong Road and Mahaphrom Road, is 'The Monastery North of the Plaza', a neglected *wat* with little funding. The main building, which faces south, is a combined *viharn* and *ubosot*, a feature of several *wat* in the Nan valley. It was built around about the same time as Wat Phumin was renovated (approximately the 1860s), and the unpainted decorations of the gable have been carved separately and then attached to the plain wood surface. The pediment is in a floral design that follows the triangular frame, with a strip of overlapping lotus leaves below, while the deep curved eyebrow pelmet underneath this is decorated with bunches of flowers hanging straight down, over a *kanok* leaf design framing the pelmet. Unusually, the *makara-naga* balustrades extend forward from the side walls instead of from the front.

The National Museum's prize exhibit, an 18-kilo black elephant tusk supported by a painted garuda.

The four-faced city pillar at Wat Ming Muang.

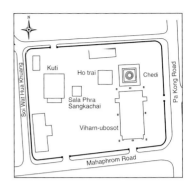

Above: plan of Wat Hua Khuang.

Above left: the ho trai, chedi and viharn of Wat Hua Khuang.

Inside, the principal seated Buddha image is in the Sukhothai style, as is the modern copy of Phitsanulok's Chinnarat Buddha placed in front: evidence of Nan's continuing predilection for Sukhothai models. Unfortunately, the principal image is corroding badly under the onslaught of bat droppings. Behind the *viharn-ubosot*, on its north side, is a slim *chedi* with a high square base, the upper storey of which is decorated with niches and pairs of standing *thewada* at the corners. The rooves capping this storey and the three diminishing square tiers above are in a *cyma recta* curve that suggests Chinese influence. Next to this, on the west side, stands an attractive *ho trai* with a decorated wooden upper storey over a plastered brick ground floor.

The painted ho trai.

Detail of the viharn's carved eyebrow pelmet.

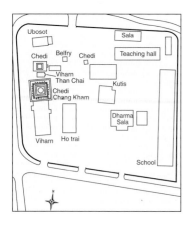

Plan of Wat Phra That Chang Kham
Vora Viharn.

The elephants which give the wat its
name, at the base of the chedi.

Wat Phra That Chang Kham Vora Viharn **

On the east side of Pha Kong Road, opposite the museum entrance, is
'The Monastery of the Relic Supported by Elephants', which you can
enter on its northern side from Mahaphrom Road or its southern side
from Suryaphong Road. As at Wat Phumin and Wat Hua Khuang, the
principal monastic buildings face south, but this major *wat* also has a
number of unique features. The *chedi* which gives the *wat* its '*chang
kham*' name was built in 1406, and has been much restored since.
Around the top of its square base stand the foreparts of twenty-four
elephants – six on each side – supporting the gilded *chedi* proper.
This design, representing the elephants which in Brahmanic and
Buddhist mythology support Mount Meru, comes from Sri Lanka via
Si Satchanalai, the sister city of Sukhothai, strongly resembling Wat
Chang Lom.

Next to the *chedi*, immediately to the south, is the principal *viharn*
of the *wat*, containing several Buddha images, including two fine,
important bronze Buddhas made in 1426-7 in the style of Sukhothai:
one walking while performing *abhaya* with the left hand, the other
standing with both hands in the same pose. These were part of a set
of five images commissioned at the same time by the then ruler, Ngua
Ran Pha Sum. One other is in Wat Na Pang, and the remaining two
are in Wat Phaya Phu nearby.

South pediment of the huge ho-trai, with garudas.

The 15th century bronze walking Buddha in the principal viharn, one of a set of five.

Next to this *viharn*, also facing south, is an even larger building with an exterior gallery of pillars in the Rattanakosin style of Rama III, with a polychromed *garuda* on its pediment and another suspended below. This is not, as you might reasonably think, another *viharn*, but Thailand's largest *ho trai*. It contains, in a glass shrine, a bronze walking Buddha image in the Sukhothai style known as the Nanthaburi Sri Sakyamuni Buddha.

North of the main *chedi* are the small east-facing Viharn Than Chai and a small *chedi* containing the remains of Chao Anantaworaritthidej, the ruler of Nan who renovated Wat Phumin and built Wat Hua Khuang. The *viharn*, which has no portico, is in local style, its wooden gable filled with rectangular *luk fak* panels. North again is a modest and plain *ubosot* built in 1857 and renovated in 1993.

Wat Phaya Phu *

To see the other two walking Buddha images that were part of the
15th century set, go east from here along Suriyaphong Road for two
blocks to the junction with Sumonthewarat Road and turn right. After
200 metres, turn right into Phaya Phu Road (actually a small lane), and
the *wat* is on your right after 100 metres. The original *wat* was built in
1413 by the then ruler, Phaya Pu, and has been patronised by all the
rulers of Nan. The *ubosot* is on the left, containing one of the largest
Buddha images in the province, in Chiang Saen style. On the right is
the *viharn*, housing the two renowned images which stand in front of
and to either side of the principal large seated image. Both are walking
while performing *abhaya*, one with the left hand, the other with the
right. The door panels of this *viharn*, which unusually faces west, are
striking, being locally carved in with ogre-like guardians known as
yama tut. Another idiosyncracy is in the eave brackets, each of which
is carved with different figures: two demons fighting, a demon on a
monkey, two monkeys fighting, and so on.

Apart from this central group of *wat* there are two others of note
within the city.

Wat Suan Tan *

Some 400 metres north of the museum and Wat Chang Kham on Pha
Kong Road is 'The Monastery of the Sugar Palm Grove', with an
unusually shaped 40-metre *chedi*. Built in the 14th century in

*Ogre-like guardians carved on the doors
of the viharn at Wat Phaya Phu.*

Sukhothai style with a lotus-bud finial, it was altered in 1914 to its present elaborate form. Above a square base with redented corners and triple-roofed niches on each side are two smaller square tiers rotated 45° so that the redenting continues up the sides; tall false roofed niches decorate the corners of the second tier, rising to four small corner spires above the third tier.

Above all this is a small bell topped with a *prang*-like finial and gilded Burmese-style parasol. The *viharn* facing the east entrance contains the bronze Phra Chao Thong Thip Buddha image, in Sukhothai style and seated in the *bhumisparsa* pose. It is 4.1 metres tall, and was supposedly cast on the order of King Tilokaraj of Chiang Mai immediately following his 1449 conquest of Nan. Compared with Sukhothai images in the classic tradition, it has a slightly provincial quality.

Wat Phaya Wat *

This monastery, situated in the south-west of town is particularly notable for its Mon-style *chedi*. To reach it, take Route 101 signposted in the direction of Phrae and, 1 kilometre south of the junction with Suriyaphong Road, turn right onto Route 1025. The *wat* is 300 metres on your left, and behind the modern *viharn* is the brick stepped pyramid, square in plan and a copy of the Chedi Mahapol at Wat Ku Kut in Lamphun.

Like the similar replicas at Wat Chedi Liam near Chiang Mai and at Wat Haripunchai in the centre of Lamphun, it was built considerably later than the Mon occupation of the area, in this case probably in the 17th or even 18th centuries. As at Lamphun, each of the five tiers has

The Phra Chao Thong Thip Buddha at Wat Suan Tan, in classic Sukhothai style.

The Mon-style stepped chedi of Wat Phaya Wat.

three niches on each side containing standing Buddha images. Behind the *chedi* is a well-preserved section of the Nan city walls: a high earthen rampart with some brick remains, backed by the deep moat.

Wat Phra That Khao Noi

A little less than 2 kilometres further west on Route 1025, the road ascends an isolated hill, on the summit of which is Wat Phra That Khao Noi, an undistinguished small *chedi* with a T-shaped combined *viharn-ubosot* and fine views over the valley if the weather is clear.

OUTSIDE THE CITY

Wat Phra That Chae Haeng **

This *wat* lies across the Nan River from the town, on a hill to the south-east. To reach it, cross the bridge at the end of Mahawong Road and follow Route 1168 for 2 kilometres, where it passes the entrance to the *wat*. It was founded in 1354-8 by the ruler of the valley kingdom, Chao Phraya Kan Muang, at a time when the capital was Pua in the north. Shortly after, in 1359, the capital was moved here and re-named Phu Phiang Chae Haeng, and stayed here on the east bank of the Nan River until 1368, when it was moved again by the next ruler Chao Pha Kong, across the river to its present location. Wat Phra That Chae Haeng fell into disuse and ruin, and it was not until 1454 that the *chedi* was rebuilt.

The approach to the enclosure is – unusually – from the west, and is flanked by two grand, 100 metre-long *naga* balustrades, added in 1806 by Chao Atthawon Panyo and rebuilt at the beginning of this century. Before entering the high-walled enclosure of the *wat*, enter the building on your left, the Viharn Saiyat, which houses a 15 metre-long reclining Buddha, its head towards the south-east. Enter the main enclosure through the small doorway in the middle of the west side, in front of a large *bodhi* tree. The 55 metre gilded *chedi* rises immediately in front of you, surrounded by a crenellated wall that encloses the path

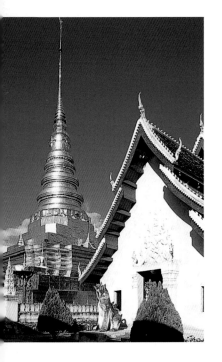

The chedi - rebuilt in 1454 - and viharn at Wat Phra That Chae Haeng.

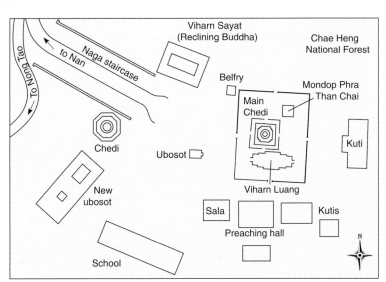

Plan of Wat Phra That Chae Haeng.

for ritual circumnambulation. Gilded *chat* stand at each corner, and the lower tiers of the base carry miniature *chedi*. On the right is the west-facing *viharn*, with massive walls in the local style pierced by very small windows, and a three-tiered roof with each tier in three sections. Eight intertwined stucco relief *nagas* decorate the whitewashed pediment over the entrances at each end.

Inside is a large seated Buddha image in *dhyana mudra* surrounded by other smaller images in front, and there is a fine *thammat*. Behind the *chedi* in the northeast corner of the enclosure stands the open-sided Mondop Phra Than Chai containing a number of images: the Phra Chao Thau Chai Buddha image, and in front of it three smaller Buddha images, on one side a footprint of the Buddha and on the other a seated *reussi* (hermit) reputed to have medical skills.

The mondop, or pavilion, at Wat Chae Haeng.

Making offerings at the chedi.

Left: statue of a revered hermit in the mondop.

THE LOWER VALLEY

South from the city, the Nan River flows towards Uttaradit and the confluence with the Yom and Ping at Nakhon Sawan, interrupted by the Sirikit Dam above the village of Tha Pla. There are few settlements along the way and no through road.

Brightly painted garuda on the gable's eyebrow pelmet, Wat Bun Yeun.

The combined ubosot and viharn at Wat Bun Yeun, built in 1797 by the then ruler of Nan.

Wat Bun Yeun

The small town of Wiang Sa is located 26 kilometres south of Nan on Route 101 to Phrae. Wat Bun Yeun is here, and has a very grand combined *ubosot* and *viharn* with a four-tiered roof that is supported inside by massive tall pillars. The *wat* was moved here in 1784 from its original crowded location by the morning market, and in 1797 the ruler of Nan, Chao Attavorapanyo, had the *viharn* built, facing north. This was followed in 1800 by the standing Buddha image inside (in the 'calling for rains' stance) and in 1802 by the *chedi* behind. Of particular note are the main door panels, reputedly made in 1789 by a member of the Chiang Khong nobility, with Brahma on the left

standing on a lotus (symbolising his birth), and Indra on the right standing on a seven-headed (instead of the more usual three-headed) elephant, both dressed in Laotian style. On the pelmet of the deep portico, note the carved *garuda* on the gable's eyebrow pelmet, painted green, yellow and white: a creature more popular in central Thailand than in the north. The eave-brackets are interesting and varied, all featuring a *naga* with an additional zodiacal animal, and in the fashion of the Nan and Yom valleys, these are polychromed. The building was restored in 1933.

THE UPPER VALLEY

The upper Nan valley has considerably more of interest than the lower valley, with some attractive Tai Lü *wat* and fine mountain scenery near the border with Laos. The main road leading out of town is Route 1080, and by combining this with the narrower Route 1081 to the east it is possible to make a circuit that can take most of a day's drive with stops along the way.

Wat Nong Bua **
The name translates as 'Lotus-pond Monastery'. A fine Tai Lü village *wat*, it was built in 1862 and contains murals executed in the same style as those at Wat Phumin, possibly by the same artists. The *wat* is 40 kilometres north of Nan; to reach it, take Route 1080 north and just after the Km. 39 marker at Ban Fai Mun, turn left. After 500 metres turn right at the T-junction, then after another 300 metres turn left. This road crosses a bridge over the Nan River and at the T-junction

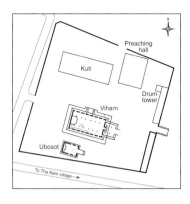

Plan of Wat Nong Bua.

The village of Nong Bua is famous for its textiles; this is a Nam Lai (flowing water) design, late 19th century.

The viharn, Wat Nong Bua, with its deep extended portico.

Opposite: in a detail from the viharn's murals, a princess in her howdah rides an elephant in procession.

Main pediment of the viharn, Wat Nong Bua.

after this, turn left and continue for 2 kilometres into the village of Ban Nong Bua. 100 metres after the road makes a sharp left, next to a bridge over a gully, you will see the *wat* on your right.

The *viharn* is notable for having an extended portico with its own two-tiered roof. This covers parts of the windows and gable of the main building in such a way that it seems to be a later addition, and one unusual effect is that there are two gables. That of the portico is treated in quite a different manner from that of the main building, and is in the same style as the *ubosot*. The pediment features boldly carved plant tendrils framing a very simplified tiger, all gilded and attached to the plain wooden background, while the main pediment on the tier above has symmetrical gilded flowers in rectangular panels, with some remaining glass mosaics. Note the topmost two roof-ridge finials, the *chofa*, which are unusual in that they are elephant-snouted *makara*, unlike the other, more usual, *garuda*.

Inside, Tai Lü *tung* banners hang from the teak pillars, and the main Buddha image sits in *bhumisparsa*. The murals were executed a few years after the building was constructed, between 1867 and 1888, and are painted in Tai Lü style illustrating the *Chanthakhat Jataka*. Although there has been considerable deterioration through damp, some scenes remain intact, including two women in a howdah

on the back of an elephant, a palace scene, a ship being loaded for a journey, and an elephant battle scene. Each of the ceiling panels between the pairs of pillars is painted and divided into large diamond lozenges. To the left of the *viharn* is the smaller *ubosot*, its pediment carved with two *garuda*, openwork vines and monkeys. The peaceful village atmosphere, which can be appreciated from the shaded seating area around the base of the large *lamyai* tree in front of the *viharn*, is a part of the *wat*'s attraction.

The village, inhabited by Tai Lü who emigrated from Yunnan in 1836, is well-known for its weaving. Formerly, each house had its own loom under the piled building, but recently the weavers have formed a co-operative under the name *Chanson Prompanya*, one of the lanes behind the *wat*. A special feature of this village is the three-day Tai Lü festival called the *Khao Kaun Muang La*, held to honour the tutelary spirits.

Route 1080 continues north to the small town of Tha Wang Pha and then 16 kilometres further on, to Pua, which was the original site of the valley's capital from the late 13th century to the mid-14th century.

Another Nam Lai design, with Pa Sin border.

Wat Ton Laeng **

Turn left off the Pua main road at the market, continue for 600 metres to a small roundabout, turn right here, and after 300 metres take the lane to the left, which in 1 kilometre reaches this traditional Tai Lü-style *wat*. About 200 years old, it comprises a single monastic building: a combined *viharn-ubosot* which is quite different in appearance from the normal gabled design seen all over Lanna. The two lower roof tiers, all with wooden shingles, are hipped and surmounted by a small

Triple naga roof finial on the unusual viharn-ubosot at Wat Ton Laeng.

*Buddha image and Tai Lü style
banners, Wat Ton Laeng.*

*Rahu over the main door of the viharn
at Wat Phra That Beng Sakat.*

pitched tier, so that the gable right at the top is very small. The lower
roof finials are in the form of three separate *naga*: another unique
feature. The interior, which houses the Luang Pho Mahani Khotareuk
Buddha image and a fine *thammat* is hung with *tung* banners in the Tai
Lü style.

Wat Phra That Beng Sakat *

Back across the main road, on a
low hill, is a *wat* which was
reputedly founded in 1283. The
front door panels of the *viharn*, set
in a gilded and painted stucco arch
that features a bizarre *Rahu*, are
carved with two fight scenes from
the Ramayana's Battle of Lanka:
one between a monkey and a
demon, the other between a
monkey and a man. There is a
distinctly Chinese influence in the
treatment of the landscape at the
base. The door panels on the north
side are more crudely carved, and

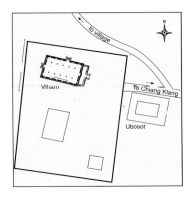

Plan of Wat Nong Daeng.

Below: one of the eave brackets, each different, at Wat Nong Dong.

Below right: the Tai Lü viharn-ubosot at Wat Nong Daeng, dating originally from 1787.

in local style, with an interesting treatment of flowing water with fish on the right-hand panel. On the south side are more scenes from the Ramayana, with Rama standing on Hanuman on the right panel.

Wat Nong Daeng **

Continue north along Route 1080, and just past the Km. 71 marker turn left, entering the village of Chiang Klang after 4 kilometres. After another 2.5 kilometres, opposite the school on the right, turn left into a lane that leads, after 500 metres, into the small village of Ban Nong Daeng. Wat Nong Daeng, another Tai Lü *wat*, is 100 metres down a side lane on the left.

Its *viharn*, like Wat Ton Laeng, is quintessentially Tai Lü, with an elegantly curving wooden shingle roof in two tiers, the lower hipped, the upper gabled. Note the unusual form of the *cho fa*, which combines a swan and elephant (both noble animals to the Tai Lü) into a mythical *hasadiling* bird. The gables are decorated with carved petalled flowers set in a pattern of rectangles, while the small glass mirror in the centre is purely Chinese, designed to drive away or reflect evil spirits. Note also the brightly-painted eave-brackets, each featuring different scenes.

The interior is hung characteristically with woven *tung* and is now much brighter than it originally was since the windows were enlarged during its restoration. The principal Buddha image sits on a Tai Lü design of pedestal known as *nak ballang* – a throne of two encircling *naga* – the rear wall of which is painted with a mural of the Three Worlds. This *wat* has, in fact, been moved several times, but dates originally from 1787. The smaller *ubosot* near the entrance was built in 1955.

Left: Buddha image in Naga throne, Wat Nong Daeng.

Above and below: the extraction of salt from local wells still continues at this village in the traditional fashion, boiling the saline water in sheds.

Below: giant Caryota palms at the summit of the pass above Bo Luang.

Bo Luang

North again from Chiang Klang, the road climbs up into the hills, gradually curving east to follow the course of the upper Nan River. Approximately 45 kilometres after Thung Chang (135 kilometres from Nan), a military checkpoint with a barrier marks the turn-off to the left toward the border with Laos, where there is a weekend market. The narrow, winding Route 1081 continues south up towards the headwaters of the Nan River and over a watershed to Bo Luang, 77 kilometres from the checkpoint.

This small town, whose name means 'Great Well', is known for its salt extraction, formerly an important rarity in a region which had very little. The source is two saline wells; clustered around each are the extraction sheds, where the water is boiled over earthen fires and the precipitated salt scooped out. Accoring to one account, annual production reached 850 tonnes in the 15th century, and was used as a tribute to King Tilokaraj in Chiang Mai.

West from Bo Luang, Route 1256 crosses a pass through the forested mountains; near the summit note the *Caryota* palms looking like tree ferns, called 'giant tufted palm' (*tao rang yak*) locally. It continues down to Pua, 49 kilometres from Bo Luang, and the Nan River.

THE KOK AND ING VALLEYS

The far north of Lanna borders both Burma and Laos, and here for a short distance flows the Mekong River, on its way through Laos to Cambodia and Vietnam. This is the part of Lanna most associated with trekking, hill-tribes and, formerly at least, the opium and heroin trade. The two provincial capitals are Chiang Rai, now bustling, and quiet Phayao looking out over its large lake.

The foothills above Mae Chan at dawn, looking towards the Mekong.

While the greater part of Lanna is occupied by the north-south valleys leading down to the Central Plains, a relatively small area – about 16% – drains north into the Mekong, most of it via the Kok and Ing Rivers and their small tributaries. The geography of ridge and valley is not quite so obvious here, and only low hills separate the two rivers. The Kok, which rises in Burma's Shan State, cuts right across the main Tanten range that forms part of the national border before reaching the plain at Chiang Rai; this happened as a result of uplift in recent geological times. The Ing, which rises in the centre of Lanna, close to the ancient town of Phayao, flows north and slightly east for not much more than 100 kilometres before it drains into the Mekong.

CHIANG RAI

Typically situated for a Lanna city of importance, with hills to the west and by a principal river, Chiang Rai commands the floodplain of the Kok River and was the first capital of Lanna, being Mangrai's first

Map of the Kok Valley and the Ing Valley to the south.

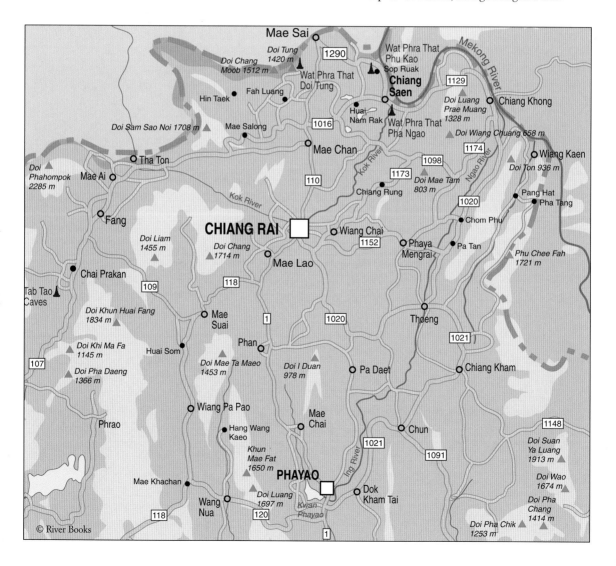

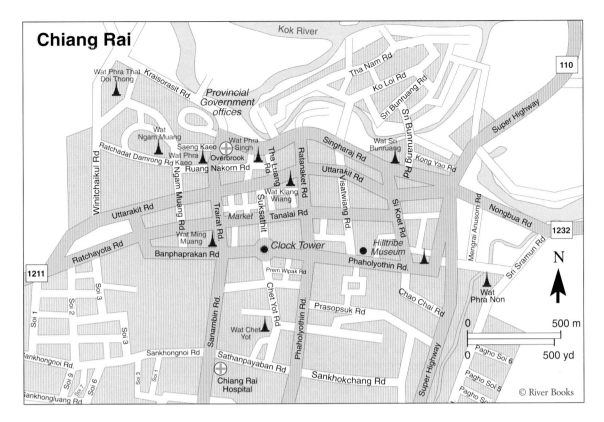

Map of the town of Chiang Rai.

choice when he moved from his birthplace, Chiang Saen, to build a kingdom through treaty and conquest. An additional attraction at that time, between 1262 and 1263, was the hill in the north-west of the present-day town, which was capable of fortification.

According to the chronicles, the *chedi* of Wat Phra That Doi Chom Thong had already been built on the summit long before, in 940, and when Mangrai surveyed the site, he had the first *wiang* constructed here, and named it after himself: '[Mang] Rai's City.' The site was actually chosen by Mangrai's auspicous elephant, which wandered up the hill by itself. According to the Chiang Mai Chronicle, Mangrai then decided, "I should make the hill the navel of the country." Astrological calculations suggest that the city was officially founded at the auspicious time of 5:48 pm on Friday, 26th January 1263.

Chiang Rai lost its political importance when Mangrai moved his capital further south, first to Wiang Kum Kam in 1286 and then to Chiang Mai proper in 1296, to follow and consolidate his conquests. However, the Lanna court did move back here for two brief periods. The first was in 1319, when Mangrai's grandson Saeng Phu was temporarily deposed at Chiang Mai and retreated here to join his father, Chai Songkhram, who had retired there the previous year. The second was in 1337, when King Pha Yu succeeded to the throne and moved here for two years. Chiang Rai regained some importance in a religious fashion in 1434 with the discovery of the Emerald Buddha at Wat Phra Kaeo.

During Lanna's struggles for independence from Burma, the town played a prominent part, rebelling in 1600 and again in 1614, provoking Burmese military reaction. It was finally placed under direct Burmese rule at the beginning of the 18th century as a dependency of Chiang Saen, not to be recaptured from them until 1786. This was acheived 11 years after Chiang Mai regained its freedom, with the help of Siam. However, as in Chiang Mai half a century earlier, the struggles and consequent devastation caused Chiang Rai to be virtually abandoned, and inhabitants had to be deliberately re-settled in 1844 from Chiang Mai, Lamphun and Lampang. The city has changed greatly in recent decades, and in the 1920s lost its walls, which were built after the refounding beginning in 1858. In 1988 two short sections were rebuilt on either side of the Yang Song Gate, but the only reference was an illsutration based on a sketch by Dr. P. Neis made in 1884.

The viharn of Wat Phra Kaeo.

Wat Phra Kaeo **

Because of its associations with the Emerald Buddha (Pra Kaeo Morakot), this is the town's principal *wat*. It is on Trairat Road opposite the old Overbrook Hospital (built in 1911 by an American missionary, Dr. Briggs). Apparently, in 1434 lightning struck the *chedi*, which cracked open to reveal the now highly revered seated image, made of dark green jasper. Howeves, how it came to be enshrined here in the first place, and more importantly what its origin were, are still unknown, although stylistically it seems unlikely to have been carved hereabouts.

From this mysterious and auspicious beginning, the Emerald Buddha acquired great importance, prompting various rulers to move it to their seat of power, or to attempt to. First, King Sam Fang Kaen ordered it to be brought to Chiang Mai, but the elephant carrying it had other ideas. This being taken as an omen, the image was instead taken to Lampang, where it was installed at Wat Phra Kaeo Don Tao (*see page 134*). King Tilokaraj moved it to Wat Chedi Luang in Chiang Mai in 1486; King Setthathirat of Luang Prabang took it back with him in 1548 when he returned from Chiang Mai; it was taken to Vientiane in 1564, and the Siamese general Taksin acquired it in 1778 when he conquered Vientiane. He then removed it to Wat Arun in Bangkok, and it was moved for the last time in 1784 across the river to Wat Phra Kaeo. It was placed in the grounds of the Grand Palace, where it presides over the *ubosot* and is considered the palladium of the Thai Kingdom.

All this has meant that Wat Phra Kaeo in Chiang Rai, despite hardly having had the honour of enshrining the image, except unknowingly before its discovery, has received considerable merit-making activity, and never more so than recently.

As you enter the main east gate of the enclosure, the building

The chedi where the Emerald Buddha was found.

Above left: the highly decorated interior of the viharn Chiang Rai.

Above: The recent copy of the Emerald Buddha.

Guardian mythical lion at Wat Phra Singh.

directly ahead is the much restored *viharn*, in true Lanna proportions but perhaps with an excess of decoration. The gilded doors are decorated in three unequal panels: *khrue thao* vine motif above, lozenges and bars below. The pelmet above is a mixture of the flowing *pak kud* design above and *khrue thao*, with blue glass in the centre. The pediment is divided into rectangular panels, all uncarved but painted with purely floral designs in gold; on close examination, you can see that these designs are quite different from the originals, some of which remain underneath. Inside is a large Buddha image, the Phra Chao Lang Thong, seated in *bhumisparsa mudra*. Behind the *viharn* is the gilded *chedi* where the Emerald Buddha was found, and behind this and to the right, in the northwest corner of the enclosure, is a new *ubosot* constructed and decorated in an amalgam of styles to enshrine a recent copy of the Emerald Buddha. This was carved from dark green Canadian jade by Chinese craftsmen in *dhyana mudra*, the meditation posture with both hands in the lap, and consecrated in 1991 by the King.

Wat Phra Singh **

This *wat* is two blocks to the east of Wat Phra Kaeo, and can be entered on foot from Tha Luang Road on the east, or by vehicle from Singharaj Road on the north. The *wat* was founded in 1385 at the beginning of the reign of King Saen Muang Ma and is so named for its principal image enshrined in the *viharn*, the Phra Sihing Buddha. This seated bronze image in the *bhumisparsa* pose is another of the Sihing type of Buddha images that attempted to recapture the supposedly purer Sinhalese lines; these are described under Wat Phra Singh, Chiang Mai *(see page 67)*.

The main building of interest, then, is the *viharn* which, like that at Wat Phra Kaeo, has been meticulously restored but also added to in its

Right: head of the Buddha Phra Chao Lang Thong, from Wat Phra Kaeo.

decoration profusely; note the peacocks filling the spaces under the eyebrow pelmets on the two winged gables. The pediment is as usual divided into rectangular panels, and these are carved with floral motifs, while the two triangular spaces at the very top have *hongse* birds. In front of the *viharn* on the south side, next to the *bodhi* tree surrounded by representations of the Buddha, is a small *Ho Phra Putthabat* ('Footprint of-the-Buddha Chapel'). Behind the *viharn* is the *chedi* on a square base, whitewashed with a Burmese-style seven-tiered *hti* on the top.

The chedi of Wat Chom Thong, dating from 1864.

Wat Phra That Doi Chom Thong *

In the north-west of town, on a hill behind the provincial government offices, is another wat with a distinguished history. It can be reached by taking Singharaj Road west past Wat Phra Singh and, at the corner where the Overbrook Hospital stands, turning right onto Kraisorasit Road, which runs alongside a branch of the river. After 600 metres turn left, go uphill 200 metres to a three-way intersection, and the foot of the staircase leading up to the *wat* is on the right. Vehicles can drive up the narrow road next to this.

Wat Phra That Doi Chom Thong ('The Monastery of the Great Gold Relic Hill') pre-dated the 1262 founding of Chiang Rai by three centuries, and the commanding location of the summit made it an attractive choice for King Mangrai's first *wiang*, or fortified settlement, here. According to the Yonok Chronicle, a *chedi* was built in 940 by Phraya Ruen Kaeo, a local prince, to house a third part of Buddha relics (the other two parts were enshrined at Wat Phra That Doi Tung and Wat Phra That Chom Kitti in Chiang Saen). The present *chedi* dates to 1864 and is octagonal from the base up to the small bell, with a prominent straight-sided indented section, and completely sheathed in gilded copper sheets.

The viharn at Wat Ming Muang.

On a lower terrace to the north is a Chinese shrine, and on the higher ground immediately to the south (the former summit that was levelled earlier this century) is the modern city pillar (*lak muang*). This was installed in 1988, and takes its dimensions from the present King Bhumiphol.

Wat Chet Yot's seven-spired chedi.

NEARBY WATS

On a neighbouring hilltop to the south is **Wat Ngam Muang**, where King Mangrai's ashes are kept. The access road to this *wat* can be entered either from Ngam Muang Road or from Ratchdet Damrong Road, but complete modernisation has left little to see of what was originally a 14th century *wat*.

Back down in the town, **Wat Ming Muang** on the corner of Trairat Road and Banphapakan Road has a renovated *viharn* with exaggeratedly low, wide proportions. Recently carved, gilded panels on the outside walls depict the zodiacal animals.

The eponymous Reclining Buddha of Wat Phra Non.

In the southern part of town, **Wat Chet Yot *** is named for its seven-spired (*chet yot*) *chedi*. This is an imitation of Wat Chet Yot in Chiang Mai, although only in the proportions; there are no stucco decorations on the walls and the *chedi* standing on the roof are different, all with lower straight-sided indented sections as at Wat Phra That Doi Chom Thong on the hill. To reach the *wat*, head south on Phaholyothin Road from the main intersection in the centre of town and turn right, after passing the Night Market on the left. However, if approaching from the west, take Sathanpayaban Road east past Chiang Rai Hospital on the right, and turn left into the narrow Chet Yot Road.

In the east of town, on Nongbua Road 300 metres south of its junction with Route 1232, is **Wat Phra Non** ('Reclining Buddha'), with a large reclining image housed in a long hall on the west side of the enclosure. Unusually, the image reclines almost on its back. The *chedi* between this building and the *viharn* is also unusual: a rectangular structure with a flat roof reminiscent of those at the two Wat Chet Yot, but with five rather than seven *chedi* on top. These *chedi* are in a Meru arrangement, with a larger central one surrounded by the four others.

THE LOWER KOK VALLEY

The Kok River flows northeast from Chiang Rai across its fertile plain to meet the Mekong River just below the historically important town of Chiang Saen, while the Ing River drains the area south and east, entering the Mekong at Chiang Khong. A little further east of this is the tiny Ngao River, rising above Chiang Kham and entering the Mekong at Wiang Kaen.

From Chiang Rai the main highway in the direction of the Mekong heads due north, following the base of the mountains to Mae Sai, a small border town of absolutely no distinction but which, like the so-called 'Golden Triangle', has been manufactured into a tourist destination. There is only one important site in this direction – Wat Phra That Doi Tung – but for those interested in visiting hill-tribe villages there are many in the mountainous area to the west (see *The Upper Valley* below).

Wat Phra That Doi Tung **

Some 61 kilometres north of Chiang Rai is the mountain-top *wat* reputed to have been founded in 911 by King Achutarat of Chiang Saen to enshrine a collar-bone fragment of the Buddha, and now a popular site of pilgrimage.

Take Route 110, the fast highway, north from Chiang Rai, passing Mae Chan after 30 kilometres. It is 13 kilometres after this town that the new road up the mountain of Doi Tung (1420 metres) is clearly signposted to the left. Although steep and winding, the 18-kilometre road is very well built, partly because it also serves as access to the palace built for the Princess Mother, who died in 1995. Along the way are Lahu and Loi Mi Akha villages and fine forested scenery. The *wat* lies just below the summit, and there is a long, curving staircase flanked by undulating *naga* balustrades leading up from a parking area or, more commonly used, a steep road that can be accessed by vehicles.

The focus of devotion here is a pair of slim gilded *chedis* believed to date from the 10th-century founding of the *wat*, although their present form owes more to their 1960s restoration. They feature prominent niches containing standing and walking Buddha

The twin chedis of Wat Phra That Doi Tung.

Footprint of the Buddha at the same temple.

images in the tall square base, and a narrow bell. Supposedly, when King Achutarat decided on the location, he first ordered a giant flag to be flown on the site (Doi Tung means 'flag peak'). As at Wat Phra Boromathat Doi Suthep near Chiang Mai, a row of bronze bells lines the terrace, and these are struck by visiting pilgrims with the short wooden sticks provided. Next to the twin *chedis* is an unsheltered Footprint of The Buddha.

HISTORY OF CHIANG SAEN

The banks of the Mekong River have a long but poorly documented history, for it was in the region around Chiang Saen that the bulk of the Tai peoples crossed over from the north. At the confluence of the Kok and Mekong Rivers, Chiang Saen has played a formative role in the culture of Lanna, and its present-day atmosphere of being a rather under-populated backwater is a legacy of more recent times. To reach it from Chiang Rai, drive 30 kilometres north to Mae Chan on Route 110, then take Route 1016 heading northwest for 32 kilometres and enter the town through the restored Chiang Saen gate.

There was a settlement here in prehistoric times, as evidence stone artefacts uncovered here and on display at the museum, but the town itself was not founded until the 14th century. Nevertheless, the surrounding area on the right bank of the Mekong was historically important for its position on a trade and migration route from Yunnan in the north (even today Chinese boats unload goods at the riverside). It seems likely, then, that a large proportion of the Tai peoples who moved south into what is now Thailand around the 12th century passed through here. The first Tai settlement of importance was Ngoen Yang, located upriver nearer Mai Sai, and there is a record of a marriage alliance around 1230 between the ruling family and that of Chiang Rung in what is now Yunnan. This marriage resulted in the birth in 1239 of a son, Prince Mangrai, who went on to conquer and rule Lanna, founding the dynasty that ruled the region for three centuries.

It was the grandson of Mangrai, King Saen Phu, who, according to the Chiang Mai chronicle, built the new city of Chiang Saen in 1329 after he emerged successfully from the vicissitudes of a family power struggle for the throne. It was originally called Muang Roi, but after Saen Phu went to live in it, the city was given his name, and it controlled a significant territory on both sides of the Mekong. Later, in the 16th-18th centuries, it suffered Burmese control along with the rest of Lanna. It was the last Burmese stronghold to be recaptured, in 1804. The fighting to capture the city was intense; as the Chiang Mai Chronicle describes it, "All of Chiang Saen was in chaos, filled with shrieks and cries of suffering and with the noise of guns that filled the skies."

By this time, Lanna had accepted Siamese suzerainty in exchange for military assistance, and it was King Rama I who ordered that Chiang Saen be destroyed as a defensive measure, leaving only the religious buildings standing. By the time that the British surveyor Holt Hallett visited Chiang Saen in 1876, the city was almost deserted. He wrote,

The chedi of Wat Phra That Chedi Luang, 58 metres high.

"we rambled through the city, about half of which was covered with the remains of fifty-three temples....Splendid bronze images of Gaudama, generally in a good state of preservation, were scattered about in every direction, and often half buried in the *debris* of fallen buildings. In 1881, by which time neither Burma nor Laos posed a military threat, King Rama V (Chulalongkorn) ordered Chao In-Ta, prince of Lamphun, to rule and re-settle Chiang Saen with people from Lamphun, Chiang Mai and Lampang, in the same way that Rama III had had Chiang Rai re-populated. Nevertheless, the population of the town to this day occupies only a small part of the original area, which is bounded by 8 kilometres of walls, and has a rather neglected air. Chiang Saen was eventually incorporated into Chiang Rai province in 1957.

The walls, of which traces remain, form an uneven rectangle bordering the Mekong River, which at this point flows from north to south. As recorded in the chronicles, Saen Phu's city measured 3 by 1.4 kilometres, but the walls as they can be traced today are a little over 2 by 1 kilometres, and the discrepancy is likely to be an error of scale. There were five gates, one each in the shorter north and south walls, and three on the west side. Of these, the Chiang Saen Gate in the middle has been restored, and it is through here that Route 1016 enters the town, becoming its main street, Phaholyothin Road.

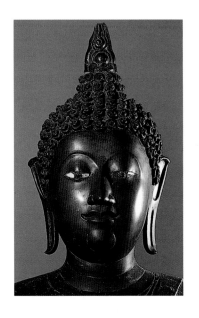

Exhibits in the national museum:

Above: head of a bronze Buddha in Chiang Saen style, 14th to 15th century.

Below: bronze hermit, 1605, from Wat Phra That Doi Tung.

Below right: bronze flame or ketmala found in the river.

Wat Phra That Chedi Luang **

100 metres east of the gate, just inside the walls and next to the museum, are the remains of Wat Phra That Chedi Luang, Chiang Saen's principal ancient *wat*. Like most of the religious monuments in the town, only the octagonal *chedi* remains standing. Built in 1331 and enlarged in 1515 to its present 58 metres, it towers over the surrounding trees. Next to it on the east side is a makeshift *viharn*.

National Museum **

This is on the other side of the giant *chedi*, and housed a small but important collection of images. Inside, facing the entrance are five Chiang Saen bronze Buddha images. Four of these, seated in the *bhumisparsa* pose, date from the 14th-15th centuries, two of them from Wat Phra Chao Lan Thong and two from Wat Pong Sanuk. The fifth, a standing Buddha in a stance holding an alms bowl (separate and now missing) was cast in 1577 and commissioned by the ruler Chao Muen Rua and his wife. Other bronzes include a small *reussi* (hermit) from Wat Phra That Doi Tung (*q.v.*) cast in 1605, and a 15th century bronze *ketmala* (flame surmounting the *ushnisha*) from a large but so far undiscovered Buddha image.

Further important exhibits are 14th-century stucco pieces from Wat Pa Sak nearby *(see below)*, including a fine, animated *kala* head and a standing stucco Buddha image, and 15th century stone inscriptions and heads. There are also ethnographic displays.

Wat Pa Sak **

'The Teak Forest Monastery' is architecturally and artistically the most important monument in the area, and is located just outside the walls, 200 metres to the right once you have left the Chiang Saen gate from the museum. Still surrounded by teak trees, of which 300 were originally planted around the walls, it is generally believed to have been founded in 1319, but there are doubts about the date. The Chiang Saen chronicle records that it was 1295, but this would put it well before the founding of the city acording to the Chiang Mai chronicles. Stylistically, some Sukhothai features in the decorative stucco work suggest a later date or later restoration. It consists today of the principal *chedi*, the foundations and bases of pillars of the *viharn* and one other building to its east, and six other ruins on the north and south sides.

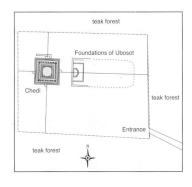

Plan of Wat Pa Sak.

The stuccoed brick *chedi*, which was built to enshrine a relic brought from Pataliputra in India, is partly influenced by the Mon style (the square diminishing tiers with niches for standing Buddhas, as at the Mahapol Chedi at Wat Ku Kut near Lamphun), and partly by Sukhothai and Pagan. The square base is lined with seven niches on

Above: standing Buddha in a niche at Wat Pa Sak.

Left: the chedi, Wat Pa Sak.

Stucco kirtimukha in the National Museum at Chiang Saen.

each side: that is, three large niches containing stucco standing Buddha images alternating with *thewada* in the four smaller ones. Above this, three diminishing steps support the main body of the *chedi*, beginning with a smaller square tier elaborated with a niche for a standing Buddha image on each side and pilasters framing the niches and at the corners. The best surviving stucco decoration is on this level, and is very lively, featuring *garuda*, *makara*, *kala* and squatting demonic figures, all reminiscent of stucco work at Sukhothai. Specifically, the small squatting figures are essentially the same as those at the base of the Ha Yot *chedi* at Wat Mahathat in Sukhothai, while the vertical projections around the top of the arch are similar to the flame motifs that can be seen at Wat Chedi Chet Thaeo in Si Satchanalai. At the same time, the floral motifs betray Chinese influence from the north. Another square reduction above this leads to a short octagonal section supporting a slim circular upper section ending in a spire.

Inside the city walls are a number of other, partly ruined *chedi*. On the north side of Phaholyothin Road, 200 metres east of Wat Phra That Chedi Luang, is the small 15th century *chedi* of **Wat Mung Muang**, and the foundations of its *viharn* to the east. Opposite, on the south side of the street, is the small *chedi* of **Wat Phra Buat**, also 15th century.

Wat Phra Chao Lan Thong

This is situated on the left halfway between Wat Phra Buat and the river, and was founded in the reign of King Tilokaraj; there are the remains of a brick *chedi* and a modern *viharn* containing the eponymous bronze Buddha image, Phra Chao Lan Thong. To the right of this principal image is a smaller bronze image from 1726 called the Phra Chao Saen Swae ('Lord Buddha of a Hundred Thousand Pins') because pins were used to assemble the different parts in which it was cast.

Wat Pha Khao Pan

On the riverfront 400 metres north of Phaholyothin Road are the remains of the 16th century *chedi* of Wat Pha Khao Pan, with niches containing images of the Buddha walking, in *abhaya*.

The bronze model of a viharn at left, 102 centimetres high and cast in 1726, now in the Ayutthaya National Museum, was made at the same time as the original, a donation for Wat Pha Khao Pan by a local dignitary and his wife.

Outside the city walls, towards the north-west, is a hill with commanding views over the river. At its top are two temples, which can be reached by driving out through the Chiang Saen Gate, turning left after half a kilometre onto Route 1290, and continuing north for 2.5 kilometres to the base of the hill. Turn left and continue up.

Wat Phra That Chom Kitti *

The higher of the two temples, on the west, is notable for its 25 metre-high *chedi* in the centre of a terrace. Leaning to one side because of subsidence, it has a high square redented base with a niche containing a standing stucco Buddha image on each side. The upper part is

This bronze model viharn is in the Lanna style, a votive offering for Wat ‘Phra Khao Nan.

sheathed in gilded copper sheets, and is distinctive for the three 12-sided mouldings below the bell. It was, according to the Yonok Chronicle, the recipient of Buddha relics that were split into three and sent also to Wat Phra That Doi Chom Tong in Chiang Rai and to Wat Phra That Doi Tung.

Wat Chom Chaeng
Down the steps from this terrace and a few metres to the east is the small *chedi* of Wat Chom Chaeng, with a modern *viharn* on a new marble terrace overlooking the town and river. An old, overgrown staircase of 350 steps leads down east to the town.

Wat Ku Tao
1 kilometre west of the Chiang Saen gate are the ruins of Wat Ku Tao, set back from Route 1016 on the south side immediately west of the Km. 29 marker. Apart from the foundations of buildings, there is a round tilted brick *chedi* with some stucco remaining near the top.

Wat Phra That Pha Ngao *
East of Chiang Saen on the road to Chiang Khong (*see page 208*) a prominent forested hill rises on the right side 4 kilometres out of town along Route 1129, a white *chedi* clearly visible at the top. At its foot is the new *viharn* of Pha Ngao, reputedly founded in 462. At the Km. 49 marker, turn right and you will be in front of the *viharn*, which contains the remains of a stuccoed brick Buddha image, the Luang Phor Pha Ngao, that was discovered during the 1976 restoration of the building. It is displayed, half excavated, below and in front of a more recent seated image. There are photographs which document its discovery.

To the left of the *viharn*, against the hillside, is a large boulder on which has been built a small octagonal brick *chedi*. A road continues up the hill, past a new, over-decorated *viharn* to the large white-tiled modern *chedi*, built in the 1980s, called the Phra Boromathat Puttha Nimit Chedi. The views are more interesting than the architecture.

Wat Song Phi Nong
Continuing along Route 1129 eastwards, and after one kilometre on the left are the ruins of 'The Two Brothers Monastery'. Apart from the small recent monastic buildings, the remains comprise two overgrown *chedi* in stuccoed brick, with the one on the side nearest the road being in better condition than the other. In front of each are the foundations of *viharn*, on one of which sits a large and rather crude modern Buddha image. The mouth of the Kok river lies immediately to the east of here, and somewhere in this area, according to the Chiang Mai Chronicle, was the predecessor to Chiang Saen, "the old city, north of the mouth of the Kok" where King Saen Phu was buried "near the market landing".

Wat Mae Kham
A simple village monastery, this only comprises one building, a small *viharn* built in 1890, and is situated 48 kilometres from Chiang Khong, just before the village of Ban Mae Rai. Architecturally it is

The crooked chedi of Wat Phra That Chom Kitti.

Chedi on a boulder at Wat Phra That Pha Ngao.

The rustic viharn at Wat Mae Kham, with its Buddha image.

undistinguished, certainly, but pleasantly unpretentious, decorated and maintained locally without the benefit of endowments which, all too often and particularly in Chiang Rai province, are an excuse for excess. Inside, each pair of pillars is painted with a different floral design. The road continues east across the hills to the small port of Chiang Khong, at the mouth of the Ing (*see map*).

Wat Phra That Phu Khao

In the opposite direction from Chiang Saen, 9 kilometres north along the banks of the Mekong, is Sop Ruak, formerly a small village, now a community of shops and hotels that have grown to feed the tourist industry that is based on the wholly artificial concept of the 'Golden Triangle'. This is best avoided altogether, but if your route brings you this way, Wat Phra That Phu Khao on top of the hill has a small old brick viharn, though in poor condition. The *wat* was originally founded in 759.

For the record, 'Golden Triangle' was the American epithet for the opium-growing region that was approximately triangular, with its base a line running from around Mae Sot north-east to the border between Laos and Vietnam and its apex in the centre of Burma's Kachin State. From the end of World War II until the late 1960s, about 80 percent of the international heroin trade was supplied by Turkish poppy fields, but production fell sharply after the Turkish government banned it in 1967. The gap was filled by this hill-country straddling Burma, Laos and northern Thailand, where opium refineries began producing high-grade no. 4 heroin (90 to 99 percent pure) in late 1969, initially to meet demand among American GIs in Vietnam. After the 1970-72 troop withdrawals, production was re-directed to international trade. None of this had anything to do with this spot, where the small Sai River flows into the Mekong, marking the border of Thailand, Burma and Laos.

PHAYAO

The town of Phayao, on the shores of Kwan Phayao, faces the mountain peaks of, from left to right, Doi Luang (1697 metres), Doi Khun Mae Fat (1550 metres) and Doi Khun Mae Tam (1330 metres). It was formerly the capital of a small independent kingdom, and originally a cluster of settlements.

Founded in 1096 by Phor Khun Chom Dham, it was built on the site of an ancient settlement dating back to at least the Bronze Age, and while its control did not extend far down the valley, it was sufficiently important in at least the late 13th century for the ruler, Ngam Muang, to be considered as an equal by Ram Kamhaeng of Sukhothai and Mangrai of Chiang Mai. The three concluded a pact of friendship in

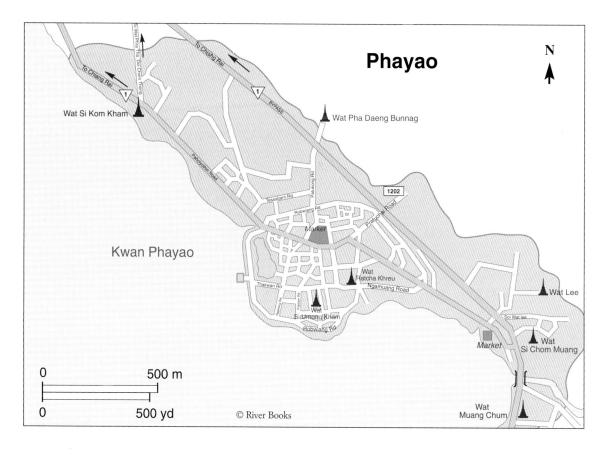

Map of the town of Phayao.

1287 and together chose the site for the city of Chiang Mai. However, such alliances tended to depend very much on personal relationships, and in about 1338 the great-grandson of Mangrai, King Kham Fu, attacked and captured Phayao, and his troops "got much plunder, such as gems and rings, silver and gold".

As a part of Lanna, Phayao then became involved in various military struggles. In 1439 Sukhothai troops besieged the city and were beaten off with the help of a cannon cast from the bronze plates covering a *chedi*, but within three decades it was, as a result of intrigue, ruled by a Sukhothai prince. During the Burmese period Phayao suffered to the extent that the small city was abandoned. Later, it was incorporated into Chiang Rai province, and only in 1977 was the province of Phayao created. Unlike the other Lanna provinces, it does not correspond to the valley, but takes in part of the upper Yom. The city retained its walls until the late 1920s.

Wat Si Khom Kham **

Phayao's principal *wat*, by the lakeshore at the northern end of town, Wat Si Khom Kham also contains Lanna's largest Buddha image (though not its most beautiful). To reach it, take Paholyothin Road north-west along the lakeshore from the old town; the *wat* is on the left 700 metres after Robwiang Road (which made the boundary of the old town).

The walled enclosure, lined with a *phra rabieng,* contains a large modern *viharn* in the centre and in front, in the north-east and south-

Plan of Wat Si Khom Kham.

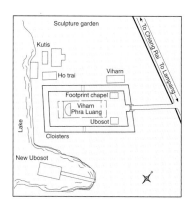

The giant Phra Chao Ton Luang Buddha image, which dates back to the 15th century.

Below: unusually styled kala, part of the ubosot's pediment.

Below right: another detail from the carved pediment.

east corners respectively, a *Ho Phra Putthabat* and *ubosot*. The *viharn*, rebuilt a number of times, most recently in 1961 and before that in 1922, contains the 16 metre-high stuccoed brick Phra Chao Ton Luang seated Buddha image. It was probably built in the 15th century, and its straight wide mouth is a development of the local Phayao school. Note the tigers on the scalloped pelmet on the west façade, carved here because the commissioning monk was born in the Year of the Tiger. Other elements include a central *garuda*, monkeys, intertwined vines and a lower edge composed of four linked *naga*. The winged gables feature monkeys fighting during the Battle of Lanka, from the Ramayana epic, and all the carving is the work of local craftsmen.

The *Ho Phra Putthabat* ('Footprint-of-the Buddha Chapel') on your right as you face the entrance of the *viharn* contains two Footprints from the 14th century, and has attractive Lanna-style pediments featuring a tiger among foliage.

The *ubosot* on the opposite side has pediments in a similar style, the one facing west depicting a striking, originally styled *kala*. This adopted Indian motif of a demon commanded by Shiva to devour itself, and so lacking a lower jaw, functions as an entrance guardian. Although normally only the face is shown with bulging eyes, this carving unusually features the rest of the body, less the jaw. Reminiscent of its treatment in Khmer lintels, where it was a very popular device, the *kala* here holds the ends of foliage stems in its mouth, although whether devouring them or issuing them (as in the Khmer style) is not clear.

The surrounding *phra rabieng* has many heads of Buddha images collected from the surrounding area, in the local Phayao style, featuring pointed noses. Historically, stone Buddha images in Lanna were virtually confined to Phayao. Beyond the monastic enclosure to the north, among trees, is one of the modern lurid sculpture gardens popular at certain Thai *wat* to illustrate the punishments of the damned in hell. Finally, built out onto the lake to the south is a modern *ubosot* of no special interest other than the modern murals.

Wat Phra That Doi Chom Thong

Due north from here is the hill-top 'Monastery of the Great Gold Relic Hill', formerly a fortified *wiang*. A long flight of steps flanked by *naga* balustrades leads to the enclosure. The *chedi*, with a high redented square base surmounted by three circular mouldings below the bell, is no longer gilded, and the *wat* has lost its former importance.

Wat Pha Daeng Bunnag

This monastery is to the east of the town, on the other side of the bypass. Its most distinguishing feature is a tall bell-shaped brick *chedi*, Sinhalese in style, on a high base.

Wat Si Chom Ruang

This is further south along the bypass, and has a *chedi* that combines a square redented Lanna base and a Burmese upper section, together with an old *bodhi* tree surrounded by shrines and offerings.

Wat Ratcha Khreu

Near the centre of town, on Ngamuang Road, is Wat Ratcha Khreu. It has a slim *chedi* that has a square redented base and octagonal mouldings and bell.

Wat Si Umong Kham *

Close to the lakeshore, in the west of town, is Wat Si Umong Kham. On a high terrace, the modern *viharn* contains a Buddha image; behind, the *chedi* with its tall redented base overlooks the western part of town and the lake.

Wat Phra That King Kaeng

To follow the Ing down to its confluence with the Mekong, take the bypass, Route 1, south from Phayao and, just past the southern end of the lake, take Route 1021 to the left. Follow this north-east through the village of Dok Kham Tai, past Doi Khun Mae Lae (1075 metres) and Doi Khun Mae Na (1048 metres) on the right. The road curves around the northern

Children in the sculpture garden of "the damned".

Chedi and tung at Wat Phra That King Kaeng.

end of this last hill and heads southeast to the small town of Chun. Here, on a low hill, is Wat Phra That King Kaeng, with a prominent *chedi* decorated with glass and gilt mosaic. Its octagonal mouldings and bell are remininiscent of those on the *chedi* at Wat Luang in Phrae.

Wat Nantharam **

Continue northwest on Route 1021, which crosses the low watershed between the Ing and Ngao Rivers, towards Chiang Kham, 30 kilometres away from Chun. On the east side of the main street is this fine Burmese monastery, formerly Wat Jongka, which had fallen into ruins by the 1920s, when a local benefactor had the multi-functional structure rebuilt. Construction took from 1925 to 1943, with the principal teak Buddha image in Mandalay style brought from another monastery and installed in 1934.

Below: interior of the Shan-style Wat Nantharam.

Right: monk's chair.

The building has been restored several times during the 1970s and has the complex multi-tiered rooves that make the Shan style monastery so appealing. Note the gable decoration over the portico featuring a peacock-tail motif in mirror inlay, surrounded by gold floral designs on a red ground. The interior is typically ornate, with a decorated coffered ceiling and three rows of gilded teak pillars in front of the altar.

Wat Sri Mana Po

North of Chiang Kham, Route 1021 leads back over the watershed to the Ing River at the small town of Thoeng 28 kilometres away. A kilometre before the bridge, on a hilltop on the right, is the *chedi* of Wat Sri Mana Po, restored in 1973 but reputedly dating from 677.

Chedi with staircase leading to it, Wat Sri Mana Po.

Wat Phra Kaeo

At Thoeng, the road meets Route 1020, heading west in the direction of Chiang Rai (69 kilometres) and north-east down the Ing Valley to Chiang Khong (76 kilometres). This latter town is a small port on the Mekong that was originally a Lawa city until its capture by King Mangrai late in the 13th century. It lies opposite the Laotian town of Huai Sai, and has two *wat*, both on the river side of the main street. Standing on an elevated terrace, the redented square base of the Wat Phra Kaeo *chedi* is also indented to give a waisted effect, while the circular mouldings and bell are decorated with coloured glass mosaic.

Wat Luang

Like the town, this monastery has lost much of its former importance. The *chedi*, however, on a very high square base, was built in the 13th century, and restored in 1881. The carved gilded wooden doors of the viharn feature a pair of *thewada*, one walking, the other standing, both on chequerboard pedestals rendered in perspective. Note the pair of *naga* serpents swimming through a lotus pond at the base. The *chedi* which, like that of Wat Phra Kaeo, stands on a high terrace, has a tall square redented base with diminishing octagonal mouldings above and a small bell.

Indented chedi on elevated terrace at Wat Phra Kaeo.

Chiang Khong is the only place on the Thai stretch of the Mekong from where the famous giant catfish *Pangasianodon gigas* (*pla beuk* in Thai) is caught. The season begins in May when the fish begin to swim upstream and continues through August; only a few are taken when they return downriver in November. Chiang Saen (*see page 208*) is a 46-kilometre drive west across a pass below Doi Luang Prae Muang (1328 metres), passing Hmong villages.

THE UPPER KOK VALLEY

The Kok Valley above Chiang Rai has fine scenery and many hill-tribe villages, but little in the way of Lanna art or architecture. The river in fact rises in Burma, 100 kilometres north of Tha Ton, and then cuts across the Taten range in an incised valley heading east-south-east towards Chiang Rai. Recent road improvements, particularly to Route 1089 between Fang and Chiang Rai and to Routes 1130 and 1234 out of Mae Salong, have opened up this formerly isolated area. It is now possible to drive between Chiang Mai and Chiang Rai using the upper valleys of the Ping and Kok respectively, and the journey is pleasant if culturally uneventful.

General view of an Akha village; the haze is from burning fields.

The small river-crossing town of Tha Ton has a beautiful scenic location at the foot of the hills that, a few kilometres to the north, marks the border with Burma. In recent years, the town has acquired a new lease of life as the departure point for boat and raft trips down the Kok River to Chiang Rai, a distance of some 80 kilometres.

Wat Tha Ton

This monastery sits on the middle slopes of a hill with a wonderful view over the valley. Apart from its small *chedi*, however, the *wat* has suffered from so many donations that the hillside has sprouted some brash concrete constructions, the least dignified of which is the

Above: the chedi at Wat Tha Ton.

Right: view of the Kok Valley.

Chinese sculpture garden on the river side. The giant white Buddha above the main *wat* is, like the majority of grandiose modern images designed to dominate the landscape, poorly conceived. There are plans, as yet unrealised, for a 49-metre *chedi* on the summit of the hill.

TRIBUTARIES OF THE KOK RIVER

One of its tributaries, the Fang, joins the Kok a short distance below Tha Ton, and its broad valley extends south in the direction of Chiang Mai. The watershed between the upper Fang and the upper Ping (which flows in exactly the opposite direction) is a little way north of Chiang Dao (*see page 129*). The town of Fang, 26 kilometres south of Tha Ton, was founded by King Mangrai in 1268 and prospered until its destruction at the hands of the Burmese at the end of the 18th century. It was abandoned until 1880, and there is now little to see of its history.

Wat Jong Paen
Located near the northern edge of town, this Burmese-style monastery has a multi-functional *viharn* featuring a multi-tiered roof.

Tab Tao Caves
Another 34 kilometres south from Fang, just after the Km 79 marker, on the west side of the road, are the Tab Tao Caves, 3 kilometres down a track. At the foot of the limestone cliffs are two sets of steps, each leading down to a cavern. On the left is Tham Pha Chak ('dark cave'), and on the right, illuminated by a shaft of daylight from the ceiling, Tham Pha Kha ('light cave'). Both contain Buddha images; the one in Tham Pha Kha has a large reclining Buddha with disciples.

   Another tributary of the Kok River, the Mae Lao, rises on the eastern side of the main north-south range, and its valley provides an older route between Chiang Mai and Chiang Rai, crossing the watershed 50 kilometres from Chiang Mai. Route 118 follows this, and at 85 kilometres from Chiang Rai passes through the small town of Wiang Pa Pao which, as its name indicates, was originally a fortified settlement (in fact, established as a Haw Chinese settlement in the mid-18th century during their campaigns against the Burmese).

Wat Sri Suthawat *
The town's principal *wat* is down a lane to the east of the road near the centre of town. Behind the tall modern *viharn* (with a mirrored ceiling!) is a Burmese-style *chedi*, and behind that is the converted old *viharn*, now a small museum with carved wooden panels and local artefacts. Close by is a wooden *ho trai* raised on round brick pillars. Its carved floral pediment is gilded and set against a blue glass background, and has an unusual small feature: a tiny carving of Indra's three-headed elephant, Erawan, executed in a naturalistic style with the god standing next to it like a mahout. A peculiar feature of this *wat* is that the *ubosot* is located outside the enclosure, among trees to the west, for extra privacy. It has its own walled enclosure, and the gate is guarded by a lion, elephant and a standing soldier.

Hill-tribes
South-east Asia's heartland, straddling the edges of Burma, China, Vietnam, Laos and Thailand, is a geographically complex mass of mountains and hills spreading out from the Tibetan Plateau and eastern Himalayas. Its outliers are the hill-country of Lanna, and along these ridges several ethnic minorities have migrated, usually escaping persecution and economic hardship. The hill-tribes, of which there are six major groups in Lanna numbering at least 500,000, are marginalised people who have, over the centuries, been forced to adapt to the difficult terrain in the face of stronger lowland peoples. Apart from the largest group, the Karen, who are found mainly on the western side of Lanna, close to Karen State in Burma, most of the hill-tribes are concentrated in Chiang Rai province.

Most began arriving in Lanna in the 19th century. Three tribes, the Lisu, Akha and Lahu, are from the same linguistic group — the Lolo sub-division of the Tibeto-Burman language family. The Hmong and Mien speak Sino-Tibetan languages. All have distinctive costume, but these are worn less and less frequently as contact increases with lowland Thais. In this respect, the Akha, and particularly Akha women, are the most conservative.

Two Lisu girls donning traditional silver costume.

Lahu woman embroidering bag.

THE PAI
AND YUAM
VALLEYS

Separated from the rest of Lanna by the largest of its
mountain ranges, these two valleys could, from their
appearance and personality, be a part of neighbouring
Burma. The small population is largely Shan, the
result of historically recent migration from Shan State,
and the inspiration for making these valleys a part of
Lanna in the nineteenth century was their elephants
and teak forests.

*The two Burmese-style chedis at the hill-top monastery Wat Phra
That Doi Kong Mu.*

THE PAI AND YUAM VALLEYS

The western flank of the Lanna highlands is the most isolated, not just physically but ethno-linguistically and culturally. Two rivers, the Pai and the Yuam, drain west into the River Salween, which for all but a short stretch of a little over 100 kilometres, to the west of Mae Sariang, is a Burmese river. A complex of mountain ranges, on a north-south axis, form the watershed between the Salween system and the Ping, and the provincial boundary follows the ridge line, but until recently there was no easy route across the range from Chiang Mai. Now, road improvements have made the Pai and Yuam valleys more accessible, and combining Route 1095 west of Mae Taeng with Route 108, which crosses the mountains west of Hot, makes a 597-kilometre circuit that is one of the most scenically attractive in Lanna. This comprises a 239-kilometre stretch from Chiang Mai north through Mae Taeng and then west through Pai to Mae Hong Son, a 168-kilometre stretch due south from Mae Hong Son to Mae Sariang, and a 190-kilometre stretch east and north-east back to Chiang Mai via Hot and Chom Thong.

The Pai River drains the northern part of these highlands, rising in the far north close to the border with Burma's Shan State and first flowing south through the town of Pai, then west toward Mae Hong Son and across the Burmese border to meet the Salween River. Smaller tributaries extend the drainage south to the small town of Khun Yuam, where a relatively low watershed separates it from the Yuam Valley. From here, the Yuam River flows due south through the town of Mae Sariang, before turning west to meet the Salween. The generally rugged topography left little opportunity for the rivers to build up fertile flood plains, with the result that cultivatable land is scarce and the population correspondingly small.

The valley of the Pai River between Mae Hong Son and Pai, as it crosses the northern end of the Thanon Thong Chai mountains.

The physical isolation of these two valleys from the rest of Lanna has strongly affected their history of settlement, and long before they came under the control of Chiang Mai they were inhabited by the Shan, albeit sparsely. Also known as the Tai Yai, and mainly concentrated in the north-east of Burma, they form one of the major sub-groups of the Tai peoples. However, settlement of any significance did not take place until the middle of the 19th century, following Mae Hong Son's emergence as an elephant centre (*see below*), and by this time the Shan who moved here were heavily influenced by Burmese Theravada Buddhism.

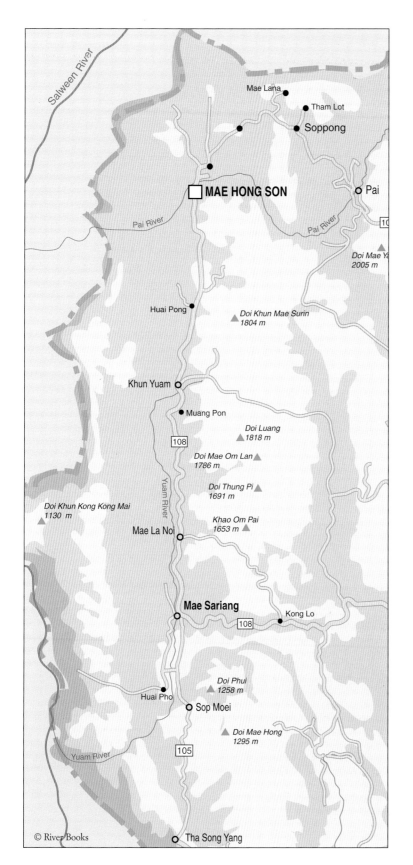

Map of the Pai and Yuam valleys.

The Shan

The majority of the population of the province is Shan, also known as Tai Yai or Tai Khun, and one of the major ethnic groups. The majority live in Burma's Shan State, in what were until 1959 feudal principalities ruled by hereditary princes known as *sawbwas*. Most are Buddhist, and the distinctive feature of their traditional dress is the turban worn by men and married women. The ordination of Shan boys is a particularly colourful ceremony, and in Mae Hong Son there is a mass ordination held in late March to early April, called the Poi Sang Long.

Shan boy dressed for shin pyu: ordination as a monk

Shan zat pwe peformer at a wat inauguration festival in Mae Hong Son.

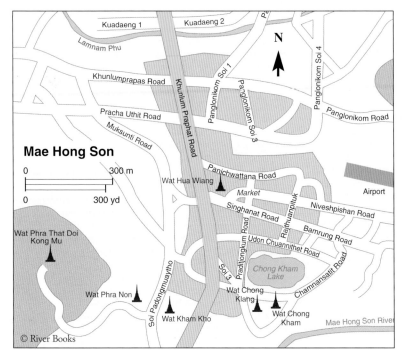

Plan of Mae Hong Son.

MAE HONG SON

The principal town of the region – despite its small size – Mae Hong Son was founded in 1831, when Chao Kaeo Muang, a Chiang Mai prince, led an elephant-catching expedition here for the ruler. A corral for trapping the animals was built here, and the camp became a training centre, gradually growing into a permanent settlement for Shan *mahouts*, and later other settlers. In 1874 it was made a city, with a ruler appointed from Chaing Mai, and in 1893 the area was designated a province. Even until the 1980s Mae Hong Son retained much of the appearance of a 19th century market town, although recent improvement in communications and consequent tourism have begun to change it. Nevertheless, the town still has many Shan-style teak houses and shop-houses, and the morning market, directly east of Wat Hua Wiang, is worth visiting for its Shan atmosphere. The physical setting is also particularly attractive, best seen from the two *chedi* on the hill above the town. Set on the edge of the rice fields of the narrow Pai Valley, it is surrounded in all directions by forested hills, with the small circular Chong Kham Lake near its centre. This is the setting for Mae Hong Son's two most picturesque *wat*, which are next to each other on the south side.

Wat Chong Kham *
Situated next to Wat Chong Klang, this is the older of the two *wat* – founded in 1827 by the Shan ruler of Mae Hong Son, Phaya Singhanataraj – although it was rebuilt after a fire in the 1970s. The multi-functional *viharn* is notable chiefly for the tall 7-tiered *pyatthat* that rises from the centre of its roof complex. To the left is a smaller *viharn* built between 1932 and 1936 to house the principal Buddha image called Luang Pho To, 5 metres tall, Burmese in style and seated. On the right is the rectangular whitewashed brick *ubosot*, with a small white-and-gold *chedi* on the roof.

Wat Chong Klang **
Built in the 1860s, its Burmese-style *chedi* can be clearly seen from the shores of the lake. It is painted white and gold, and niches extend from all four sides, each surmounted by a small brick and stucco *pyatthat*. Three of these contain Buddha images, while that on the east side connects to a fine 5-tiered *pyatthat*, its metal roof decorated with intricate filigree. The multiple rooves of the large *viharn* in green-

Plan of Wat Chong Klang.

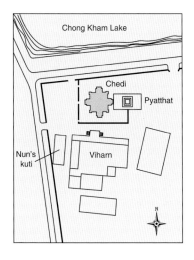

Wat Chong Kham and Wat Chong Klang from across the small Chong Kham Lake in the centre of town.

Scenes from the jataka tales painted on a wall of 200 glass panels: one of the treasures of Wat Chong Klang.

Carved wooden figures in Burmese style at Wat Chong Klang, illustrating scenes from the jataka tales.

painted corrugated sheeting are also trimmed with filigree, and the interior is typically elaborate. To the left of the altar carrying the Burmese-style images of the Buddha is the most notable feature of this *wat*: almost 200 glass paintings illustrating scenes from the *jataka* tales. These are set into the painted and gilded walls of the abbot's private room, to the left of the altar. Next to these, a door leads to a back room containing 33 large wooden figures of characters in the *Vessantara Jataka*. They were brought from Burma in 1857.

Wat Hua Wiang *

This is the town's principal *wat*, situated on the south side of Phanit Wattana Road east of the intersection with Mae Hong Son's main street, Khunlum Praphat Road. The Burmese-style *viharn* in the centre of the enclosure was restored in 1993, but retains a fine multi-tiered roof and also contains the large seated bronze Buddha image known as Phra Chao Phala Lakhaeng. Cast in Mandalay in the 1930s in sections, it was then transported here, where it was assembled. A new *ubosot* was built

At the inauguration of a new ubosot for Wat Hua Wiang, a worshipper prays to one of the nine sacred marker spheres, luk nimit, before they are all buried at a special ceremony.

Offerings made to the principal Buddha image of Wat Hua Wiang, the Phra Chao Phala Lakhaeng, in the main viharn.

on the east side of the enclosure in 1998, sadly replacing the old wooden ruin with a design in central Thai style of little architectural merit.

Wat Phra Non *

In the south-west of town, at the foot of Doi Kong Mu Hill, is Wat Phra Non ('Monastery of the Reclining Buddha'). The large (12 metre-long) image in question was built in 1875 of brick covered with plaster, but the building of principal interest here is the Burmese-style *mondop* standing alone on a terrace on the south side of the enclosure. The lower section of its walls is in brick, the upper parts wood, and the roof, decorated with silver-painted metal filigree, is outstanding. Note the *bai sema* which are natural stones arranged in pairs radiating from the building. The long staircase up the hill to Wat Phra That Doi Kong Mu begins here but is overgrown. An old tree in front of the *wat*, on the road, has two attractive spirit houses, one unusually in iron.

The mondop of Wat Phra Non, with its exquisite Burmese-style filigree roof.

Wat Kham Kho

Directly opposite Wat Kham Kho, this *wat* is on the west side of Khunlum Praphat Road. Its viharn was built in 1890, and has a portico with a multi-tiered roof at the

230

An evening festival, complete with outdoor cinema, at the hilltop Wat Phra That Doi Kong Mu.

end of a long covered walkway. It houses five Buddha images, the principal one in Burmese style, the others Thai, and an ornate peacock throne from the beginning of the century with coloured glass inlay.

Wat Phra That Doi Kong Mu *
The road running by the south side of Wat Phra Non climbs the hill of Doi Kong Mu. Near the top are the two whitewashed *chedi* of Wat Phra That Doi Kong Mu, the larger built in 1860, the smaller in 1874. Behind and higher is a recent and unattractive large standing Buddha: yet another failed attempt to create an imposing image on the landscape. Although often shrouded by morning mist, the hill-top offers fine views over the Pai Valley.

THE PAI VALLEY

For a short distance upriver from Mae Hong Son, Route 1095 follows the winding, narrow valley and the forested hills on either side reaching right to the edges of the rice fields. These are dotted with many traditional thatched huts, used as day-time shelters by farmers, who because of the scarcity of arable often have a long walk from their village. After the village of Pang Mu, the road leaves the valley and crosses the hills via Soppong (64 kilometres from Mae Hong Son, where there is one of the largest case systems in the region, Tham Lot) to rejoin the river at the small town of Pai.

Formerly a remote backwater, Pai now receives a small but steady stream of visitors along the newly paved Route 1095, and is a base for trekking to nearby Lisu and Lahu hill-tribe villages. The distance from Mae Hong Son is 106 kilometres, and from Chiang Mai 133 kilometres. Unfortunately, none of its few *wat* is of great interest; **Wat Luang**, on the west side of Route 1095 near the centre of town, opposite the District offices, is Pai's principal *wat*, and has a large Burmese-style *chedi*, painted white and surrounded by 12 smaller *chedi*. **Wat Hua Na** near the hospital has a similar *chedi,* and immediately east of the bus station, on the north side of the street that runs down to the river, perpendicular to Route 1095, is **Wat Klang**.

THE YUAM VALLEY

The southern half of Mae Hong Son province is drained by the Yuam River, and the valley is accessible from three directions. At the southern end, Route 105 enters the principal town, Mae Sariang, from the direction of Mae Sot. From the east, Route 108 crosses the hills

Teak and logging
The combination of the Thai government's ban on logging in 1989, extensive teak forests in the hills near the Burmese border, and the often strained relationship between the two nations is a recipe for illegal logging and frequent skirmishes involving the army and rangers. As a result, the Forest Industry Organisation, a state enterprise, maintains a base in Mae Sariang with elephants to haul out confiscated logs, but even deploying these is a frustrating experience. As one ranger observed, referring to illegal loggers, "When I'm over on the other side of that hill, they're here. When I'm here, they're there."

from Hot to Mae Sariang, a distance of 103 kilometres. From the north, Route 108 leads directly from Mae Hong Son, entering the upper Yuam Valley at Khun Yuam and continuing due south to Mae Sariang.

Mae Sariang

This is the main market town for the valley, and until the 1989 ban on logging in the country, was a centre for teak. The government Forest Industry Organisation still maintains an operation here, with elephants, but they are now mainly employed recovering illegally cut teak logs when these are discovered by rangers of the Forestry Department. There is still considerable clandestine logging in the border area to the west, and occasional clashes between loggers (often from the Burmese side) and the Thai authorities.

A field shack in the Pai Valley above Mae Hong Son.

Again, the town's *wat* are only of moderate interest. **Wat Chong Sung** (also known as Wat Utthayarom), built in 1896, has three gold-painted *chedi* and Burmese-style Buddha images, which include a small reclining Buddha in a beautifully carved and gilded *phyatthat*. **Wat Si Bunruang**, built in 1939, features elaborate fretwork rooves on both the *viharn* and the smaller *ubosot* opposite.

In the upper Yuam Valley north of Mae Sariang are a number of traditional Shan villages maintaining a largely unchanged rural existence. Muang Pon, 85 kilometres to the north on the east side of Route 108, from which it can be seen very clearly as the road climbs, is typical. The population of the village subsists on the agricultural produce of its surrounding fields, which fill the narrow valley floor.

Threading leaves together to make traditional roof thatching in Muang Pon, the Yuam Valley.

The altar with Buddhas at Wat Chong Sung, including an ornate phyatthat housing a Reclining Buddha.

CHRONOLOGY

early 800s Founding of Haripunchai, with Princess Chammadevi as ruler (in 661 according to the chronicles)

1096 Phayao founded as the capital of a small independent kingdom by Pho Khun Chom Dham

mid–1100s Chiang Saen area ruled by Khun Chüang

1220s Unrest in southern Yunnan stimulates movement of Tai peoples southward, across the Mekong

1239 Mangrai born in Ngoen Yang

mid–1200s Tai population dominates the region

1258 Ngam Müang succeeds his father as ruler of Phayao

1259 Beginning of King Mangrai's reign at Chiang Saen

1262 Mangrai founds Chiang Rai as capital of Lanna, around Wat Phra That Doi Chom Thong

1279 Ram Kamhaeng becomes third king of Sukhothai

1281 Mangrai captures Haripunchai from the Mon king Yi Ba

c 1282 Muang Pua (Varanagara) founded in the upper Nan Valley as the capital of a small independent kingdom

c 1286 Wat Chedi Liam's Haripunchai-style *chedi* built near Chiang Mai

1287 Ram Kamhaeng, Mangrai and Ngam Muang of Phayao conclude treaty. Kublai Khan captures Pagan

1288 Mangrai moves capital to Wiang Kum Kam, near presentday Chiang Mai, and sends emissary to Haripunchai to undermine the ruler

1289 Mangrai concludes treaty with king of Pegu, marrying the king's daughter

1290 Mangrai settles 500 families of goldsmiths, silversmiths & coppersmiths from Ava in Lanna

1292 With advice from Ram Kamhaeng and Ngam Müang, Mangrai chooses the site for Chiang Mai, his capital

1296 Mangrai founds Chiang Mai. Yi Ba rebels and is exiled

1297 Wat Chiang Man founded in Chiang Mai

1298 Death of Ram Kamhaeng. Sukhothai's rule extended to Phrae, Phayao, Nan & Luang Prabang, but rapidly contracts after this date

1317 Death of Mangrai. His son Chai Songkhram succeeds him briefly

1318 Chai Songkhram hands over the throne of Chiang Mai to his son Saen Phu and retires to Chiang Rai

1319 The prince of Muang Nai seizes the throne from Saen Phu, who retreats to Chiang Rai. Wat Pa Sak founded at Chiang Saen

c 1322 Saen Phu's brother, Nam Thuam, overthrows the invader

1324 Saen Phu re-installed on the throne of Chiang Mai by his father

1328 On the death of Saen Phu, his son Kham Fu takes the throne. A new city is founded at Chaing Saen

1337 Kahm Fu dies, succeeded by his son Pha Yu, who is crowned and rules at Chiang Rai

1338 The independent kingdom of Phayao absorbed into Lanna

1339 Chiang Mai once more, and finally, established as capital of Lanna

c 1341 City walls of Chiang Mai built in brick

1345	Wat Phra Singh, Chiang Mai, founded as Wat Li Chiang Phra by Pha Yu, to enshrine his father's ashes
1347	Foundation of Ayutthaya by U Thong
1349	Sukhothai submits to U Thong of Ayutthaya without a struggle
1353	The Laotian Kingdom of Lan Xang founded by King Fa Ngum (a Tai chieftain, married to a Khmer princess)
1355	Pha Yu's son, Ku Na, becomes king. Sukhothai art begins to influence Lanna styles
1359	The city of Muang Pua moved to Wat Phra That Chae Haeng, on the east bank of the Nan River, and re-named Phu Phiang Chae Haeng
1367	The Phra Sihing Buddha image installed in the (re-named) Wat Phra Singh. Wat Umong Maha Therachan built
1368	Phu Phiang Chae Haeng re-named Nan, and moved to its present location
1370	Wat Phra Yeun built at Lamphun for the Sukhothai monk Phra Sumana
1371	Wat Suan Dok, Chiang Mai, founded by Ku Na for Phra Sumana. Also Wat Boromathat Doi Suthep
1378	Sukhothai becomes vassal of Ayutthaya
1385	King Saen Muang Ma begins reign, defends Chiang Mai against Ayutthya. Wat Phra Singh built in Chiang Rai
1387	Saen Muang Ma unsuccessfully attacks Sukhothai
1390	Chiang Mai is attacked by Ayutthaya and submits to King Ramesuan
1401	King Sam Fang Kaen succeeds Saen Muang Ma on the latter's death
1405	Sam Fang Kaen repels attack from Yunnan
1409	Tilokaraj born
1434	The Emerald Buddha discovered in the *chedi* of Chiang Rai's Wat Phra Kaeo, after a lightning strike. Taken to Lampang
1441	Sam Fang Kaen overthrown by a palace official. King Tilokaraj crowned in his place
1450	Tilokaraj captures Nan, consolidating Lanna
1451	Wat Phra That Sri Chom Thong's *chedi* built
1455	Wat Chet Yot built in Chiang Mai as King Tilokaraj's funerary temple and to commemorate the 2000th year of Buddhism
1459	Tilokaraj conquers Si Satchanalai
1461	Chiang Mai forces capture Sukhothai and lay siege to Phitsanulok, but a Yunnanese invasion forces them to retire
1464	Chiang Mai's third attack on Ayutthaya is repulsed; peace follows for three decades
1467	Trailoknat of Ayutthaya sends a Burmese monk to Chiang Mai to foment disputes at the court
1468	The Emerald Buddha brought from Lampang and installed in the *chedi* of Wat Chedi Luang
1477	Eighth World Buddhist Council convenes at Wat Chet Yot, Chiang Mai. Wat Phra Singh's *ho trai* built
c 1480s	Sukhothai styles and techniques begin to appear in Chiang Mai sculpture and ceramics, as a result of Tiloka's capture of Si Satchanalai.
1486	The principal *viharn* built at Wat Phra That Lampang Luang

1487	Death of Tilokaraj. Succeeded by Yot Chiang Rai
1494	War resumes between Chiang Mai and Ayutthaya
1495	King Muang Kaeo begins reign
1496	The *chedi* of Wat Phra That Lampang Luang enlarged to its present shape and size
1508	A Chiang Mai attack provokes a Siamese invasion, which is repulsed
1510	Another Chiang Mai attack, with the same result
1513	Chiang Mai forces raid and loot Sukhothai
1515	Chiang Mai forces take Sukhothai and Kamphaeng Phet, but are driven back by a Siamese army under the king & defeated near Lampang
1526	King Chettarat succeeds King Muang Kaeo
c 1530	Peace treaty between Chiang Mai & Ayutthaya
1538	Chettarat deposed by his son
c 1540	Lanna kingdom extends to Salween in W (Muang Nai NW corner), Keng Tung & Jing Hong in N, Chiang Khong & Nan Valley in E, just above Tak & Uttaradit in S
1543	Chettarat retakes throne
1545	Chettarat assassinated, Queen Chiraprapha enthroned Earthquake damages Chedi Luang. Unsuccessful attacks on Chiang Mai by Ayutthaya and Shan prince
1546	King Setthathirat of Luang Phrabang accepts invitation to rule Lanna
1547	King Setthathirat returns to Luang Prabang on the death of his father. Civil war in Lanna
1551	Phra Mekuti, a Shan prince, is accepted as ruler of Chiang Mai by local princes. The Emerald Buddha taken from Chiang Mai to Luang Prabang. The warlike Bayinnaung crowned at Pegu and begins subjugation of all surrounding Tai states
1558	Chiang Mai and the rest of Lanna taken by Burmese army, beginning two centuries of Burmese suzerainty
1564	Ayutthaya falls to Burmese, who also mount a punitive expedition to Chiang Mai due to previous lack of cooperation. Mekuti deposed by Burmese.
1565	Mekuti is deposed by the Burmese. Princess Wisutthithewi installed as regent of Chiang Mai, with Burmese garrison
1569	Ayutthaya falls again, after 7-month siege, to the Burmese, who use Chiang Mai as a base for attacks
1578	Mangrai's dynasty ends with the death of Queen Wisutthithewi. Burmese King Bayinnaung places son Tharawaddy Min on throne of Chiang Mai
1598	King Naresuan of Ayutthaya retakes Chiang Mai from the Burmese
1600	Chiang Rai revolts against the Burmese, but is subdued
1614	Chiang Rai revolts against the Burmese again, provoking a Burmese expedition that recaptures both it and Chiang Mai
1661	King Narai of Ayutthaya briefy retakes Chiang Mai
1701–5	Chiang Saen, and Chiang Rai as its dependency, placed under direct Burmese rule
1703	The city of Nan sacked by the Burmese
1714	Chao Fa Meow Sa, a Burmese prince, sent to rule Nan

1726	On the death of Chao Fa Meow Sa, local prince Luang Tin Mahawong appointed to rule Nan under Burmese suzerainty
1767	Ayutthaya captured and razed by the Birmese
1774	With Siamese help, Phraya Chaban of Chiang Mai and Chao Kawila of Lampang defeating the Burmese in Lampang
1776	Chiang Mai recaptured, but abandoned for 20 years after counter-attacks
1781	Chao Kawila, prince of Lampang, takes control of Chiang Mai under Siamese suzerainty
1786	Chiang Rai recaptured from the Burmese
1788	Nan placed under Siamese suzerainty
1796	Chiang Mai resettled by Chao Kawila
1802	Chao Kawila appointed ruler of Chiang Mai by King Rama I. Keng Tung raided to capture Shan families to resettle Lanna
1804	Chiang Saen, the last Burmese stronghold in Lanna, recaptured, then razed as a defensive measure. Tai Lue from Sipsongpanna taken to repopulate Lanna, particularly the Nan valley
1815	Death of Chao Kawila
1830	Mae Hong Son begins to be used as an elephant capture and training centre for Chiang Mai princes
1844	The re-founding of Chiang Rai, which has lost much of its population to conflict with the Burmese
1871	Chao Inthawichayanon is last semi-independent ruler of Chiang Mai
1874	Siamese high commissioner appointed to Lanna
1881	Chiang Saen re-settled on orders of King Chulalongkorn
1885	Telegraph reaches Chiang Mai. British conquest of Upper Burma.
1892	Lanna incorporated into Siam as Monthon Phayap
1893	Siam cedes the east bank of the Mekong, including Laos and part of Lanna, to France
1902	Shan rebellion
1904	Siam cedes the west bank of the Mekong to France, apart from a short stretch around Chiang Saen
1910	First Akha village established in Chiang Rai province
1921	Railway reaches Chiang Mai
1925	Second Akha village established in Chiang Rai province
1926	King Rama VII is first Siamese ruler to visit Lanna
1931	Nan incorporated into Siam, on the death of the local dynasty's last ruler
1932	Chiang Mai becomes a province of Siam. Overthrow of the absolute monarchy

BIBLIOGRAPHY

Charoensupkul, A.,
*The Elements of Thai
Architecture.*
Bangkok: Satri Sarn, 1978.

Coedes, G.,
The Making of South East Asia.
Berkeley and Los Angeles:
University of Los Angeles, 1983.

Davies, R. B.,
*Muang Metaphysics: A Study in
Northern Thai Myth and Ritual.*
Bangkok: Poindorra, 1984.

Gooden, C.,
Around Lan-na.
Halesworth: Jungle Books, 1999.

Griswold, A. B.,
Wat Pra Yun Reconsidered.
Monograph No. 4. Bangkok:
Siam Society, 1975.

Hall, D. G. E. A.,
History of South-East Asia.
London: Macmillan, 1958.

Hallet, H., A.
*Thousand Miles on an Elephant in
the Shan States.*
Bangkok: White Lotus, 1988.

Hargreave, O.,
*Exploring Chiang Mai. City, Valley
& Mountains.*
Chiang Mai: Within Books, 1997.

Jumsai, S.,
*Naga: Cultural Origins in Siam
and the West Pacific.*
Singapore: Oxford University
Press, 1988.

Jumsai, S.,
*Seen: Architectural Forms of
Northern Siam and Old Siamese
Fortifications.*
Bangkok: The Fine Arts
Commission, The Association of
Siamese Architects, 1970.

Krug, S. and Duboff, S.,
The Kamthieng House.
Bangkok: Siam Society, 1982.

le May, R.,
An Asian Arcady.
Cambridge: W. Heffer & Sons,
1926.

Lewis, E. and L.,
Peoples of the Golden Triangle.
Bangkok: River Books, 1998.

Lair, R.,
*Gone Astray: The Care and
Management of the Asian
Elephant in Domesticity.*
Rome: FAO, 1997.

Marchal, H.,
l'Art D'coratif au Laos.
Paris: Arts Asiatiques, 1964.

Panjabhan, N.,
Wichienkeeo, A. and Na Nakhon
Phanom, S.,
*The Charm of Lanna Wood
Carving.*
Bangkok: Rerngrom Publishing,
1994.

Penth, H.,
*A Brief History of Lan Na:
Civilizations of North Thailand.*
Chiang Mai: Silkworm Books,
1994.

Prangwatthanakun, S. and
Naenna, P.,
Chiangmai's Textile Heritage.

Shan, J. C.,
Northern Thai Ceramics.
Oxford, 1981.

Woodward, Jr., H. W.,
The Sacred Sculpture of Thailand.
Bangkok: River Books, 1997.

Wyatt, D. K.,
Thailand: A Short History.
New Haven: Yale University Press,
1984.

INDEX

Page reference in **bold** refer to illustrations.